Aggression
and
Violence

Aggression and Violence

Edited by
Peter Marsh and Anne Campbell

St. Martin's Press · New York

© Basil Blackwell Publisher 1982

St. Martin's Press, Inc., 175 Fifth Avenue, New York, NY 10010
Printed in Great Britain
First published in the United States of America in 1982

ISBN 0–312–01402–3

Library of Congress Cataloging in Publication Data
Main entry under title:

Aggression and violence
Includes index.
1. Violence—Addresses, essays, lectures. 2. Aggression—
Addresses, essays, lectures. I. Marsh, Peter E. II. Campbell,
Anne.
HM281.A34 1981   303.6′2   81–14342
ISBN 0–312–01402–3   AACR2

pd
8-15-83

Contents

vi

Acknowledgements

We would like to acknowledge our debt to Whitbread Ltd, who funded the Contemporary Violence Research Centre, University of Oxford, with considerable generosity between 1977 and 1979. The Centre no longer exists. Peter Marsh is now Senior Lecturer in Psychology at Oxford Polytechnic. Anne Campbell is doing research with the help of a Harkness Fellowship in New York. Thanks are also due to Janet Gallagher for typing and retyping the various drafts.

P.E.M., Oxford
A.C.C., New York

CHAPTER 1

Introduction

Peter Marsh and Anne Campbell

Aggression and violence are aspects of human life that, quite understandably, give rise to considerable alarm and concern. In recent years social scientists have been called upon to provide 'answers' and 'cures' for aspects of human behaviour that might in earlier times have been seen as unremarkable, but are now construed as novel and dangerous. Such demands, of course, are not easy to meet. Indeed, one could argue very strongly that it is not the job of a researcher to study 'problems' at all, but rather to look at aspects of human behaviour in a rather calmer way than is possible if one has a particular moral axe to grind. At the same time, a case could be made that the contribution of the academic world to our understanding of man's aggressiveness towards his fellow man has been, at best, limited.

There would seem to be a number of reasons for this state of affairs. It is fair to say that the subject area is an extremely difficult one to investigate. It is almost impossible to simulate aggression and violence in a laboratory in a way that is in the slightest bit realistic or likely to illuminate real-life behaviour. In the real world the problems are greater, because by and large violence is covert, fleeting and rarely performed for the analytical benefit of social researchers.

Second, the climate of general opinion in Western societies is that violence is increasing with great rapidity in both frequency and severity. The age in which we live, it is felt, is altogether less pleasant and safe than that of our youth or the youth of our parents. As a result, a reasonable concern is transformed into an almost universal near-obsession which precludes a more discriminating approach. Mugging old ladies, beating wives and children – such acts are seen as belonging in the same category as fist fights in the playgrounds or 'bother' at soccer games. In reality, it could be argued that such sets of activities have so little in common that a single explanation of violence cannot possibly apply to both of them.

The third reason is perhaps most significant in the context of this particular book. It concerns the high level of compartmentalization within the academic world itself. Traditionally, psychologists and sociologists, for example, have little regard for each other's approach to the study of social issues. Rarely do they read the journals of the other discipline. And within each of the fields there are further seldom-breached subdivisions. The same is true for the splits between other fields, such as anthropology, genetics, physiology and so on. And yet all profess to be concerned with the same subject matter – aggression.

Such divisions are unproductive, and the result is a proliferation of narrow theoretical and methodological approaches which fail because of their lack of concern for a wider perspective. A possible integration of such approaches is ruled out because they are couched in idiosyncratic terms or are based on fundamentally different assumptions and frames of reference. The small amount of professional contact between members of different academic departments ensures the maintenance of this highly unsatisfactory *status quo*.

Reversing these trends will never be easy. Certain theoretical stances are so distant from each other that integration of any kind is quite out of the question. But there is a large area of common ground where a multi-disciplinary approach can be very fruitful indeed. A necessary condition for enabling such an approach, however, is clarification of the *levels* of explanation to which disciplines contribute, and of how such levels are nested and ordered. A social–psychological explanation of aggression, for example, will rarely be of much value unless placed within the context of a wider sociological theory which pays attention to the genesis of the societal frames in which the social action under scrutiny takes place. Similarly, a broad 'environmental' theory will be inadequate unless it can also be posited alongside an explanation of how individuals perceive and construe their physical and social world and endow it with meaning. While we can allow an element of job demarcation in this quest, it is foolish to perpetuate the myth that any one branch of the social sciences is going to succeed single-handed in fully accounting for the many varied aspects of human activity that can reasonably be termed aggressive or violent.

There is no suggestion here that simple eclecticism is the answer. There have been many attempts to place an assortment of rather poor theories and bits of evidence on the table and force them all into a rather badly shaped frame. That achieves very little except further confusion. A proper multi-disciplinary approach aims at something rather better. And its crucial significance is to allow individual contributions to draw strength and support by being placed around or within other ways of looking at and accounting for a given social phenomenon.

A realistic approach to aggression and violence is one that establishes a number of levels of explanation. At the end of the day, one must suppose, the 'final' explanation will be a neuro-physiological one. Action and interaction result from the complex machinations of the grey tissue that rests inside our heads. The content of our heads, however, is shaped both by diffuse genetic factors and by the interaction, via sensory organs, with objects and events in the outside world. For the world to have an effect, it must be rendered meaningful. Different heads have different ways of seeing, and the manner in which the world is perceived dictates the manner in which we act in the world.

The constraints on an inter-disciplinary approach are, therefore, quite straightforward. Physiological theories, which do not fall into the trap of assuming that human organisms simply react mechan-istically to purely objective environmental stimulation in a fixed manner, can be integrated with, say, sociological approaches, which in turn do not assume that social institutions and cultural frameworks spawn each other without the active participation of individual persons. In fact, it is possible to view each of the major disciplines contributing at the levels of explanation shown in figure 1.1. Thus, we might begin an explanation of aggression by con-sidering genetic factors but without assuming that such factors *cause* aggressive behaviour in a direct sense. A more rational approach would be to examine how such diffuse influences are mediated through cultural evolution, societal development and micro-social elaboration. The central idea here is that cultures might actually build upon nature, and that, while biological factors in no way predetermine cultural development, they might well serve to reduce the element of randomness. Approached in this way, anthropological and macro-sociological theories might derive some support from evolutionary considerations and, in turn, embrace theories couched in micro-sociological or psychological terms.

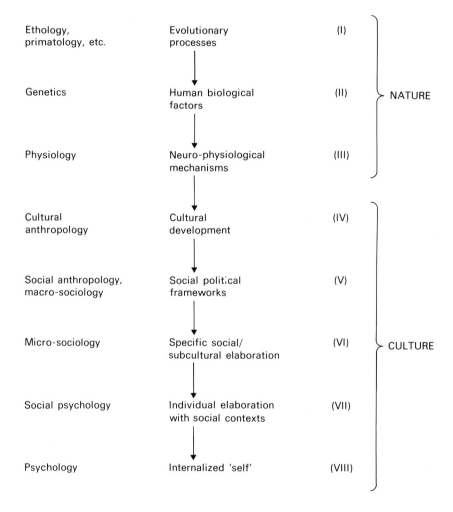

Figure 1.1 Inter-disciplinary approach to the study of violence and aggression.

This might sound rather idealistic and, indeed, the level of mutual recriminations that self-styled Marxist sociologists and neo-Darwinists heap upon each other is sometimes rather extreme. (They seem to forget that Marx and Darwin were more engaged in mutual admiration.) The selection of papers in this book, however, is in keeping with our growing dissatisfaction with the understandable but often frustrating compartmentalization in research on aggression. Indeed not only have we selected across academic disciplines, but we also have views from elsewhere. The contributions made by a New York police officer with the special talents of John Galea, an ex long-term prisoner and a man faced with the problems of aggressive adolescent boys in a community school are considerable. They added that quality of experience and practice that is often marked by its absence in academic debates. And while we may disagree with some of the points they make, or the standpoint from which they make them, we are obliged, I think, to give them serious attention.

No attempt is made in this book to force all the contributions into a single coherent framework. They are varied perspectives, which focus on an issue and contribute at different levels to an explanation of aggression and violence in various contexts. Individuals will undoubtedly differ in their perception of the contributions as significant, ideologically acceptable or applicable to their conception of the real world. If however, the various views and approaches presented here contribute in any way to a widening of one's own perspective on this undeniably important subject, the book will have achieved its aim.

CHAPTER 2

The Violent Imagination

Robin Fox

We hear a great deal today about the problem of violence, but if man has a problem of violence, it is a problem only because he makes it so. Nature knows no such problems. In nature violence is commonplace; aggression is commonplace. Both are undoubtedly necessary. The lion knows no problem. The lion knows when to be violent; when to assert itself; when to kill; when to run. It knows these things in a sense that perhaps no human being knows. Its knowledge is the same as the body's knowledge of digestion and movement, flight and sleep. For man there is a problem of violence in much the same way as there is a problem of eating, of sleeping, of making love, of worshipping the gods. There is a problem because man imbues violence with *meaning*. Without meaning there is no problem; with meaning there are a host of problems, problems that are largely symbolic, organizational, semantic, comprehensible, and avoidable – but problems none the less.

In the same way, no animal has a problem about eating. The animal knows what it eats: if it is a hunting animal it kills its prey and devours it; if it is a scavenging animal it follows the killer to the prey and eats the leavings. With man, in the earliest years of his truly human existence, there was also no problem: he ate what it was his destiny to eat; he killed what he knew he should kill; he asserted himself against that which he knew he should overcome.

The problem arises not out of the desire to kill, any more than out of the desire to eat. The desire to kill is certainly different from the desire to eat, and this is something we must examine. But it is as

real as the desire to eat; as natural as the desire to eat; as unavoid-
able as the desire to eat. If one considers that the desire to kill is in
itself a problem, it is a little like saying that the desire to eat or the
desire to copulate is a problem. In what sense is it a problem? There
is no problem for the lion: it is certainly no problem for the theory of
natural selection that the lion should desire to kill, in the same way
that it should desire to eat or copulate. The same is true for man.
Only if one wishfully decides that there should be no killing does
the very existence of the desire to kill become a problem. In and of
itself, the desire (and the killing) is neutral. It is a problem only if
one chooses to make it so. For many animals killing is reasonable
within the framework of their experience and their need to survive.
It makes as much sense to say that killing *per se* is a problem as it
does to say that the herbivore's desire to eat grass is a problem
because it destroys the grass: it is a problem not for the herbivore,
but only for those who can imbue behaviour with meaning. The
herbivore and the carnivore do not do this: omnivorous man does.
And the problem exists because he is the animal that creates
problems, not because he is the animal that kills, or eats, or
copulates.

Since man evolved as a hunting, omnivorous species, it follows
that he will destroy animals, plants, and even other members of his
species who threaten him. He is right to do so. All these things are
totally natural, totally within a comprehensible scheme of evolution. They are not problems. That man is on occasion both
aggressive and violent presents no more of a problem, in a scientific
sense, than the violence of the lion: it is the same. Many herbivores,
even, can be aggressive and violent, although they kill only rarely
and accidentally. They were mostly created for flight, not fight. But
even then, their violence against their predators is natural and
explicable. It is the other side of the coin of altruism. The most
pacific of animals will be furious, for example, in the defence of
their young, or in the battle for mates. And this is totally comprehensible within the explanatory theory of natural selection. The
animals protect their genes; protect their reproductive efficiency;
protect their fitness – in Darwinian terms. To do this, they must
alternate between altruism and aggression. This is explicable,
natural and unproblematic.

There is really no point and no future in trying to prove that man
is *not* an aggressive or a violent animal. It makes as much sense as

trying to prove that he is not an altruistic, kind and self-sacrificing animal. Even if he is all these things, he is an animal. And when he lived on a scale that was the same as that of other animals, there was no problem. He defended his territories; he hunted his prey; he devastated the vegetable environment; he killed his enemies. In this he differed not a bit from other similar animals, for example, wolves, lions, hunting dogs, or even the occasionally predatory baboons or chimpanzees, his closest relatives. There was no problem. He killed his fellows; so do lions. He killed his prey; so do baboons. He defended his territory; so do wolves. He fought his fellows for status and the right to reproductive success; so do other animals. There was no problem. There would have been a problem for some tender-minded god who preferred a system in which there was no killing, in which there was no aggression, in which there was no status, in which there was no struggle for reproductive success; in the absence of such a tender-minded deity no problem existed, any more than it exists now for the lion and the elephant, for the walrus, for the dolphin, for the giraffe or the baboon. All animals have difficulties, but they do not have problems.

It is not even enough to say that the problems stem from man's consciousness of his own existence. Consciousness was a necessary but not a sufficient cause of the problems. In the stage of his existence when he lived in much the same kind of balance with nature as his fellow hunting animals, exploiting much the same kind of territory as the wolf pack, for example, and employing much the same means of hunting as the wild dog, he was as conscious of his existence as he is now, and it is highly likely that as a consequence he created certain problems for himself. But these were not problems that were out of scale with his mode of existence. They did not in any real sense interfere with it; they did not prevent him from successfully attacking and competing with his fellows – they may even have helped him to do so.

But man began to believe that his own unaided efforts were not enough. Unlike his fellow hunting animals, he was aware of the vagaries of nature. His memory storage and his conceptual ability had made him understand that the seasons differed vastly from each other; that nature was not instantly bountiful; that hunts might not succeed; and that there were forces beyond his comprehension and immediate control. So he created systems of magic and religion to aid him in controlling this probabilistic universe. He created systems of artistic endeavour to enable him to comprehend it as a whole rather than piecemeal; and, of course, he always had language in which to cache all his doubts and all his approaches to magical certainty. There was no real problem – no real intellectual problem – about the nature of what he was doing. He was surviving. He was competing with other animals, with other groups of his own species and, in a sense, with the total environment. And in this gamble he used such means as were at hand. There would have been no future in doubts, questions and concerns about the very mechanisms that his magical and religious systems supported and expanded. He did not use magic and religion to *question* the very nature of violence, or to ask whether it was necessary, but merely to supplement it and help it, and also to comprehend it in a sense very different from that which we mean today. He meant to comprehend violence as a potentiality; as something to help him survive; as something he knew was both natural and necessary – as natural and necessary as sex and eating, artistic expression and language. It was not therefore to him a problem, any more than sleeping, waking, walking, hunting and singing were problems. He knew why he did these things, knew it immediately, in a way that we cannot know today, simply because they are not in the same way necessary for survival. We can comprehend the possibility of living without violence. We have even, in certain of our communities, and in many personal lives, evolved ways of living without reproductive sex. We certainly live without hunting. And we certainly, in most cases, live without an immediate fear of the vagaries of the universe. We are cushioned against all these things.

But in a paradoxical sense, it is because we are cut off from the roots of violence – from the roots of the reproductive struggle – that we make these things into problems. It is true that the lion, cut off from all these things, as for example when caged in a zoo, does not in the same sense make them into problems, because it lacks consciousness. What it does is to ritualize its behaviour in much the same way as the inmates of lunatic asylums, who have also cut themselves off, even from such rudiments of their natural existence as civilization leaves them. But man's self-consciousness, his awareness of his own existence, does not in and of itself create the problems unless he is placed in a position where that self-consciousness is not being employed directly as an adjunct to those natural propensities to violence and copulatory success.

It is not then the self-consciousness in and of itself that creates the problem, but the context in which the self-consciousness has to operate. And the major context in which it has operated has been that of 'early man': 99 per cent of our existence as a distinct genus. (It is really an absurd term – we should rather refer to ourselves as 'late man', since so-called 'early man' is the true representative of the species; civilized man is a mere afterthought.) Early man utilized his self-consciousness largely to deal with difficulties rather than create and solve problems. For example, his self-awareness led him to understand that the end result of violence could be death. (It is possible in some sense that some animals understand this, but certainly not in the same way that man does.) But this very knowledge is a difficulty; because the knowledge that in, for example, tackling an enemy or large prey the possible outcome might be death may very well cause fear, cowardice and failure. In magic and religion, therefore, the strength of group sentiment and a whole host of rituals could be employed to bolster individual males against the possible consequences of their own fragility. This was not a case of attempting to understand the problem of violence, but of understanding the difficulty that might arise from individual weakness or failure of nerve. There was never any question that violence was both necessary and useful, and in a very positive sense good – as good as eating, copulating, singing. Only obviously it created more difficulties, because the possible outcome was the loss of an individual life – which is clearly a difficulty for the individual – and the loss of a member, which was a difficulty for the group. But when I say this was not a problem, I meant it was not an intellectual problem. If one likes one can say it was a practical problem. I prefer simply to call it a difficulty. One tried to overcome practical difficulties; one did not try to solve intellectual problems.

Again, I am not saying that early man never tried to solve intellectual problems. I am merely saying that, unquestionably, he did not create unnecessary intellectual problems where they did not exist. There was for him no *intellectual* problem of violence; there was for him no intellectual problem of sex. These are later inventions of human self-consciousness, not a necessary conse- quence of human self-consciousness.

What I am arguing is that in a sense – in some natural and

non-teleological sense – there is an intended balance of nature in which even man's self-consciousness is in harmony with the environment because it is being *used* by him as part of his struggle for existence, as part of the adaptational process. It is being used in a very positive sense to advance the reproductive interest of the individual and, as a necessary by-product, the reproductive success of the population and ultimately of the species – even if, paradoxically, this involves a great deal of killing between members of the species, and between the species and its prey.

These things are not at all imcompatible, however unpleasant they may appear to the tender-hearted god that we have posited as the original problem-maker in this otherwise happily Darwinian universe. In this stage of human existence, where men lived in small hunting groups scattered over the face of the earth with plenty of room in which to move, plenty of space for manoeuvre in the chase and in the skirmishing that in those days passed for warfare – in this stage of existence there was no problem of violence, no problem of aggression. There *was* aggression, and there *was* violence. Both had consequences. But they were not problems. There was eating, and there was copulation. Each equally had consequences. Each equally was not a problem. There were many difficulties (indeed, it may have been a precarious time for the species), and if the difficulties had not been adequately handled, and if those attributes of consciousness – language, art, religion, science, conceptual and classificatory ability and the like – had not been brought freely into play, we would not be here to create problems. True, if all that apparatus had been devoted to problem-solving, we might not be here to solve any more problems; instead, it was devoted to overcoming adaptational difficulties.

The problems arise, therefore, not because of man's self-consciousness; not because of the relationship between that self-consciousness – that thinking, concentrating, classifying aspect of cerebral activity – and the lower brain with its emotional demands; not in conflicts between supergo, ego and id; not in any real evolutionary disjunction between different aspects of man's personality, or between the forebrain and the nervous system. They arise simply from the rapid and bewildering change of context that occurred as a result of the neolithic revolution: the invention of agriculture, the expansion of population, the growth of dense

communities, the beginnings of coercive economies, the origina-
tion of social classes, the founding of nations, and the advent of
industrial society. Nothing in man's nature changed, and nothing
in man's nature is basically at fault – contrary to what many contemporary thinkers would have us believe. There is no war
between the higher sensibilities and mental capacities and the basic
aggressive, instinctive violent perturbations of some unwanted
reptilian pre-existence. When we lived in small hunting groups,
there was a perfect harmony between all these aspects of consciousness and the higher brain: between art, religion, science and
conceptual and mathematical thinking on the one hand, and
hunting, killing and the pursuit of men and animals on the other.
All these higher attributes enabled this curiously successful beast to
be more and more successful. And of course therein lies a paradox.
The very nature of its success meant that it would overreach itself;
and in so doing rapidly destroy, recreate, change – change utterly –
the whole environment for which its violence, its aggression, its
copulation, its eating, its art, science, technology and religion had
been adapted. Neither its violence nor its most exalted religious
thought had developed in order to enable man to live with cities,
armies, industries and social classes. They had been intended for
face-to-face status competition, for rapid skirmishing between
small groups, and for all the intimate, ebullient complexities of the
small-scale tribal existence. The brain that painted the caves of
Altamira was quite good enough to invent moon rockets; it has not
changed in the meantime. The violence in man that drove herds of
horses and ungulates over cliffs by the hundreds, or fought for
diminishing hunting grounds during the glacial periods, was also
quite good enough to win the battle of Waterloo or conduct the
Second World War. That brain could have invented the hydrogen
bomb, and that capacity for violence could have used it. What
presents the problem here is neither the brain nor the capacity for
violence, which when dealing with other small groups of human
beings, and even with herds of mammoths, was acting within its
evolutionary range: what creates the problem is the atom bomb and
the armies and the industrial technology, which are outside this
evolutionary range. Because if the upper paleolithic hunters that
we are continue to behave as though huge armies are skirmishing
bands, as though atom bombs are stone arrowheads, and as
though the destruction of three-quarters of mankind is a raiding

expedition against the next tribe, then we have problems.

But it is not our very nature that is the problem, for that is totally unproblematical. It is not violence that is the problem, for this is part of the unproblematical nature. It is not aggressiveness or killing that are the problem, for these are as natural as copulation and eating. It is the *new context* in which these totally natural activities have to operate that is the problem. The problem is not violence, but warfare; the problem is not aggression, but the stratified societies in which aggression is manifested; the problem is not weapons, but the very scale of the weapons, which if used will destroy even the user. The problem is not even man's capacity for illusion, or his greater capacity for evil; for, again, in the small-scale context both of these are explicable, understandable, useful. It is the scale on which they must operate that makes the illusions dangerous and the evil cruelly destructive instead of merely exciting.

Above all it must be understood, and the need for this understanding is rather desperate, that the problem is not in any way one of violence, but one of human imagination. The human imagination can create incredible systems of symbols because it can imbue natural processes with meaning. It can, for example, create extraordinary gastronomic schemes and rules and rituals of food usage, because it can take a natural activity and out of it create symbolic meaning. Similarly with sex: rules, interdictions, magical incantations, art (or pornography, as we call it), elaborate beliefs and practices can make the simple process of reproductive success into a vast system of meaning. In either, it can create both problems and difficulties for the individuals enmeshed in these systems. By and large, these do not have wholly disastrous consequences, unless the systems get out of hand and, for example, eating or sex is totally forbidden. After all, whatever the systems of meanings, as long as people copulate and eat the species will survive. Similarly, when it comes to the sheer business of making symbols, the human imagination can weave symbolic systems out of symbolic systems. A great deal of religion must be understood as precisely this. In the same way as food and sex can be woven into systems of meaning, so can symbols themselves, because symbol-making is as much a human attribute, and in a curious sense more so, than sex or eating.

But what is perhaps most difficult to grasp is that exactly the same reasoning applies to violence. Like sex, eating or symbol-making, violence is natural and explicable. But the human imagination can take violence in all its natural aspects and, using it like the colours from a painter's palette, create from it elaborate systems of understanding – systems as complex as the sexual intricacies of the Kamasutra, the sexual complexities of protestantism; systems sometimes as baffling as the most intricate philosophy, or religious rituals; systems maybe even as beautiful as those of art, music or dance; systems that, indeed, employ all these others, but culminate in a consummatory act of violence on a scale and magnificence that exceeds anything in any other sphere because it is more terrible, and more profound.

 The problem for the species is not violence itself. The fascination of violence is as real and as profound as the fascination with sex, with food, with the supernatural, and with knowledge, exploration and discovery. And its satisfactions are of much the same kind. The problem lies with the capacity of the human imagination to create its encompassing, consummatory systems with violence as their focus and purpose. We call these systems battles, wars, pogroms, feuds, conquests, revolutions or whatever, and therefore what we must understand is that the problem is not violence, but war; the problem is not aggression, but genocide; the problem is not killing, but battle. And into the organization of war, of battle, of genocide, goes far more by way of imaginative energy than physical violence. Indeed, if one were to do an inventory of the energy expended in a war, the actual physical violence would probably amount to very little. And with modern war this is even more striking. Modern war is almost better understood as an aspect of complex bureaucracy on the one hand and artistic capacity on the other. A quartermaster is as important as a general. A quartermaster – the logistics man – is the super-bureaucrat. He must insure that the battle equipment, and all the men, are in the right place at the right time. Without this the relatively little violence involved would be useless. The general often never sees the field of battle and spends most of his time with maps and communiqués. He is perhaps best likened to a conductor of a vast orchestra of a rather modern piece, in which the tune is hinted at and the orchestration only partially developed, and in which a great deal is left to the conductor himself. (Maybe an even better analogy would be that of a chef who knows roughly what dish he is going to prepare, and so invents a stroganoff as he goes along, and in the end produces something the like of which has never been seen before, mistakes and all.)

The problem here is not violence. The problem here is the use to which violence is put. The problem with puritanism is not sex, but the uses to which sex is put in the control of people. The problem for orthodox jews is not eating, but the imaginative restructuring of the conditions of eating that the religion demands. The problem is not our violent nature, or even the nature of violence, but our violent imaginations, and our imaginative use of violence: an imaginative use that no longer bears any close relation to the evolved conditions of violence – the conditions in which violence is a contained, normal, explicable and unproblematical aspect of our adaptational history as a species.

In thus recreating violence in another image, we are at our most magnificent, most terrible, most inventive and most destructive. We are using at one and the same time the highest intellectual and the highest imaginative capacities. We are also utilizing our deepest resources of compassion, co-operation, courage, love and self-sacrifice, along with our capacities for destruction, hatred, xenophobia, sadism and revenge. But it is the canvas on which these are painted, their orchestration and reorganization, the use to which they are put, the scale on which they operate, the context in which they are organized that is the problem. Neither violence nor compassion are the problem, in and of themselves. When they become caught in the great symphony of war, and large-scale corporate conflict generally; when they become built into the code of the Mafia, or written into the Geneva convention, or woven into the elaborate framework of the rules of warfare of the eighteenth century, then they may become a problem in their own right. This problem cannot be understood by a simple reference to the roots of human nature, to the desire of man to dominate and kill other men, to simple human evil, to innate aggressivity or any other such inborn tendencies, sure as it is that these exist. For 99 per cent of our existence there was and has been a context in which all these could operate and without problems, because this orchestration was pre-ordained, and their imaginative use was therefore constrained. It is only within the last few thousand years that they have become problematical and have caused man to regret his own nature. And, after all, this is an extremely foolish thing to do. Man's nature is all that he has. The lion does not sit about regretting his nature, nor did self-conscious and aware man for 99 per cent of his existence.

He may have bewailed his difficulties, but he saw these not as stemming from his own nature as much as from problems he had in struggling with the total environment, which included, of course, his fellow men.

This bewailing of our own nature is the true alienation of modern man; and by 'modern man' I mean man since the neolithic revolution, and probably even later than that – probably man since the advent of cities and conquest; man particularly since the advent of literacy and class society. For all these are in a very profound sense unnatural to man. Status, hierarchy, aggression, killing – these are in no sense unnatural to him. Armies, warfare, classes, exploitation, alienation – these are all unnatural, in a sense that we must explore more fully. This is not to say that the natural attributes of animals, like the weight of the dinosaur, might not often get them into extreme difficulties. Had such an animal been endowed with self-consciousness, the dinosaur might have bewailed its fate. And there may indeed be a lesson in that. For we have done for ourselves what nature did for the dinosaur: we have created our own weight problem – literally, since it is sheer weight of numbers that is at the root of all our problems and present difficulties. The dinosaur evolved a huge bulk but could not adapt to changing conditions. We have evolved a huge population which is in danger of not being able to do the same. We have evolved along with it a weight of armaments and of ideas that are as dangerous to our survival as the bulk of the dinosaur. That is what our capacity for self-consciousness has managed to do with our natural resources.

This argument does create something of a paradox, because if it is in our nature to be imaginative then we can argue that, in using our imagination to create unnatural conditions, we are only acting in accordance with our nature. This is something like the Cretan liar paradox. I am not too sure how it can be resolved, but in saying that it is not our nature that is at fault, what I am saying is that conditions can be imagined – and, indeed, for that precious 99 per cent of our existence, did exist – in which this nature could operate without problems. Then it was comprehensible and adaptive, and within the natural scheme of things. But because, paradoxically, of one aspect of that nature, we have changed that context for ourselves, and we have added the bulk and weight that threaten to drag us down, that cause our present troubles, and that give rise to the so-called problem of violence. Possibly I will have to admit that our nature is at fault. But it need not have happened. It was certainly not inevitable. We existed for long enough without this albatross around the species's neck.

To return to the crux of my argument, even if we are to blame and bewail our nature, what we should blame and bewail is not the violence *per se*, not aggression *per se*, or hatred, or evil, or sadism *per se*, but man's violent imagination, which enables us to use these in unprecedented, unforeseen and unintended ways – unintended, in the sense that they are not ways appropriate to the small-scale hunting existence for which we were evolved. The flaw in the scheme, then (if we are to look for a flaw, and it seems that, like the Greek dramatists, this is what we are to do) – the Achilles' heel – is our violent imagination. Again, I insist that, in and of itself, this can operate within a context where it is constructive: the orchestration of a paleolithic hunt or a Red Indian raiding party did not threaten any species. But of course the potential was there – the potential for organizing this entirely constructive violence on a scale that threatened not only the species itself, but all the other species as well.

We often hear about the problem of violence in the modern world, about the problem of violence in cities, in the ghetto, in schools; about the problem of seemingly endemic violence in such places as the Middle East and Northern Ireland; about the problem of the apparently ever greater willingness to resort to violence. But, this is not a problem of violence: it is a problem of ghettos, of xenophobia, of capitalism, of economic exploitation, of racial prejudice and a whole host of other things. *These* are the problems. (There is really no problem involved if, when, for example, a person is standing on my foot and refuses, despite all my exhortations, to move, I push him off. After all, I'm faced with only two alternatives: I can either grin and bear it or I can knock him off. If I choose the latter there is no problem involved.) A problem is created when, in our infinite capacity for problem-making, we insist that those who resort to violence to redress grievances have no right to do so because, for example, there are many other channels open to them to right their wrongs.

This argument, of course, can be used endlessly to bolster exploitation. It was an argument used against the followers of George Washington and Padraig Pearse. It is an argument used today against ghetto blacks and Palestinian guerrillas. I am not saying that in all these cases violence is in any abstract sense wholly

justified – I am not interested in justification. This is part of the
elaborate symbol system. To some people violence is never justified. But this is nothing to do with violence. This is to do with
schemes of abstract ideas. The point that I am trying to make is that
in none of these cases does the violence itself present the problem.
The violence is a perfectly natural and useful response. One is at
liberty not to like the response; one is at liberty to prefer some other
response; but one is not at liberty to say that the problem is the
violence as such. In many cases this is simply a way of dodging the
real issues, or dodging the issues to which the violence was a
response.

The violence can be a response in two ways. As a rational,
calculated response it is simply one alternative among others, and
sometimes the only effective one for achieving whatever an individual or a group wants. We have to consider this rational aspect of
violence. Too often, to hide from the problems, we look only at the
purely expressive side of violence. That is another kind of
response: not a rational attempt to gain power or to force a solution
on an opponent, but simply an expression of a state of frustrated
oppression. Even here there is no problem of violence. It is perfectly reasonable in some evolutionary and natural sense for a
cornered animal to strike. To those who deplore this, one can only
quote the French:

Cet animal est très méchant
Quand on l'attaque, il se défend.

To the retort that in many cases these people have not been
physically attacked, one can always say that there are attacks and
attacks. Constant humiliation, constant psychological castration,
constant denial of basic rights and needs is as much an attack as a
smack in the face; insolence is as much an attack as a jab with a
cattle prod.

This may appear to sound like something along the lines of the
aggression–frustration hypothesis, and it is something like that.
But frustration is not the only thing that provokes violence.
Violence itself begets violence, and in perfectly unfrustrated
people. The example of violence is easily imitated. We also know
how easily violence can become endemic – can become a cult. This
business of routinization can apply to almost any human emotion

or activity. Under such circumstances one does not need to be in any way frustrated in order to be attracted by violent activity. The problem lies not with violence but with the human capacity to create cults, and with the context in which these cults must operate. Our dispersed, primitive tribes were not particularly frustrated, but their males – at least a considerable number of their males – certainly enjoyed going on the warpath, and they made of this an elaborate cult activity, connected, as we know, with status within the group. As a consequence of this routinization, this transformation of a natural activity into a symbolic one, young men are enormously attracted to these violent escapades because they expect considerable rewards; because the activity is itself rewarding and pleasurable. It has to do with excitement, the sense of danger, the sense of achievement. As I have emphasized, within its proper context this is, as far as the species is concerned – or even as far as considerable populations of the species that are involved are concerned – a perfectly harmless activity. If some males get killed, it will not affect the breeding potential of the group very much, if at all. In fact, the net effect may be to increase the sexual activity, the spread of genes, and the fertility of the groups concerned. It may even be part of the process of selection within populations which improves their general stock, intelligence, strength and all-round ability.

Again, it is only when this cult activity of violence, which has nothing whatsoever to do with frustration, is taken totally out of context and placed in, for example, the supposedly orderly, rational, law-abiding framework of a modern city that it has the disruptive effect of a Mafia gang or a street mob. In the absence of police, city hall, school systems, welfare services and all the other paraphernalia of a modern, bureaucratic, industrial city, street gangs rapidly reach accommodation with each other, and their system of cultic violence achieves some sort of equilibrium and steady state. Again, it is not the violence. The context of articulation, the new orchestration – the gun, the city block, the police, the politician, the alcohol merchants, the dope pushers – rather than the violence itself, is the real problem. And I am talking now about a problem of understanding, not what I have previously dubbed a 'difficulty'. Certainly, all this violence is a 'difficulty', but it is not in the intellectual sense a problem, whether it be the response in various forms – crude or sophisticated – to frustration and exploitation; whether it is expressive or rational; or whether it is cultic organization of violence which seems self-rewarding and exciting on the one hand, and rationally rewarding in terms of status on the other. It is all perfectly understandable, and presents no problem. It is what men do. If you take a group of men and oppose them in some way to another group of men, the likelihood of their coming up with a violent way of distinguishing themselves the one from the other, and of organizing themselves internally, is very high. This is not to say that in many cases groups do not exist that have other than violent solutions: we are talking here about probabilities, and the probabilities are extremely high. If a violent solution is not sought, it is usually because of a threat of even greater violence from some other source. Then again, throughout, the problem is not one of violence, and to pose it as such is to avoid asking the real questions.

And this leads us on to a further consideration, since I have been talking repeatedly about *provoking*, or calling forth, violence: the extent to which violence is an appetite, like hunger or sex. First we must consider whether hunger and sex are even comparable. We must remember that all these three activities are located in the same circuit of the brain and, indeed, the sparking off of one of these three often leads to the arousal of another. But with sex and hunger we have a problem; for, as far as the individual organism is concerned, whereas it can do without sex and still survive, it cannot, clearly, do without food. Sex could perhaps be considered as an appetite like hunger if we consider the species, rather than the individual: the species will not survive unless it reproduces itself, and in this sense, the individual must reproduce to survive in the same way that he must eat to live.

If one is deprived of food for long enough, a great need for it is aroused, much stronger than the need for it if one is being regularly fed. Similarly with sex. This will be disputed, and, of course, individual capacities differ enormously. Sex may be desperately necessary to some people and not necessary at all to others, with the vast majority lying somewhere in between. Of course, sex must differ in some profound way from hunger since it is possible, as Freud pointed out so brilliantly, to sublimate sexuality; that is, to substitute other activities for sex, which would be difficult to do for very long in the case of food. But we can see that, although unlike hunger sex does not impose a constant daily demand on the individual, the individual must be motivated to want to reproduce in order for the species to survive.

A well-fed individual can be aroused by the thought of a delicious meal, or the sight of a particularly tasty dish. Similarly with sex: even in the absence of any craving or frustration, an individual can be aroused by fairly straightforward erotic stimuli. On the other hand, if systematically frustrated and subjected to erotic stimuli, an individual is likely to burst out in rather violent sexual activity. It seems to me that there is really no harm, and a good deal of common sense, in regarding violence similarly. To some extent, the individual has to be capable of, and easily aroused to, violence in order to survive. But this is more like sex than like hunger: one does not need it all day and every day, but on the occasions that one does need it, it has to be easily facilitated. Both sexual desire and the lust for combat, as it were, have to lie somewhere near the surface.

These basic motivations can be tampered with and deeply interfered with, since there is nothing rigid or instinctive, in the old sense, about them. They are highly malleable drives. They can be reflected, suppressed, sublimated and subjected to all the other manipulations psychologists describe so well. But they cannot be eradicated. With sufficient punishment, or with sufficient bribery, one can suppress them, but one could do so in the long run only with great damage to the integration and stability of the rest of the organism's behaviour. To use the modern slang expression that is extremely expressive, we can say that the human animal is very easily 'turned on' to sex and violence. And while not every human animal is exactly the same in this respect, it would be very rare human beings indeed who had *no* propensity to violence and *no* attraction to sexual activity. Critics to this point of view are very fond of pointing out that the wickedness of its proponents is subtly visited upon the whole species: because, for example, my friends and I are easily turned on by violence, we assume the rest of the world is the same. I have a great many friends who are not all that easily turned on by violence, but none who are not turned on at all, although such people must exist; I have some friends who are extremely timid about sex, but none who would maintain that they are not turned on somewhat by the appropriate erotic stimuli. But then, no one suggests that sex drives and sex needs do not exist, as a great many people wish to do with violent drives and violent needs. (I am always very curious about the lives of these loquacious pacifists who, certainly in print and very often in their personal behaviour, are most extraordinarily violent people.)

The human capacity for illusion, the human imagination, the human conceptual schemes certainly allow us to arrange communities of people who deplore violence, and maybe even deny its reality, and certainly outlaw it. Similar communities have existed that have outlawed sex, and it is obvious that they cannot survive by the normal processes of reproduction. They tend, in fact, not to survive as viable communities. But we recognize the absurdity of hoping to produce any kind of organic community (as opposed for example to some kind of association like a monastery) by outlawing sex. It is probably equally self-evident, if we really look it in the face, that it is very difficult for communities to exist that totally outlaw violence, and indeed, the very fact that they need these elaborate precautions suggests, as do the elaborate precautions that surround any attempts to suppress sexual activity, that what is being dealt with and denied is real and persistent.

This way of looking at violence, as very similar in some respects to sex, gives us a hope for dealing with it. For if we see it as something with appetitive elements, but which basically requires 'turning on' for full arousal, then it is open to us to engineer a low-key system of arousal. Thus, in any ongoing community we can expect a certain amount of sexual activity, because people enjoy it and, even if not particularly stimulated, will still want it. We also know that cultures that bombard members with erotic stimuli will produce high levels of sexual activity, far beyond what is necessary for pleasure or reproduction. Similarly, we can expect that in any normal ongoing organic community there will be a certain level of violence, both among the members of the community and towards others. We can also recognize communities that have effected the institutionalization of violence, its elevation to a cult status, its glorification, its frequent representation in symbolic forms and artistic performances, its constant evocation, and its justification at the highest religious and philosophical levels. In such a community, because its members as a result of their evolutionary history must be easily turned on to violence, we would indeed find many times the normal level of violent activity.

Thus to insist that violence is normal, natural and unproblematical when seen in its proper evolutionary perspective is not to say that extremely high levels of destructive, pointless, irrational, emotive, cruel and barbaric violence are normal, necessary or in any sense desirable any more than to say that, since sex is a normal, explicable and unproblematical evolutionary activity, constant orgies and elaborate but non-reproductive perversions are also normal, or to be expected in every organic community of humans. Man needs sex, not orgies; in the same way man needs violence, but not the massacre of innocents. Therefore to accept the nature of violence in the way I am suggesting it should be accepted is not at all to accept the inevitability of certain extreme forms of violence. Which brings us to the question of the control and the regulation of violence, the rules of violence – perhaps what one might even call the *inherent* rules of violence.

In much the same way as violence itself is a natural attribute, so the regulation of violence is an equally natural attribute. Again, the analogy with sex may be argued. The propensity for sexual activity is of course natural, but so is the propensity to regulate it. There is a long evolutionary argument behind this argument which states, briefly, that it is a major characteristic of man that he will formulate rules about the things which most concern him. Food, sex and violence are of course high on this list. But it may go deeper than this; for it may be that the conscious and even elaborate rules that men make are not something that self-conscious and aware culture imposes on a crude and vicious nature, but are themselves a product of that nature. These rules and regulations, in other words, are the labels that speaking men use for the kinds of behaviour that non-language men would have indulged in anyway. Roughly, the issue is that even non-language men did not fight without rules, any more than they copulated without codes. These may not have been explicit, but they existed; and when he came to speak and to symbolize man gave them expression. In other words, the rules of fighting are as natural as the fighting itself. Given symbolic capacity, men can play elaborate games with these rules, in a way that a non-symbolizing animal could not. But the fact that he is moved as strongly to regulate as he is to fight is another intriguing source of hope. Because man is as turned on by rules and regulations, even when he opposes them, as he is by sex, food and the joy of combat. Left to his own devices, in other words, man would regulate his sex and violence with as much relish as he copulates and fights.

I have said that this goes deeper than cultural and symbolic activity, and indeed it is perhaps one of the greatest contributions of the ethologists to show us how animals 'ritualize' their violent behaviour. They can perhaps be criticized for over-emphasizing this ritualization and for ignoring the real violence that does occur; but what they have pointed out is that within a species there are strong tendencies to turn potentially sanguinary and death-dealing combat into a ritualized game. It does not always work, but the tendency is there and it is strong, and the more violent and better armed the species, the greater the tendency. It all works within limits – real violence is still prevalent – but the limits are interesting. The fact that they should exist is hopeful. For in man also, by nature a creature easily aroused to violence and obviously gaining enormous satisfactions from its expression, the same tendency exists, and exists strongly. And what is perhaps amazing about this violent species of ours is not that we kill so many, but that, given our potential, we kill so few and so infrequently. And this is not because we are not violent, or because we can easily substitute passivity for violent activity, but because we inherently develop ritualized means to regulate violence. And we perhaps now should ask how this operates. We should address ourselves, in other words, not to the question of violence, the so-called 'problem of violence' which we understand really very well, but to the question of the *regulation* of violence – equally basic, and equally natural. The real question for research is: why, if this regulation is so basic and so natural, do we seem to find such difficulty with it?

We must then ask about the conditions for the ritualization of violence; that is, about any processes that serve to minimize the sanguinary outcome of violent conflict. Under many circumstances this reaches almost absurd heights, whereby the conflict, even involving hundreds of thousands of people, has virtually no sanguinary outcome whatsoever, despite all the panoply of war, and the seemingly savage intentions of the participants. At the other extreme, there seem to be no regulations whatsoever, and the outcome is mayhem, massacre, and the slaughter of millions. Which, we might ask, is nearer to that 'normal' state which is always at the back of our discussion? I think there is no doubt that a relatively highly regulated state is a normal one. It is a state in which violence and killing occur, but in which the degree of regulation is high, and the sanguinary outcome relatively minor. I must repeat that this is not to deny the violent nature of man, but to add this extraordinarily important qualification: that in his natural setting he'll eat his violent cake and have it. He will have all the benefits of violence without excessive mortuary consequences – all the excitement, the danger, the exploration, the comradeship, the compassion, the daring, the beauty and the glory, but as little as possible of the death. Even so, the reality of death must always be present, for this is never a mere game, much as it may often approach one. (That is why, whatever its popularity, football can never have the religious fascination of bullfighting.)

What then are the conditions of successful ritualization? This is always relative. When we say that the outcome is only a 'minor' amount of killing, this depends on the scale involved. When two armies of 100,000 are facing each other, and after the supposed battle is over 2,000 or 3,000 are left dead, one must suppose this to be a relatively small number in terms of what might have been the case. But it is not usually upon such a scale that violence operates, but rather upon a very small scale — a scale, in fact, on which we evolved. Within any small community, there cannot be too much sanguinary conflict without draining the population of its re-sources and its manpower, and eventually effectively injuring its chances of survival as a community. Therefore, within community boundaries there is a strong immediate urge to regulate the violence that is bound to occur.

There is always the tendency to regulate, even though it does not always work. No one would want to claim that these regulatory activities were all successful. But there is a persistent tendency for them to operate. In all communities there are some standard ways of engaging in relatively violent conflict, while limiting its incidence and modifying its outcome. The duel and single combat are the prototypes. In some communities, like the Pueblo Indian, where these forms of ritualized violence are not allowed – where the regulatory attempt is a blanket prohibition of violent activity – the result is a high level of personal, expressive violence, which, from its very unregulated nature, can be very dangerous. Also, there are often extremely high levels of communal violence, as in the persecution and beating to death of witches. The Pueblos might turn out to be excellent examples not of the perfectly harmonious pacifist communities they are often taken to be, but of precisely how *not* to deal with violence. We should look rather to those many examples of communities in which fighting of one sort or another occurs but within an explicitly or implicitly defined and often sanctified set of rules and regulations that allow the combatants all they need by way of expressive violent activity. When does this work, and when does it break down?

Moving from the small to the large scale, we can reinterpret the history and current state of warfare to try to understand the ratio of negotiation to combat, and the conditions under which the elaborate regulation and restriction of warfare evolves. This approach would not so much look for the 'causes' of war – it would assume that wars occur for many reasons – but would concentrate on searching out the factors that lead to the regulation and restriction and ultimately containment of war. Its assumption would be perhaps a variation of Clausewitz's dictum: it would assume that war is diplomacy's way of creating more diplomacy, since men love the treaties and negotiations at least as much and probably more than they love the combat. To this end, wars cannot be allowed to get out of hand, or diplomacy would suffer.

I venture a rough-hewn hypothesis: where 'pure dominance' is involved – a simple matter of who is top nation, tribe or kingdom – the rules, negotiations and displays proliferate; where 'real interests' (territory, population, women) are involved, the rules break down and we approach mayhem. The basic hypothesis behind this one – that men are as attached to the rules as to the killing, and that other things being equal they will minimize the killing in favour of the display – is precariously hopeful. Other things are equal more often than we imagine; it could be much worse; and, given the awesome possibilities, we may be living in something close to the best of all possible worlds.

Note

On the evolutionary argument behind the role of the neo-cortex as an inhibitor, not only of the capacity but of the *drive* to make rules about basic behaviours, see Robin Fox, *The Red Lamp of Incest*, New York: Dutton, 1980; London: Hutchinson, 1981 – particularly chapters 6 and 7.

CHAPTER 3

The Language of Violence

Sociological perspectives on adolescent aggression

David Downes

Violence has rarely been singled out as a theme in the sociology of crime and delinquency. Sociological definitions of violence rarely stray beyond that of lay common sense: it consists of the inflicting of injury on persons or property in a manner proscribed by the criminal law. In accounting for violence, however, sociologists in general share a presumption frequently at odds with lay theory: that violence (to adapt Clausewitz, on war) is an extension of communication by other means. Violence is presumed to share with other forms of social behaviour the properties of rationality, motive and meaning: to presume their absence is to abdicate the sociological task. Its many forms have in general been addressed as one element (albeit the most dramatic feature) of what has been taken to be the *real* problem, that is, the 'way of life' that entails the commission of many kinds of law- and rule-breaking.[1]

The sources of knowledge about violence, unfortunately, lend themselves only fitfully to the discovery and analysis of these

[1] Limited support for this assumption can be found in a recent study from the Vera Institute of Justice: 'Violent acts appear, for the most part, to be occasional occurrences within a random pattern of deviant behaviour, rather than a "speciality" of juveniles. . . . The great majority of violent delinquents are not psychotic or otherwise seriously disturbed emotionally, although many are neurotic and characterised by poor impulse controls.' Paul A. Strasburg, *Violent Delinquents*, Monarch Books, 1978, pp. 78–9.

properties. Documentary sources, such as official criminal statistics, are now viewed with such grave suspicion for their errors of omission and commission[2] that there is a danger that even their more reliable aspects[3] will be dismissed out of hand. Even were they to be granted full validity, however, they cannot yield those properties essential for an understanding of the meanings of violence. The retrospective eliciting of accounts of violence, by the use of self-report, victim surveys or interviews from the actors involved or observers, takes us nearer that goal; but such accounts, depending on the skill of the researcher, are still subject to the vagaries of recall, impression management and selective memory. Accounts of violence at first hand would seem to offer all the ingredients missing from these approaches: a sense of immediate context, violence as an 'emergent property' of interaction, and so forth. Sadly, even with all participants assembled for scrutiny, seemingly intractable problems abound: the accounts of what led to violence rarely match and often differ quite markedly; disagreements can obtain even on 'what happened' a few minutes before; the observer may be faced with a quite genuine ignorance about why or how the violence had occurred at all. Moreover, such accounts of violence on the move are uncommonly hard to find, and there are perfectly straightforward reasons why this should be so: the very presence of an 'observer' may inhibit the expression of violence; for the great majority of so-called delinquent groups, violence may be exceedingly rare; and some sites of violence (the family being the obvious example) are effectively off-stage and out-of-reach of coventional observational work.[4] Sociologists have

[2] See in particular Steven Box, *Deviance, Reality and Society,* Holt, Rinehart & Winston, 1971, chs. 3 and 6.
[3] For a revaluation of the 'reality' of the official criminal statistics, see R. Mawby (ed.) *Policing the City,* Saxon House, 1979. For a trenchant critique of self-report studies of delinquency, see Albert J. Reiss, Jr, 'Inappropriate theories and inadequate methods as policy plagues: self-reported delinquency and the law', in N.J. Demerath III *et al.* (eds), *Social Policy and Sociology,* Academic Press, 1975, pp. 211–22.
[4] See, for example, the account by James Patrick of a pub fight (pp. 30–1) and his discussion of its implications (pp. 202 et seq.) in *A Glasgow Gang Observed,* Eyre Methuen, 1973, 'The boys responsible for the assault could think of no motive of any kind to explain their actions, and neither could I. . . . Not only were the marginals terrified by the core members of the gang, but the leaders were disturbed by aspects of their own behaviour

of late begun to grapple more effectively with these problems; but in the face of them, it is not too surprising that theoretical ingenuity has characteristically outstripped the capacity of empirical work to support or refute them.

The starting point for sociological theories of adolescent aggression, therefore, is the assumption that violence can be read, appreciated, decoded – in short, understood – and that theories cast in terms of irrationality, mob psychology, individual pathology and simple instrumentality are to be rejected as incapable of explaining the social meanings of violence. This assumption alone lends consistency to what is otherwise a bewildering array of competing perspectives. It is, needless to say, open to challenge on a number of counts; for example that much violence emanates from the mentally ill, whose hold on rationality is arguably tenuous; or that such an approach involves what Gellner[5] has elsewhere termed 'contextual over-charitability' (i.e. the presumption that some semblance of rationality can be adduced to account for all acts of violence, however bizarre, rules out all possibility of sheer absurdity or ambiguity in social life). All that can be said here is that the various perspectives meet such criticisms in varying ways, but that ultimately no perspective adequately disposes of them. Thus far, sociological theories can claim little more than that the assumption of rationality has generated insights into violence more illuminating than those that have flowed from the reverse proposition. It should be added that, in evaluating the worth of these insights, reference may be made to the capacity of theories to account for *variations* in the character and extent of adolescent aggression, both over time and between societies. The difficulty

for which they could find no rational explanation. . . .' (p. 202). Since Patrick's book, some attention has been given to the intense significance attached to 'body talk' and the elaboration of licensed 'nutter' roles in youth groups – but to make sense of violence after the event often involves a marked stretching of accounts to fit interpretive schemes. In general, however, sociologists reject the 'sociopathic' explanations of youth violence in the work of Patrick and Yablonsky, if only because of the circularity involved in accounting for violence by recourse to a 'condition' that is manifested primarily in the violence it is intended to explain.

[5] Emert Gellner, 'Concepts and society', in I.C. Jarvie and J. Agassi (eds), *Cause and Meaning in the Social Sciences*, Routledge & Kegan Paul, 1973.

involved in elucidating these variations compound those involved in inferring motivation at a particular place and time.

Without wanting to assert that what follows is an exhaustive taxonomy of theorizing in the juvenile delinquency and youthful violence field, there seem to be five perspectives that offer distinctive causal models, images of deviance, theories of meaning and motives, assumptions about the relations between the individual and society and – finally – implications for policy and/or praxis. Each imbue violence with a different *expressive* yield for the actors concerned. The distinctive concerns of these perspectives can be traced back to 'parent' theories in mainstream sociology, which in turn bear different preference and aversions for various methods of research. Few theorists, however, adhere stringently to one perspective alone, and usually they take elements from two or more in attempting syntheses of previously disparate accounts. The perspectives concerned are grouped under the following terms: strain, labelling, control, culture conflict and class conflict.

STRAIN

Strain theories are built on the assumption that industrial political democracies harness their entire populations into striving after certain common ends, notably what Merton termed 'money success', though other theorists, such as Albert Cohen, substituted social status in much the same model. Anomie (i.e. deviance of various kinds) enters in because only a minority of the populations can attain this culturally prescribed goal. Acquisitive crime, especially of the organized quasi-business variety, which would entail the instrumental use of violence, was seen by Merton as one of the principal ways in which individuals would seek to attain it, albeit by illegal means. Merton's basic argument was that anomie prevails because, despite the propensity to conform, ultimately a large minority find the tension born of the discrepancy between ends and means intolerable. They seek to redress the balance by juggling with one or the other, by rejecting both, or by seeking an alternative social order.

Anomie theory held sway for almost two decades. It seemed to fit the problems of the Depression years in America, in which unemployment rose to 12 million while the Hollywood Dream

Factory poured out images of glittering prizes effortlessly attained. A decade after 1945, moreover, not only had youth gang violence stubbornly refused to disappear: it had apparently assumed more virulent forms. Albert Cohen noted the inability of anomie theory to account for what seemed the cardinal feature of most serious delinquency: its *expressive* and *collective* qualities. He characterized what he termed the delinquent subculture as non-utilitarian, malicious, negativistic, hedonistic, versatile and built on prime loyalty to the gang. Fighting, vandalism and general hell-raising were just as prominent as theft: even theft lacked the purposive character of adult crime. Cohen sought the rationale for this apparently motiveless and meaningless behaviour in the problems faced by the sector of society apparently most involved: lower-class, male, urban adolescents. He found their source in the Catch 22, many-are-called-but-few-are-chosen character of democratic schooling. Schools exist to make children care about status and achievement, but then deny it to all but a minority of working-class children. The delinquent gang enables the rejected both to acquire status in a form more accessible to them *and* to hit back at the system that branded them as failures. The rules of the gang are those of respectable society turned upside down: the D-stream's revenge. By contrast, the middle class generally 'make it'; for girls, occupational success is less salient; and in non-urban areas it has less sway.

Cohen's subcultural theory quickly provoked variants and alternatives. The most immediately relevent were those of Cloward and Ohlin, and Matza. Cloward and Ohlin's study was arguably the most influential academic source of the American 'War on Poverty' strategy, which sought to expand the 'opportunity structure' of the inner city and therby reduce delinquency and allied social problems. (As such, it also indirectly led to the Lilliputian Community Development Projects in Britain later in the 1960s.) They proposed much the same structurally based 'frustration–aggression' model of delinquency causation as Cohen, but argued that three tyes of delinquent subculture arose in different types of neighbourhood: criminal (gangs pursuing utilitarian forms of theft); conflict (the fighting gang) and retreatist (drug-using gangs). They also argued that the school was largely irrelevant to those most involved in serious gang delinquency: far more central was the economic pursuit of 'money–success' earlier stressed by Merton, which they reinstated as the primary source of embittered frustration in the downtown slum areas of metropolitan America.[6]

Matza equivocates in his handling of strain theory, both roundly condemning it (along with all prior work) for 'over-predicting delinquency', for accounting for far more of it than exists, and at the same time retaining some of its most central features, notably the stress on group processes, and – in his assertion that 'preparation' and 'desperation' are preludes to delinquency in certain areas – conjuring up a sense of strain just as marked as those theorists he rejects. Matza's major achievement is to build his theory of delinquency around the axiom that it is *willed* behaviour, and in general intermittent and mundane. Boys *drift* into delinquency rather than being propelled into it by circumstances; instead, a 'subculture of delinquency' is a set of precepts that facilitate rather than bind, as the delinquent caricatures commonly held values rather than adhering to oppositional ones. Central to his theory of delinquency is the view that 'subterranean' values are common property rather than a minority cult. The pursuit of excitement, the disdain for routine work and the equation of toughness and masculinity are in combination enough for males in the limbo of adolescence to manufacture excitement by law-breaking. In attempting to assess the relevance of the American theories to the situation in East London in the early 1960s, it seemed to me that Matza came closest to capturing the general run of delinquency: the sporadic joy-riding, petty thefts, occasional fights and acts of vandalism. All that needed chaning was to emphasize the class-based character of youth culture, and to stress the intense charge that working class adolescents bring to their leisure (even when, as Corrigan has so vividly perceived, 'nothing' is going on).

Whether or not, or just how fully, Matza's theory fits run-of-the-mill delinquency, there is little doubt that it characteristically 'under-predicts' the most serious youth violence. Far too elliptically,

---

[6] James F. Short and F.L. Strodtbeck's *Group Process and Gang Delinquency*, Chicago University Press, 1965, is the most rigorous of the many attempts to test these propositions. Then Chicago research confirmed the existence of 'conflict' and 'retreatist' subculture, though 'pure' criminal subcultures were not found even in the worst delinquency areas. Their main conclusion was that gang boys did not adhere to a clear-cut oppositional system of values, but struggled to align their basically lower-class culture with affirmations of the desirability of certain middle-class alternatives.

'desperation' is weighed in to account for it. That will not do as an explanation of, for example,

> [the] fact that homicide is the leading cause of death among young black males in the U.S.A.; indeed, it continues to be a significant cause of death right up through middle age. Thus, if you are a 15 year old black American male, your chances of being a homicide victim sometime before you reach 55 are 30 out of a thousand – more than triple the risk of your dying from tuberculosis. . . . Accidents, suicide, homicide: deaths from violence in one form or another account for three out of four male deaths in this age group.[7]

I do not have comparable figures for the UK, but, as Ian Taylor has recently reminded us, 'the winter of 1978–9 has involved at least five homicides [of blacks living in the East End of London]'.[8] And Willis notes in his study of motorbike boys, that the club showed 'fantastic' death rates.[9] Obviously, even allowing for Northern Ireland, the rates of violence between the two societies are vastly different. But it may be that the historic conditions that underwrote those differences are shifting with what look like the beginnings of a long-term deterioration in youth employment, especially in the inner city; and with black minority groups at risk of being used as scapegoats for what are fundamentally structural changes.

LABELLING

Labelling theories in some ways complement, in others radically contradict, strain theories. Becker, Lemert, Cicourel and other theorists in the labelling tradition, broadly conceived, were the first to approach the societal reaction to deviant behaviour as a *variable*, not a constant; and to argue that the relationships that developed between deviants and social controllers are in themselves important influences that help to shape and transform deviant pheno-

---

[7] Victor R. Fuchs, *Who Shall Live?* Basic Books, 1974, pp. 41–2. I am indebted to Robert Scott for this reference.
[8] Ian Taylor, 'Two new departures in the analysis of youth violence', *British Journal of Criminology*, July 1979, p. 276.
[9] Paul Willis, *Profane Culture*, Routledge & Kegan Paul, 1978, p. 205, n. 4.

mena. Dramatic analogies played a major part in the models of
deviance and control that flowed from his perspective: the process
of *becoming* deviant was conceived in terms of the gradual
construction of a role and an identity that mirrored the conventional career. The early emphasis was on the amplificatory
potential of social control on deviance: the maladroit agencies of the
state created far more deviance than would otherwise exist by
criminalizing morally disturbing activities (e.g. certain forms of
drug use); by mobilizing bias and unduly heavy penalties against
groups low in power and status; and by attributing quite spurious
and stigmatizing features to deviant groups. As Young stressed,
the media in particular could be singled out as promoting stereo-
typical images of the deviant, which are then contrasted with a
picture of 'normality' that is over-typical. The result is to polarize
society into a conforming majority and a deviant minority, a
dynamic process that helps create a self-fulfilling prophecy, since
those to whom deviance is attributed become both objectively and
subjectively more at risk: they are subjected to forms of exclusion
(from jobs, housing, recreation) that worsen their situation; and are
under pressure to collude with the majority view that they are
'essentially' deviant.

British sociologists have contributed strongly to this perspective,
and in Stan Cohen's study of the 'moral panic' induced by the
Mods and Rockers conflict in the mid-1960s we have a repository of
the nuances of social control of at least one moment in British social
history. Loose stylistic associations were metaphorically transformed into tightly knit gangs. Ideal-typical 'folk-devils' were
created: the youth who offered to pay his fine by cheque was
extolled as a symbol of youthful affluence, defiance and indifference to authority. Even non-events became news: towns
'held their breath' for invasions that did not materialize. Cohen
argues that the sensationalistic treatment of the initial events
sensitized far more adolescents on the fringes of the Mods and
Rockers scene to a novel form of action than would have been the
case with more modest and realistic reportage.

More recent work in this perspective had tended to align it with
class and culture conflict theories (Hall *et al.*; Gill) or with functional
approaches (Marsh). All stress the inadequacy of labelling theory
alone to account for the phenomena concerned, but see it as
addressing an essential dimension missing from previous theo-

rizing. Thus, Gill is concerned to trace the emergence of 'Luke St' as a delinquency area from the initial policy, which concentrated the largest available publicly owned housing into one small neighbour-hood and then decanted into it families already classified as 'problems', who faced considerable difficulties owing to large family size, low incomes and high unemployment. Adverse label-ling impinged on the lives of the relatively large number of adolescents who came of age together in this context in various cumulative ways. Coming from the 'worst' area of Liverpool, they found even 'dead end' jobs withheld; episodes of street delin-quency were given wide press coverage, which reinforced the stereotype; local youth clubs banned them; they were, or at least *felt*, subject to unusually fierce police harrassment. Gross exclusion fuelled a sense of local territoriality, which in one episode – Bonfire Night – escalated into a running battle with the police.

In *Policing the Crisis*, Hall and his colleagues see the 'mugging' scare of the early and mid-1970s as a classic instance of the 'moral panic'. The novelty of the term 'mugging' in an English context gave it wide journalistic currency; and the conflation of disparate offences of robbery with violence gave the crime figures for certain areas a dramatic if short-lived increase. The combination of black assailants and white victims aroused particular alarm. Hall *et al.* argue that the rise was largely spurious, yet came at a conjuncture of economic and political crisis which led to its adoption as a symbol of declining law-and-order. This in turn was held to justify tough ,policing measures, and deflected attention from deeper structural issues. At the same time, they argue, 'Crime is one perfectly pre-dictable and quite comprehensible consequence of this process [the deteriorating position of black labour]'. [10] If this proposition is valid, there is little need to invoke the 'crisis of hegemony' to account for the reaction.

In their study of soccer hooliganism, Marsh and his colleagues argue that it is basically a ritualized form of aggression ('aggro') which would escalate into real violence only rarely were it not for the disruption of group-controlled processes by outside agencies, particularly the police. In a shrewd assessment of the dynamics of such hooliganism, they explain the apparently 'schizoid' accounts of their behaviour in terms of a 'conspiracy' by soccer fans. Fans

[10] Stuart Hall *et al.*, *Policing the Crisis*, Macmillan, 1978, p. 390.

claim that those they oppose 'get their heads kicked in': but miraculously the victims are 'all right – usually, anyway'.[11]

> In conspiring to construct a reality which seems to be at variance with their tacit knowledge of orderly and rule-governed action, fans are engaged in the active creation . . .of excitement. For fans, regularity and safety are things to be avoided. . . . What the soccer terraces offer is a chance to escape from the dreariness of the weekday world of work or school to something which is adventurous and stimulating. But in order to achieve the contrast it is necessary to construe, at least at one level, the soccer terraces as being radically different from the weekday world.

The media collude with the conspiracy. The police play a more complicated role, since the fans script them in to defuse a situation without loss of face to themselves. Should the police either over- or under-react, by implication, things go awry. This chimes extremely well with Matza's notion of delinquency as the 'manufacture of excitement', as a contrast to the routine of everyday life.

As yet, labelling theorists seem to be most at home in instances where social control resembles over-kill, deviance is largely spurious, and the media offer easy analytic meat with hopelessly over-written editorials. But what about cases where the boot really does go in, where the police behave with exemplary restraint, where people really are victimized? Would a total ban on all crime reporting make the slightest difference? Phil Cohen and Dave Robins assert the vitality of a soccer hooliganism folk-lore that by-passes the media altogether. Scull has documented the extent to which the changes in drug use in Britain preceded any media or control culture reaction. One need not labour the point, but it does recur in studies that take too 'mediacentric' a view of deviancy. That said, the labelling perspective has transformed deviancy studies from a somewhat naive and almost exclusive focus on deviant events to a far more realistic inclusion of the highly variable reactions that such events elicit.

[11] P. Marsh *et al.*, *The Rules of Disorder*, Routledge & Kegan Paul, 1978, pp. 83–4 *et seq.*

CONTROL

Control theories are only slightly concerned with accounting for the character of and motivation underlying delinquency and aggression: they are assumed to be immanent properties of mankind, welling up whenever the psychological and social controls that curb them are absent, weak, or for any reason disturbed. In the field of behavioural psychology, the theory of crime and personality of Eysenck is a good example: the neurotic extrovert is most resistant to conditioning; therefore is most likely to be criminal. In sociology, Durkheim is probably the classic instance: anomie blossoms in the pursuit of 'infinite aspirations', to which men are doomed when social regulation is weakened (as in economic boom or slump). Of late, control theories have had a considerable revival: in the work of Hirschi, Nettler and Box; in the 'defensible space' theory of Oscar Newman; in the onslaught against labelling theory by Patricia Morgan; and in empirical work on crime and technical opportunity. In a sense, we are all control theorists, in so far as we lock our doors at night, prefer a car with a steering lock to one without an anti-theft device, and so on. The assumption is that the quantum of crime can be reduced by a combination of increased surveillance and diminished opportunity. Oscar Newman argues that technology militates against social processes of control in the high-rise type of housing development, which destroys the scope for informal control of the street, and creates instead deserted under-passes and bleak throughways, architectural equivalents of 'no man's land'. In such terrain, crime can flourish unchecked (a view that echoes the concern some years ago about 'indifference phenomena' in the USA – people ignoring cries for help but turning up the TV). In the work of the control theorists in general, violence is a resource people withhold as long as their attachments to society are secure, and/or the controls governing its expression are strong: however, not much attempt is made to account for the *nature* of the aggression that occurs, except in terms very similar to those of strain and labelling theories.

CULTURE CONFLICT

Culture conflict theories explain aggressive delinquency mainly by

reference to the sheer magnitude of the cultural differences
between the middle and working classes (without implying any
necessary built-in antagonism, as do class conflict theories, and
without implying that working-class adolescents are significantly
influenced by middle-class culture, as do strain theorists). They
share with control theorists a view of the dominant society as
unable to gain any effective purchase on the hearts and minds of
the working class: but in their view, this is because working-class
culture is so profoundly lodged as (in Miller's view) the result of a
'generations-old, shaking-down process' born of industrialization
and urbanization, and little affected as yet by the changes and
reforms so often heralded as tending towards classlessness.

Miller's theory (in many ways the inheritance of Thrasher's view
of the gang in the work of the Chicago School) simply argues that
lower-class group delinquency, far from representing a 'counter-
culture', is the direct, intensified expression of the dominant
culture pattern of the lower-class community: 'a long established,
distinctively patterned tradition with an integrity of its own'. This
culture comprises six 'focal concerns': *trouble* (the tension between
law-abiding and law-violating behaviour); *toughness* (masculinity–
effeminancy); *smartness* (sharp-wittedness–dull-wittedness);
excitement (activity–passivity); *fate* (luck–being unlucky); *autonomy*
(independence–dependency). To Miller, engagement with these
'concerns' tends to involve lower-class adolescents in a head-on
clash with the dominant society, whose legal code is underwritten
by middle-class values. Moreover, since its members are likely to
be brought up in female-based households, where little reliance is
placed on the stability and earning power of the male, the gang
helps resolve problems of sexual identification by providing a
framework for the pursuit of masculine status and reassurance.

Miller claims much empirical support for his theory; notably, a
high proportion of aggressive acts in street-corner groups that take
place within the group are verbally but not physically aggressive,
and rarely hit against middle-class or even adult targets – signs that
ambivalence about status in those terms in negligible. Most delinquency is non-violent, and theft accounts for a higher proportion
than any kind of assault: such delinquency is, however, rare in
itself. Violence, when it does occur, is a response to perceived
insults and/or rejection by other groups (at times local institutions),
not a random outpouring of senseless aggression. It is a source of

group cohesion, and an affirmation of group values, rather than a springboard for hostility against 'society', the 'adult world' or 'middle-class values'. An age-old culture conflict is being played out which is largely immune to surface changes to do with political radicalism, youth culture and drug use. His most recent analysis of such delinquency concludes:

> At the beginning of the period [the 1950s] youth gangs, some quite violent, flourished throughout the nation, particularly in slum areas of the largest cities. At the end [the 1970s] the basic forms and characteristic pursuits of these gangs, while certainly reflecting the changing fashions of the larger adolescent subculture, showed a high degree of continuity.[12]

A similar type of explanation is afforded by Oscar Lewis's concept of the culture of poverty. Generated by the experience of poverty, this culture allegedly takes much the same form whatever the national or structural context. Whether it is studied in Buenos Aires, Glasgow or New York, the same combination of values is observed: a refusal, amounting to an inability, to defer gratification; a stress on machismo, a combination of sexual virility and masculine honour, and a profound fatalism about the possibility of influencing events. Violence, particularly as a result of the impugning of masculinity and honour, finds fertile soil in this culture.

There are several counterparts to these theories, and the theme of masculine consciousness as lending aggression real legitimacy recurs from the work of the Chicago School onwards. The work of John Mays in Liverpool resembles that of Miller. John McVicar refers to 'crude machismatic values' as central to the delinquent subculture to which he was attracted. Paul Willis discerns throughout the culture of motorbike boys a concern with the elaboration of masculine imagery, of a kind that

> owed nothing to the conventional notion of the healthy masculine life. . . . Valued traits of this code . . . such as impudence before authority, domination of women, humilia-

[12] W. Miller, 'Youth gangs in the urban crisis era', in J.F. Short, Jr, *Delinquency, Crime and Society,* Chicago University Press, 1976, p. 118.

tion of the weaker, aggression towards the different, would be abhorrent to *traditional* proponents of honour, and would be labelled criminal by agents of social control. [13]

In early rock and roll, they find a musical form that corresponds perfectly to their self-image. The motorbike is culturally appropriated rather than just mechanically used.

There are naturally a host of criticisms that can be made against the view of working-class culture propounded by Miller *et al.*, and it is clearly highly dubious to over-generalize the toughness and defiance of authority found among the 'roughest' such communities to the working class in general. Nor is there much to be said for the implication, quite strong in Willis's work, that the middle class are a bunch of pastel-shaded softies, whose culture lacks the authenticity of profane experience (unless they opt for the hippy solution). There is also an element of tautology in inferring cultural trails from behaviour. Nevertheless, and unsatisfying scientifically as such a criterion may be, these approaches do 'resonate' with the more serious forms of violence in a way the more abstract Mertonian theories do not.

CLASS CONFLICT

Class conflict theories apply much the same set of ideas to the question of aggressive delinquency as do other theorists: but they do so within a broad Marxian framework which takes it for granted that class conflict is inevitable in capitalist societies, and that the dynamics of such conflict will be related to issues of deviance and control. This does not necessarily mean that delinquency is simply decoded as a symptom of class warfare; or that delinquents are seen as fighting 'the system', albeit in a regressive way. But these theories undoubtedly loom large in the interpretation of delinquency and violence from this perspective.

The concept of subculture, for example has been applied by Phil Cohen to innovations in youth culture which are seen as emerging where the contradictions of capitalist political economy bite most sharply: in the working-class inner city. Postwar changes in housing, transport and technology have, despite some gains in

[13] Willis, *Profane Culture*, p. 30.

affluence, served to fragment the working-class community. The costs of the faltering of the machinery of prosperity have fallen quite disproportionately on working-class youth and on immigrant minorities. The inability of the 'parent' working-class generation to cope with these problems means what they are deflected on to the young, whose response to the resulting family tensions, fragmented community and economic insecurity is to create a succession of subcultural styles that 'express and resolve, albeit "magically", the contradictions which remain hidden in the parent culture'. Thus, for example, the Mod style could be interpreted as an 'attempt to realise, but in an imaginary relation, the conditions of existence of the socially mobile white-collar worker. While their argot and ritual forms stressed many of the values of their parent [i.e. working-class] culture, their dress and music reflected the hedonistic image of the affluent consumer'.[14] The Skinhead style was an attempt to recover and assert the traits associated with hard manual labour under threat from technological change. And if there is a certain uniform pattern to the rise and fall of successive styles – Teds, Mods, Rockers, Skinheads, Punks – this is because revolts into style (in Melly's phrase)[15] can only ever re-transcribe, and not resolve, in any structural sense, the set of contradictions that give rise to them.

Stuart Hall and his colleagues have applied much the same analysis to the issue of delinquency in general, and to middle-class expressive movements since the war. The rise of the hippy 'counter-culture' is traced to the growing incompatibility between the traditional puritan ethic and the newfound affluence and consumerism of the expanding middle class. The breakdown of traditional middle-class constraints began from *within* the domi-

[14] Philip Cohen, 'Working-class youth cultures in East London', *Working Papers in Cultural Studies*, 2, 1972.
[15] George Melly, *Revolt into Style*, Allen Lane, 1972. Though Dick Hebdige notes (in *Subculture: The Meaning of Style*, Methuen, 1979), in his study of these 'spectacular subcultures', that 'we should be hard pressed to find in the punk subculture any symbolic attempts to "retrieve some of the socially cohesive elements destroyed in the parent (i.e. adult working class) culture" (Cohen, 1972). . . . Rather, the punks seemed to be parodying the alienation and emptiness which have caused sociologists so much concern. . . .' (p. 79) – and, it might be added, in a highly media-conscious way.

nant class, and was then transformed and pushed to expressive lengths, in both the hippy and student protest movements, which were perceived as a threat to social order. The authors are aware of the dangers of giving too ideological a reading to youthful styles. 'Disaffiliation' is frequently short-lived, and some phenomena are so ephemeral that it is straining credulity to invest them with much symbolic significance. Thus, class conflict theories are as likely to 'over-predict' as strain and culture conflict approaches.

In his study of 'how working-class kids get working-class jobs', Willis tackles a subject that is almost worn out by the sociological repetition of the nostrum that schooling is perceived by such youth as a massive irrelevancy, but gains a wealth of insight by the use of overlapping interviews and observation with a small group of boys in a typical comprehensive over a period of time that took in their last year at school and first year in work. What they revealed above all was their clear sense of their limited life chances in the industrial division of labour, and the implications of that sense for their resistance to schooling. Their own hidden curriculum was a time-table for skyving, dossing and 'having a laff'. Their culture stressed 'the perennial themes of symbolic and physical violence, rough presence, and the pressure of a certain kind of masculinity'.[16] Sexism and racism are part of the price to be paid for the accomplishment of a form of masculine self-image which renders the prospect of routine manual work palatable, and which sets off the alternative major grouping in the school, the 'ear 'oles', who are destined for superior skilled manual-cum-technical jobs, as cowed conformists. Willis undercuts the moral condemnation of their culture by making the profound point that only such a willed appropriation of labouring saves a liberal society from forced labour.

Corrigan adds a historical dimension to the seeming paradox that the long struggle to win the right to schooling for working-class children is so largely wasted on the supposed beneficiaries. We should not be too surprised about the result, he argues, in view of the fact that what has been won is the right to form a schooling originally *imposed on* the working class (the term used by Forster was 'gentling the masses') in a struggle that robbed them of their own emergent educational institutions. This argument neverthe-

---

[16] Paul Willis, *Learning to Labour*, Saxon House, 1977, p. 36.

less finesses vital questions about the most appropriate form that working-class education should take in the future. Corrigan also proposed a different interpretation of the idea of Matza that much street delinquency is the 'manufacture of excitement' in a context of 'nothing going on'. The elaboration of 'weird ideas' as a feature of apparently 'doing nothing' involves frequent rule-breaking. But the 'rules are not broken *specifically because they are rules;* rules are broken for the most part as a by-product of the flow of activity engaged in by the boys'.[17] This account presumes an innocence about 'the rules' that is open to question; but it offers an alternative to interpretations that perhaps adopt too cramped an image of delinquency as stressed and conflict-ridden.

OUTSTANDING PROBLEMS

1. The sheer proliferation of accounts of delinquency and violence over the past three decades have perhaps sown an undue amount of confusion, which might have been avoided if theorists had specified more carefully what they have been trying to explain. One commentator has noted that

> work on juvenile delinquency has been managed as if it were a single, prolonged assault on one essential problem. An article written on New York gangs in the 1950s can be celebrated as a refutation of assertions made about Chicago in the 1920s. Observations on Californian delinquents can in turn upset conjectures about East Coast society. British examples are flourished to counter American theories.[18]

While this criticism is not altogether fair, in that many theorists attempt to accommodate *variations* in delinquency within the same analytical framework, theories that account quite well for, say, run-of-the-mill vandalism hardly begin to account for the most

[17] Paul Corrigan, *Schooling the Smash Street Kids,* Macmillan, 1979, p. 140.
[18] Paul Rock, 'The sociology of crime, symbolic interactionism, and some problematic qualities of radical criminology', in D.M. Downes and P. Rock (eds), *Deviant Interpretations,* Martin Robertson, 1979, p. 57.

damaging kinds of gang violence. A more rigorous use of the comparative method might help on this score.[19]

2. Another problem endemic in this field is what might be termed the 'fiddling while Rome burns' syndrome.[20] On this view, sociologists spin while others weave to ill effect. In sum, what use are all these theories? In part, sociologists have only themselves to blame for this attack, since all too often the very complexity of the theory highlights the paucity of practical and policy inferences that are drawn from it. This criticism would carry more weight, however, if those instances that *had* produced strong policy implications had been acted on or even taken up in debate. For example, Gill's work on housing policies and delinquency, which echoes that of Morris 20 years earlier, could hardly be more relevant to public housing management policies.[21] The extent, if any, to which such work has led to changes in public policy remains obscure, and the interplay between theories and policies should figure more centrally on the agenda, as should the monitoring of policy changes where they do occur. The main limitation of this criticism, however, is that it over-simplifies the correspondence between sociological and social problems.

3. Perhaps more serious than either problem is the danger that sociologists, in their concern to render delinquency intelligible, may be constructing nothing more than a series of intentional fallacies. The constructing of behaviour as ordered and rational, when considered from a particular standpoint of the sociologists's making, is clearly a procedure that must be related, at some point, to the actors' own definition of the situation. 'Somewhere along the line, symbolic language implies a knowing subject, a subject at least dimly aware of what the symbols are supposed to mean'.[22] If that touchstone is abandoned, the most ingenious explanations will prove a barrier, and not a means, to understanding.

[19] For a discussion of particular issues, see Roland Robertson and Laurie Taylor, 'Problems in the comparative analysis of deviance', in P. Rock and M. McIntosh (eds), *Deviance and Social Control*, Tavistock, 1974.

[20] See, for example, 'Comment' by Anthony Bottoms to D.M. Downes, 'Promise and performance in British criminology', *British Journal of Sociology*, December 1978.

[21] Owen Gill, *Luke St*, Macmillan, 1977; Terence Morris, *The Criminal Area*, Routledge & Kegan Paul, 1958, esp. ch. 11.

[22] Stanley Cohen, 'Symbols of trouble', Introduction to new edition of *Folk Devils and Moral Panics*, Martin Robertson, 1980.

BIBLIOGRAPHY

General

Morris, Terence 1958: *The Criminal Area*, London: Routledge & Kegan Paul.
Patrick, James 1973: *A Glasgow Gang Observed*, London: Eyre Methuen.
Short, James F. Jr and Strodtbeck, F.L. 1965: *Group Process and Gang Delinquency*, Chicago: University Press.
Yablonsky, Lewis 1962: *The Violent Gang*, Harmondsworth: Penguin.

Strain Theories

Cloward, R.A. and Ohlin, L.E. 1960: *Delinquency and Opportunity*, New York: Free Press.
Cohen, A.K. 1955: *Delinquent Boys: The Culture of the Gang*, New York: Free Press.
Downes, D.M. 1966: *The Delinquent Solution*, London: Routledge & Kegan Paul.
Fuchs, V.R. 1974: *Who Shall Live?* New York: Basic Books.
Matza, D. 1964: *Delinquency and Drift*, New York: John Wiley.
Merton, R.K. 1957: *Social Theory and Social Structure*, 2nd edn, Glencoe, Illinois: Free Press.

Labelling Theories

Becker, Howard 1971: *Outsiders*, New York: Free Press.
Cicourel, Aaron 1968: *Social Organization of Juvenile Justice*, New York: Wiley.
Cohen, Stanley 1972: *Folk Devils and Moral Panics*, London: McGibbon and Kee/Paladin.
Gill, Owen 1977: *Luke St*, London: Macmillan.
Hall, Stuart *et al.* 1978: *Policing the Crisis*, London: Macmillan.
Lemert, E. 1967: *Human Deviance, Social Problems and Social Control*, Englewood Cliffs, NJ: Prentice-Hall.
Marsh, P. *et al.* 1978: *The Rules of Disorder*, London: Routledge & Kegan Paul.
Parker, Howard 1974: *The View from the Boys*, Newton Abbott, Devon: David & Charles.
Robins, D. and Cohen, P. 1978: *Knuckle Sandwich*, Harmondsworth: Penguin.
Scull, Andrew 1972: 'Social control and the amplification of deviance', in *Theoretical Perspectives on Deviance*, ed. J. Douglas and R. Scott, New York: Basic Books.
Young, Jock 1974: 'Mass media, drugs and deviance' in *Deviance and Social Control*, ed. P. Rock and M. McIntosh, London: Tavistock.

Control Theories

Box, Stephen 1971: *Deviance, Reality and Society*, New York: Holt, Rinehart & Winston.
Eysenck, H.J. 1963: *Crime and Personality*, London: Routledge & Kegan Paul.
Hirschi, Travis 1969: *Causes of Delinquency*, Berkeley: University of California Press.
Morgan, Patricia 1978: *Delinquent Fantasies*, London: Temple Smith.
Newman, Oscar 1974: *Defensible Space*, London: Architectural Press.
Nettler, G. 1974: *Explaining Crime*, New York: McGraw-Hill.

Culture Conflict Theories

Lewis, Oscar 1961: *The Children of Sanchez*, New York: Random House.
Lewis, Oscar 1966: *La Vida*, St Albans: Panther.
Mays, John 1954: *Growing Up In the City*, Liverpool: University Press.
Miller, W.B. 1958: 'Lower-class culture as a generating milieu of gang delinquency', *Journal Social Issues* 14(3): 3–19.
Miller, W.B. 1966: 'Violent crimes in city gangs', *Annals of the American Academy of Political and Social Science*, March 1966, no. 364.
Miller, W. *et al.* 1961: 'Aggression in a boy street-corner group', *Psychiatry: Journal for the Study of Interpersonal Processes*, 24(4): 283–98.
Miller, W. 1976: 'Youth gangs in the urban crisis era', in *Delinquency, Crime and Society*, ed. J.F. Short, Jr, Chicago: University Press.
McVicar, John 1974: *McVicar by Himself*, London: Hutchinson.
Thrasher, Frederick 1927: *The Gang*, Chicago: University Press.

Class Conflict Theories

Clarke, J. *et al.* (eds.) 1976: *Resistance through rituals*, London: Hutchinson.
Cohen, Philip 1972: 'Working-class youth cultures in East London', *Working Papers in Cultural Studies*, 2.
Cohen, Philip and Robins, Dave 1978: *Knuckle Sandwich*, Harmondsworth: Penguin.
Corrigan, Paul 1979: *Schooling the Smash Street Kids*, London: Macmillan.
Hebdige, Dick 1979: *Subculture: The Meaning of Style*, London: Methuen.
Willis, Paul 1977: *Learning to Labour*, Farnborough: Saxon House.
Willis, Paul 1978: *Profane Culture*, London: Routledge & Kegan Paul.
Taylor, Ian 1979: 'The new departures in the analysis of youth violence', *British Journal of Criminology*, 270–8.

CHAPTER 4

Anthropology, Violence and Catharsis

Paul Heelas

The concept of war belongs *essentially*
to my behaviour. [Winch 1971:128]

Anthropology is the comparative discipline *par excellence*, so our attention is immediately directed to whether it is possible to order societies according to the degree of violence they tolerate or manifest. The majority of anthropologists – together with psychologists and human ethologists – assume that it is not difficult to show that some societies are less violent or aggressive than others, differences being attributed to child-rearing practices or features of social organization and religion. My main theme is that violence is not so easily placed under comparative, and thus anthropological, scrutiny. In fact, I want to take a controversial line, arguing that it is impossible to devise an objective measure or definition that can be applied cross-culturally.

This argument has a number of consequences. It helps explain why there is controversy over the extent to which violence is an inherent feature of human nature. Thus the disagreement between Montague (1978) and Eibl-Eibesfeldt (1979) over the existence of non-aggressive peoples surely owes much to the absence of adequate criteria for assessment. Another consequence is that those anthropological theories that purport to demonstrate that religious systems either encourage or minimize violence lack adequate empirical basis. The impact of the systems in question cannot be properly assessed by reference to cross-cultural measures of the incidence of violence.

The argument has other consequences, including how it bears on experimental (cross-cultural) psychological research. However, I shall limit myself, in the second section of the paper, to a topic of considerable contemporary interest: the theory that a wide range of rituals functions cathartically. Thus my demonstration of the consequences of the argument that violence cannot be objectively compared cross-culturally will be to show why there is lack of consensus over whether or not some rituals function cathartically – thereby minimizing violence.

THE QUESTION OF COMPARISON

Because the argument leading to the conclusion that the incidence of violence cannot be compared cross-culturally in an objective fashion involves a number of steps, I indicate them as they are reached.

Differences in Conceptualization

Notions of what counts as violence show radical cross-cultural variation. Chagnon's study of the South American Yanomamö provides a by no means exceptional illustration. From our point of view, these are one of the most fierce and aggressive of peoples: husbands, for example, treat their wives abominably – they beat them, hold glowing sticks against them, even kill them. Yet women 'measure their husband's concern in terms of the frequency of minor beatings they sustain', and the ethnographer overheard a woman commenting 'that the other's husband must really care for her since he has beaten her on the head so frequently' (1968:83). What for us counts as violent wife-battering is seen by Yanomamö women as a sign of care, perhaps even endearment.

Discrepancies

Thus, purported instances of violence can be approached from two points of view: that of the participant, and that of the observer. Tension arises when what counts as violence in one frame of reference is not so construed in the other. Discrepancies are thrown into starker relief when the observer attempts to develop 'objective' criteria of what counts as violence in any particular society. Anthropologists often work with objective definitions of the kind, 'violence is that which disrupts the established social order';

psychologists, as Eibl-Eibesfeldt summarizes the situation, 'in general describe behavior as aggressive if it leads to another party's being hurt; this includes not only physical hurt (injury or destruction) but any kind of hurt, including annoyance, taunts, or insults' (1979:29). Let us apply this last definition to the renowned mortuary ceremonies of Dinka (southern Sudan) masters of the fishing-spear. One of Lienhardt's informants told him: 'when a master of the fishing-spear has fallen sick and is becoming weak, he will call all his people and tell them to bring his whole camp to his home and bury him whilst he lives' (1961:300). Does Dinka religion encourage violent 'suicide' (as our objectivist might conclude), or should we not follow Lienhardt's participant-based interpretation and see the event as the Dinka asserting their autonomy *vis à vis* death?

Two Types of Comparison

We have seen that the incidence of violence in various cultures can be assessed from two points of view (by reference to 'objective' or participant criteria) and that a different picture emerges depending on which is adopted. Objective criteria are meant to provide a way of classifying societies along a scale from low to high incidence of violence. A measure is devised – say, the infliction of physical hurt – which is held to apply to all the cases under consideration. With this base line, this universally applicable criterion, violence can be spotted and compared in various cultures. Like is compared with like. The base line makes comparison *absolute*: it is simply a matter of adding up the number of times physical hurt is inflicted in various societies.

Comparison by reference to participant criteria results in a very different picture. As we have seen, what counts as violence shows very considerable cross-cultural variation. Jains regard the inadvertent destruction of any sentient being (including insects) as violent; in other societies, including many in highland New Guinea, the destruction of strangers does not appear to be thought of as violent. In our own society, an act seen as violent during a middle-class dinner party is not so regarded on the building site, and types of questioning normal in university-educated circles are treated as insulting transgressions in working-men's clubs.

This *relativism* – that what counts as violence in one context is not seen as such in another – means that it is no longer possible to build up a neat comparative scale. Each case is distinctive, there being no base line in common to allow cross-cultural assessment. Thus, if the claim is made that middle-class society is generally less violent than life among the male working class, because there is less physical aggression, the fact that working men do not see violence in the same way is ignored.

Adopting the view that what counts as violence is relative to particular socio-cultural frameworks means that the most the comparativist can now do is compare cultures according to how they use terms such as 'violence'. In this connection, it is probable that the Yanomamö are much less violent than they appear to us (in terms of our opinions of what counts as violent). But because our use of the term is so different to that found among the Yanomamö, neat scale ordering is out of the question. It could be objected that there must be some states of affairs – such as what we call homicide or violent death – that are universally construed as violent and that therefore allow comparison within the participants' frame of reference. I argue against this later.

Conditions

What conditions have to be fulfilled for objective comparison to work? Granted the relativism inherent in the use of participant criteria, the relativist cannot readily seek his objective criteria in this domain. His obvious strategy is to seek an understanding of what counts as violence in the domain of the *natural*, rather than the *cultural*, world.

This distinction needs clarification. I do not want to fall into the trap of claiming that violence can be conceived of as *existing* in the world in two ways – either as belonging to the natural world or as an inherently culture- or meaning-dependent phenomenon – because it seems evident that violence is in measure inherently biological or psychological. (I return to this.) But I do want to claim that there is a difference between the two domains when it comes to establishing what *counts* as violence. Thus, if the first option is valid – that violence can be spotted by reference to genetic or psychological processes or states of affairs that exist regardless of participant conceptualizations – violence can justifiably be spotted independently of these conceptualizations. The objectivist can base his definitions on what he knows to exist in the natural world, and so can get to work without fear of distorting ethnographic evidence by contradicting what participants *happen* to call violent. However, if violence belongs to the world of cultural meanings in the sense that states of affairs can be treated as cases of violence only if they are conceptualized as such within the participants' frame of reference, objective comparison runs into the relativist problem already outlined.

An analogy will help explain what I mean by the strategy of seeking criteria in the natural world. Members of many societies hold what are for us erroneous ideas about age, but this does not prevent objective comparisons of longevity. Comparison is facilitated by the fact that ageing and death belong to the natural world: how participants might happen to conceptualize the processes can be ignored, because the comparative base line is embedded in processes that operate regardless of participant conceptualizations. Returning to violence, the justification for treating at least some states of mind and acts as violent when participants do not regard them as such must rest on the objectivist seeking a foothold in the natural world. Only in this way can some universally applicable base line be applied, and only in this way can participant criteria be ignored if necessary.

A Foothold in the Natural World?

Unable to use relativistic participant criteria, the objectivist, we have seen, has to turn elsewhere for his measures. It is not simply that participant criteria are too diverse; it is also because, if one is to be justified in ignoring or contradicting participant criteria, one can scarcely infer one's objective criteria from these same conceptualizations. The question, then, is whether it is possible to arrive at objective measures.

Consider the hypothesis that violence exists as an innate, inherent, proclivity of human nature, manifesting itself in the natural tendency of people to fall into violent or aggressive states of mind and to act in violent or aggressive fashion. This hypothesis can be subdivided into those theories that hold that violence is genetically programmed or physiologically indentifiable, that violence is an inherent state of mind or emotion (for example, anger or aggression), or that violence is a natural way of behaving under specifiable conditions. I do not think that we are yet in the position to use genetic or physiological measures as criteria of the variety I introduced in the analogy of longevity, and criteria based on inner states are, as we shall see, of dubious value. That leaves behavioural criteria – which, as Eibl-Eibesfeldt indicates, are the ones most commonly employed.

Attempts to develop an objective vantage point on the basis of behavioural criteria founder because human action does not, in the main, belong to the natural world of simply physical or behavioural events. When objectivists claim that violence can be defined as the infliction of physical hurt (or whatever), they are basically saying that the infliction of physical hurt is a *natural sign* of violence. But acts of this kind belong to human life, which means that their significance is pervaded by *conventional* factors.[1] To the extent that this is true, they cannot function as natural signs of violence. The same item of behaviour – such as what we call wife-battering – can be a sign of violence and as the Yanomamö example shows us, also a sign of endearment.

Sticking my neck out, I would go so far as to claim that the cross-cultural variety of what counts as violent behaviour rules out the possibility of there being any natural behavioural signs. If there are, what exactly are they, and why is there so much cross-cultural variation? Almost any behaviour can, in appropriate circumstances, indicate violence – or something else. Mutilation might indicate violence, or it might enter into initiation ceremonies as an indication of bravery and values of manhood. The raw behaviour, in other words, on which the objectivist bases his definitions, is related to violence conventionally, not naturally. The nature of human action depends on how raw behaviour is interpreted; what meaning systems it enters into. Perhaps this is putting it rather strongly, for it would be rash to deny that violence is an inherent aspect of human nature and that it is more closely allied to some kinds of behaviour than others. However, it remains the case that no particular behaviour need be 'naturally' violent, the consequence being that behaviour provides a poor basis for objective definition.

My conclusion is that the objectivist cannot find an adequate foothold in the natural world: violence has not been adequately charted as an aspect of the natural, biological, genetic or behavioural world to function as a basis for objective comparison and an overruling or participant conceptualizations. Violence is almost

[1] For a general discussion of this distinction and its bearing on the cross-cultural study of human nature see Needham (1972:esp. 136–51).

certainly an inherent aspect of human nature, but this is not to say that it belongs to the natural world as a definable entity. It is both too inaccessible and too modifiable in expression for that to be possible.

Violence as Culture-dependent

I do not deny that violence is almost certainly based in the natural world; I do deny that at least to date this fact can provide the basis for objective measures. But what of the future? Will it ever be possible to specify genetic or physiological criteria in order to spot instances of violence regardless of participant conceptualizations? I want to tackle this question by arguing that participant criteria of what counts as violence must necessarily take precedence over objective criteria. I want to argue that it makes no sense to describe a state of mind or act as violent unless one has, so to speak, the permission of participants. In other words, to admit that violence exists as an inherent aspect of human nature is not to deny that there are important ways in which it is also culture-dependent.

There are two features of this. The first pertains to violent states of mind or emotions. Applying Schachter's (1971) plausible, if ultimately inconclusive, argument that such states are in measure culture-dependent, violent emotions are not simply given in physiological nature: they are also constituted by conceptual appraisal. Dependent on cognitive appraisal, the existence of violent emotions is co-terminous with what participants count as such. Participants, so to speak, cannot be wrong. The second sense in which violence is inherently culture-dependent involves denying that even the most apparently violent behaviour (for example, what we know of as homicide) need be a sign of violence if participants think otherwise. Let me draw another analogy. A mark on a piece of paper might be a vote or simply a tick. The nature of this event, or what counts as a vote, is meaning or culture-dependent. In similar fashion, a visit to the dentist in our society might involve the infliction of physical hurt but does not count as a violent or aggressive act on the part of the dentist, because of the meanings and intentions involved. To give another example, killing an animal in a painful fashion belongs to the natural world (the animal dies in pain). But if all such cases are regarded as exemplifying violence (as the objectivist might conclude), a crucially important distinction is ignored: that between killing an animal for the sake of sadistic or violent pleasure, and killing an animal in sacrifice.

Summary

It is time to draw together the threads and to place the argument in broader perspective. Winch has claimed that social life does not exist in the natural world; in other words, that it does not exist independently of the ideas that inform or constitute it: 'social relations between men exist only in and through their ideas' (1971:123). Hence the observation with which I began – 'the concept of war belongs *essentially* to my behaviour' – and hence his claim that 'it is impossible to go far in *specifying* the attitudes, expectations and relations of individuals without referring to concepts which enter into those attitudes, etc. . .' (1971:128, my emphasis). Sacrifice is culture-dependent by virtue of the meanings attached to what would perhaps otherwise be acts of brutal violence.

I have admitted, however, that it cannot be argued that violence exists solely as a cultural phenomenon. Because violence is almost certainly embedded in the natural world, one cannot simply claim that its cultural aspects mean that it only exists if it is conceptualized as such. Thus I have had to go further than Winch by considering the possibility of specifying – and thus comparing – the incidence of violence by reference to natural criteria.

This possibility has been rejected. Violence has to be specified *via* the cultural world (and in that sense belongs to it), the natural world providing no adequate criteria. Behaviour is only violent if participants agree, for since no particular behaviour need be violent, behavioural criteria cannot be used to overrule participant conceptualizations. Emotions do not provide a basis for objective comparison; for, apart from the Schachter argument that emotional states are partly constituted by how they are conceptualized, we shall see how difficult it is to compare and isolate aggressive or violent states of mind cross-culturally. As for genetic and physiological criteria, our knowledge is not as yet very advanced, and in any case it is not clear how additional knowledge could help us identify and compare manifestations of violence in behaviour. Yanomamö wife-'battering' might involve similar states of physiological arousal as wife-battering in our own culture, but this surely cannot justify our ignoring the Yanomamö assessment.

The natural world provides an inherent proclivity or tendency, not the specific states of affairs or manifestations that the comparativist is generally interested in. What counts as violence is culturally organized and articulated, and so must provide the basis for comparison. Participant conceptualizations are vital for charting violence because the natural world provides no useful criteria of whether a *specific* act (or emotion) is violent, and because how we conceptualize violence belongs essentially to what counts as it. As a phenomenon bridging the nature/culture dichotomy, the modifiable manifestations of the former means that the latter is what matters in identifying what has to be compared. Objective, natural, criteria cannot rule the comparative enterprise. A bang on the head is not a bang on the head and a case of violence – it could even be a sign of endearment.

THE QUESTION OF CATHARSIS

Anthropologists have not been disinclined to emphasize the powers of ritual, frequent appeal being made to the notion of catharsis. Gluckman's (1963) account of 'rituals of rebellion' in south-east Africa provides a classic illustration. When the Swazi king walks into his sanctuary, women sing songs expressing their hatred of him. The ritualized aggression is held to control violence because it is a surrogate of the real thing, that is, of psychological tensions engendered by conflicts inherent in the social order. In Gluckman's words, 'Clearly we are dealing with the general problem of *catharsis* set by Aristotle in his *Politics* and his *Tragedy* – the purging of emotion through "pity, fear and inspiration" ' (1963:126).

The underlying assumption is that the impact of ritual on violent and socially disruptive psychological states can be assessed. I have argued that the absence of objective criteria and the relativistic nature of cultural criteria means that objective cross-cultural comparison is impossible. Granted the importance of participant criteria, reliance on objective criteria results in a distorted and inaccurate picture, violence being found where none exists or going unrecognized when participants acknowledge it. Even if objective measures were somehow obtained of a kind broad enough to allow cross-cultural comparison, they would inevitably result in participant notions being sometimes ignored: and this is not justified; for, unlike things in the natural world, manifestations of violence depend on what participants think of as such.

There is so much controversy over the nature and existence of catharsis that it would be ill-advised to make full use of the argument I have just summarized. In particular, I do not know what to say about the question of whether catharsis occurs independently of participant conceptualizations. What can be argued, however, is that satisfactory ways of assessing the impact of supposedly cathartic mechanisms have not yet been devised, and, indeed, are unlikely to be devised in the future. The psychological evidence is inconclusive because contradictory, this in turn being due largely to the inaccessibility of emotional states. Having discussed this, I return to the anthropological, cross-cultural, perspective to show that assessment is here even more difficult.

Types

It is first necessary to distinguish between different types of catharsis, it not being fair to create contradictions by applying findings that bear on one species to those that belong to another. The most inclusive definition I can envisage is of catharsis as the release or transformation of emotional pressure or impulses via activity and expression. The idea of release is important because no one would want to describe all expressions of emotion (such as love) as cathartic. Catharsis has its home with emotions that somehow build up in us or that require expression if we are to feel right. Thus the notion bears on unpleasant, disruptive or negative emotions: in a recent article, Scheff lists four 'distressful' emotions; grief, fear, embarrassment and anger (1977:485).

The greatly simplified model illustrated here subdivides theories of catharsis by reference to what happens to the self when catharsis occurs (the cathartic effect), and to the mechanisms whereby the effect is obtained (the method of discharge).

The cathartic effect	*Methods of discharge*
Purification: the reduction of internal tensions and associated improvements in subjective feelings	*Vicarious:* catharsis occuring via substitute forms of the initial cause of the repressed emotions or via indirect means. Repression important

Purgation: simple decrease of remaining instigation of aggression

Direct: catharsis occuring via direct action on the cause of the distressful emotion. Repression less important

In the first type, vicarious purification, rituals, films, games and the like provide surrogate, vicarious or mimetic expressions of violence and aggression. Repressed emotions are evoked and then purified, rituals functioning as models of how they should be regarded. The second main type, direct purgation, does not provide sophisticated methods of discharge and so rituals purge rather than purify. As for the remaining two possibilities, direct purification and vicarious purgation, the former is not often encountered (because purification requires sophisticated models) although the second is quite popular (it being perfectly possible to hold that vicarious means can diminish distressful emotions).

Contradictions

Given the very considerable experimental literature on catharsis, I limit myself to a schematic presentation of a handful of recent studies. A more comprehensive survey would, however, only further emphasize the point I am making: that the evidence is inconclusive because contradictory.

Vicarious methods of discharge: purification? The experimental evidence is increasing on this question, largely because of the popularity of ritualized self-improvement emotive psycho-therapies such as Gestalt or primal therapy. In so far as the evidence bears on purification (and that is not very clear), contradictory findings are emerging: compare Glas *et al.* (1977) with the positive findings of Bierenbaum *et al.* (1976) and Nichols and Bierenbaum (1978).

Direct methods of discharge: purgation? A classic confrontation in this respect is that between Konečni and Ebbesen (1976) and Geen *et al.* (1975). The latter had argued for the disinhibitory effect of aggression, angered subjects engaging in more subsequent aggression than non-angered. Konečni and Ebbesen found that angered subjects' aggression may be reduced by aggression.

Vicarious methods of discharge: purgation? Kaplan and Singer, in their useful review, ask: 'Does the fantasy violence shown on television cause people to behave more aggressively?' (1976:35).

Having summarized what they call activation and catharsis theories, they side with the 'null view'. Their conclusion, that 'such violence on television has not been demonstrated to have significant effects on aggressive behavior', stands in contrast to the apparent ease with which other investigators have found either stimulation or purgation evidence.

Explanation

A number of considerations have been adduced to explain the contradictory nature of the evidence, including problems with experimental design and in handling the many variables involved. However, the main reason must surely be due to difficulties encountered in isolating, distinguishing, comparing and measuring emotional states. These difficulties, it is important to note, cannot be by-passed by using behavioural criteria, for reduction in aggressive behaviour after supposed catharsis might indicate factors other than reduced aggressive arousal. As Geen and Quanty put it 'Lowered aggressiveness may be the result not only of reduced arousal but of other processes as well, such as the creation of active restraints against aggressing' (1977:5). To show that direct purgation has occurred, it is thus necessary to show that *the performance of aggressive acts brings about a reduction in aggressive arousal,* this alone explaining subsequent diminishment in direct aggression.

Decrease in aggressive behaviour might indicate decrease in arousal, or it might indicate the operation of other factors, including social inhibition and guilt. So how are we to get at the arousal factor to establish – in the case of direct purgation – whether there is a correlation between reduction in aggressive emotions and performance of aggressive acts (when the end result is the reduction of such acts)? Physiological criteria provide the obvious avenue. But this is what Geen and Quanty conclude:

> In view of the conflicting evidence on the relationship of the various measures of arousal to experimental conditions associated with frustration and aggression, and lacking any clear theory of the psychophysiological significance of the various measures, we would perhaps be well advised not to generalize too liberally across experiments in which a

catharsis-like physiological recovery, or its absence, is reported. [1977:17][2]

Back to Anthropology

We have here a good illustration of an aspect of the argument of the first part of this chapter, namely, that the main reason why there is so little consensus over whether specified rituals function cathartically is because it is difficult, if not impossible, to devise an objective scale for assessing the incidence of violent emotions within one culture (the experiments cited use Western subjects) let alone cross-culturally. There seem to be no natural signs of catharsis, which makes it difficult to see, for example, how one could distinguish between the role of ritual in actually diminishing the violent impulses or in channelling it into relatively safe (because symbolic) forms of expression.[3] And it does little good to rely on participant reports such as 'I felt relieved'. For, apart from the obvious objection that reports might simply be made, for example, in accordance with a desire to be culturally conformist, members of some societies are simply not able to report catharsis even though it could be perhaps occurring. They might well not assume that emotions are *discrete inner states*, which can be stored in the self, and which require release if the individual is to be at peace with himself (c.f. Lienhardt 1961). So how is the anthropologist to proceed in those cases where participants cannot use the language of catharsis? What signs should he rely on?

[2] Many other points could be raised about assessing catharsis and aggression levels (see e.g. Kaplan and Singer 1976:esp. 40). Thus I have not discussed ways of establishing 'discharge', the question of whether an increase in aggressive behaviour need rule out catharsis of a direct purgation variety, ways of handling the possibility that diminished arousal might simply be due to time-lag, and questions raised when one tries to establish the aggression-inducing content of films or rituals. There is also the issue of whether disinhibition is not in fact ultimately cathartic, allowing the full expression of emotions and so releasing them.
[3] A related alternative, raised by Bandura (1965:28), is that vicarious processes might diminish psysiological arousal by attention shifts, not via the release of pent-up emotions. Yet another is obviously between ritual as constitutive of emotions, arousing them at the very least, as opposed to releasing them. Much depends here on how Schachter's (1971) theory is viewed.

Paul Heelas

Difficulties with physiological, behavioural and verbal criteria mean that the hypothetically cathartic impact of ritual on violent emotions cannot be assessed within a scientific frame of reference. The hypothesis cannot be tested because of the inaccessibility of the crucial factor of emotional arousal, physiological criteria being too inconclusive, other criteria being too contingent. That anthropologists such as Gluckman or Ortner (with her theory of the vicarious purification of anger among the Sherpas (1978:149–52)) use the notion suggests the influence of our cultural heritage – specifically, the presence of the concept in our own cultural or indigenous psychology – rather than of hard evidence. The absence of objective measures, in other words, has facilitated 'psychological imperialism'. Just as our own assumptions about what counts as violence have been imposed on other cultures, so too have our own popular assumptions about the cathartic powers of many forms of ritual.

REFERENCES

Bandura, A. 1965: 'Vicarious processes: a case of no-trial learning', *Advances in Experimental Social Psychology*, ed. L. Berkowitz, London: Academic Press, Vol. 2: 1–55.
Bierenbaum, H., Nichols, M. and Schwartz, A. 1976: 'Effects of varying session length and frequency in brief emotive psychotherapy', *Journal of Consulting and Clinical Psychology* 44(5): 790–8.
Chagnon, N. 1968: *Yanomamö: The Fierce People*, New York: Holt, Rinehart & Winston.
Eibl-Eibesfeldt, I. 1979: *The Biology of Peace and War*, London: Thames & Hudson.
Geen, R., Stonner, D. and Shope, G. 1975: 'The facilitation of aggression by aggression: evidence against the catharsis hypothesis', *Journal of Personality and Social Psychology* 31(4): 721–6.
Geen, R. and Quanty, M. 1977: 'The catharsis of aggression: an evaluation of a hypothesis', *Advances in Experimental Social Psychology*, ed. L. Berkowitz, London: Academic Press, Vol. 10: 1–37.
Glas, L., Kirsch, M. and Parris, F. 1977: 'Psychiatric disturbances associated with Erhardt Seminars Training', *American Journal of Psychiatry* 134: 245–7; 1254–8.
Gluckman, M. 1963: *Order and Rebellion in Tribal Africa*, London: Cohen & West.
Kaplan, R. and Singer, R. 1976: 'Television violence and viewer aggression: a re-examination of the evidence', *Journal of Social Issues* 32(4): 35–70.

Konečni, V. and Ebbesen, E. 1976: 'Disinhibition versus the cathartic effect', *Journal of Personality and Social Psychology* 34(3): 352–65.
Lienhardt, G. 1961: *Divinity and Experience*, Oxford: University Press.
Montagu, A. 1978: *Learning Non-Aggression*, Oxford: University Press.
Needham, R. 1972: *Belief, Language and Experience*, Oxford: Basil Blackwell.
Nichols, M. and Bierenbaum, H. 1978: 'Success of cathartic therapy as a function of patient variables', *Journal of Clinical Psychology* 34(3): 726–8.
Ortner, S. 1978: *Sherpas through their Rituals*, Cambridge: University Press.
Schachter, S. 1971: *Emotion, Obesity and Crime*, New York: Academic Press.
Scheff, T. 1977: 'The distancing of emotion in ritual', *Current Anthropology* 18(3): 483–506.
Winch, P. 1971: *The Idea of a Social Science*, London: Routledge & Kegan Paul.

CHAPTER 5

Mass Communication and Social Violence
A critical review of recent research trends

Graham Murdock

This chapter sets out to review the main trends in research on the relationship between mass communication and social violence over the last decade or so, concentrating on the two issues that have dominated discussion; the long-standing debate on the role of media imagery in stimulating violent behaviour, and the more recent, but equally important, argument about the links between media presentations and the formation of public opinion and policy on questions of law and order. But first, by way of introduction, I want to outline the three major perspectives that have under-pinned these debates, which I shall call: the Individualistic, the Interactionist, and the Critical.

CURRENTS OF CONCERN, STYLES OF INVESTIGATION

The first of these perspectives locates the mainsprings of violence inside the individual. Aggression is viewed as a universal and ever-present human potential, a reservoir of animality, which is activated when the customary internal and social controls prove too weak to prevent it breaking through. Acts of violence are therefore seen as the product of two intersecting forces: the influence of external stimuli, which lower inhibitions on aggression, and the inability of individuals to withstand these inducements owing to their personal inadequacies and/or the breakdown of normal cultural controls. In casting around for

powerful stimuli, commentators soon fixed on commercial entertainment.

As Edward Thompson has shown, popular attitudes towards
crime at the beginning of the industrial era operated with an
'unwritten code' which encouraged a distrust of the forces of law
and order and made certain kinds of criminals into popular heroes
(Thompson 1968: 63–7). One of the best known was Jack Sheppard,
who was eventually hanged for theft at the age of 22 after an
audacious career which included three spectacular escapes from
Newgate Gaol. This counter-current in popular culture provided
the themes for many of the songs and plays produced for the new
urban proletariat in the first half of the nineteenth century. Not
surprisingly, these presentations caused considerable alarm
among middle- and upper-class observers, haunted as they were
by the spectre of popular insurrection. The fears mainly revolved
around the images of collective violence provided by reports of
strikes, street demonstrations and acts of terrorism. But they were
easily stretched to accommodate more mundane forms of violence,
on the grounds that all acts of vandalism and aggression challenged
the state's legitimate monopoly of force and retribution and so
threatened the *status quo*. Violence of all kinds therefore appeared
as a sign of the times, tangible proof that the moral and political
order was collapsing. And among the forces working to unpick the
social fabric, popular entertainment was assigned a central role.

The influential *Edinburgh Review,* for example, was in no doubt at
all that the popular theatres featuring melodramas of crime and
passion were 'a powerful agent for depraving the boyish classes of
our towns and cities', and that 'the boy who is led on to haunt them
becomes rapidly demoralised, and seeks to be the doer of the
infamies that have interested him as a spectator' (*Edinburgh Review*
1851: 409).

In this, and similar attacks on popular drama, we can find in
embryo most of the themes that have since come to dominate the
individualistic approach. They are:
1. the identification of social violence with interpersonal
   aggression, and the consequent neglect of institutional violence
   and repression;
2. the assumption that, since violence is a matter of personal
   behaviour, its causes are to be sought mainly at the level of the
   individual;

3. the insistence that popular entertainment is a powerful independent factor in stimulating aggressive behaviour;
4. the assumption that there is a direct causal link between
   exposure to violent imagery and subsequent behaviour via
   imitation and modelling;
5. the view that 'the problem of violence' is primarily a problem of
   street crime and working-class disorder;
6. the concentration on children and young people on the grounds
   that their relatively weak moral controls make them particularly
   suggestible and open to influence.

As I have shown elsewhere (Murdock 1979: ch. 3), panics about
the effects of popular entertainment have repeatedly connected
with wider concerns about rising rates of juvenile crime, and both
have drawn on 'storm and stress' models of adolescence. However,
as the *Edinburgh Review* extract indicates, most of this concern
centred on boys. There are two reasons for this. First, the public
and collective nature of much male deviance has linked it more
forcefully and obviously to underlying fears of social disorder.
Second, aggression and masculinity are firmly yoked together
ideologically in the dominant culture's celebration of competitive
individualism and the subordinate culture's stress on physical
competence and toughness. In contrast, concerns about the
deviant behaviour of adolescent girls have tended to focus on
sexuality and its management.

The individualistic perspective has its roots in the doctrine of
original sin, and many of its earliest promoters were clergymen or
moral entrepreneurs of one sort of another. This religious strand
continues to inform the arguments of latter-day crusaders like Mrs
Mary Whitehouse, but unlike their predecessors, they can call on a
wealth of research evidence to bolster their case.

Individualistic approaches have permeated academic work on
violence in several forms. Perspectives derived from genetics and
animal behaviour, for example, have had a substantial impact,
although so far they have made little impression on the media–
violence debate. Models derived from clinical practice have made
rather more of a dent, notably through Fredrick Wertham's influential work on the effects of horror comics and television. But it
is through behaviourist psychology, with its stimulus–response
model of action and its elevation of the controlled laboratory
experiment, that the individualistic perspective has found its most

consistent and powerful expression. And it is the behaviourist project that still dominates debate on the links between media involvements and violent behaviour.

Despite its centrality, however, behaviourism has been consistently challenged by work conducted from an interactionist perspective. These currents break with behaviourist assumptions at three crucial points.

First, and most importantly, they place individual behaviour firmly in the context of everyday life. Where behavourism searches for causal links between isolated stimuli and individual responses, interactionism explores the conditions under which people resort to violence in managing their social relations and negotiating their social environment. Hence aggression is seen as the product of social conditions rather than as individual maladjustment, and its roots are sought in social deprivation and disadvantage rather than in personal deficiency or pathology. This theoretical shift – from individual responses to social relations – is accompanied by an equally important shift in methodology. In place of the behaviourist preference for controlled experiments, interactionists rely on ethnographic studies which use interviews and observations to build up a detailed account of the role and meaning of violence in the everyday life of particular social groups. This 'naturalistic' approach was pioneered by early documentary journalists like Henry Mayhew, and it was an ex-journalist, Robert Park, who did most to promote it within academia in his capacity as head of the sociology department at the University of Chicago between the two world wars. Interactionism's first contribution, then, is to contextualize violent behaviour socially. Against the behaviourist fixation with *direct* links between specific stimuli and particular responses, it insists that the effects of media representations are always *mediated* through patterns of social relations, and cannot be adequately understood in isolation from them.

Interactionism's second contribution is to contextualize violence culturally. Whereas behaviourists treat the definition of 'violence' as unproblematic, interactionists regard it as a negotiable cultural category whose meaning varies between different social groups and in different social circumstances. This relativistic perspective has important consequences for the way people's responses to the mass media are conceptualized. Instead of seeing reaction as a one-way process through which specific stimuli produce particular responses, interactionists stress the dynamic relations between imagery and audience. They insist, first, that all media artefacts contain a range of possible meanings, which are capable of generating a variety of different and even contradictory responses, and, second, that reactions are the outcome of an *active* process of selection and interpretation grounded in the particular experiences and values of the viewer. As two other eminent Chicago sociologists put it, at the end of their research into the impact of movies on American youth in the 1930s,

> It is evident that motion pictures may exert influences in diametrically opposite directions. The movies may help to dispose or lead persons to delinquency and crime or they may fortify conventional behaviour. . . . How are these conflicting influences to be explained? As we have indicated, two conditions determine the nature and direction of the effects of motion pictures on the behaviour of a given person: first, the diversity and wide range of themes depicted on the screen; and second, the social milieu, the attitudes and interests of the observer. [Blumer and Hauser 1933: 201–2]

This pioneering Chicago work contains an idea that has been developed in some detail by later writers. This is the notion that people's responses to media imagery are bounded by their differential access to socially located meaning systems. Of central importance here is the argument that subordinate groups develop distinctive views of the world which exist underneath the 'official' culture, and that these *subcultures* provide alternative ways of relating to mass media products.

This stress on the social structuring of audience responses also provides the starting point for interactionism's third main contribution. Where behaviourists are interested solely in the links between violent imagery and violent *action*, interactionists are also concerned with the impact of media presentations on *reactions* to violence, both official and popular. They do not deny that portrayals of, say, juvenile 'muggers' may play some role in triggering initial deviance among adolescents, but they insist that it is just as relevant to look at their impact on general attitudes towards teenage crime and on the reactive policies developed by the police and the juvenile justice system. As George Gerbner has pointed out,

> Conventional wisdom. . . might stress the one or two in a thousand who imitate violence and threaten society. But it is just as important to look at the large majority of people who become more fearful, insecure, and dependent on authority, and who may grow up demanding protection and even welcoming repression in the name of security. [Gerbner, Gross *et al.* 1979: 196]

This strand in interactionism also has nineteenth-century roots, in the debates about the role of the press in forming public opinion and influencing policy-making; but it is only in the last 15 years or so that these processes have become a major topic of media research.

Interactionism, then, challenges the behaviourist paradigm on two broad fronts. If offers an alternative account of the relationship between media involvements and the commission of social violence, and it insists on the need to examine levels of impact and response, which behaviourism ignores.

Critical approaches take over these core concerns but recast them within a class analysis grounded in Marxism. From this perspective both deviant behaviour and official responses to it are presented as forms of class action. Hence working-class youth cultures appear as means of waging the class war by other means, using style and ritual to wave two fingers in the face of consumer capitalism. By the same token, reactions to these initiatives from above (including their portrayal in the mass media) are viewed as exercises in class power aimed at reasserting the core values that support the *status quo*. As a consequence, the theoretical focus shifts from the interactionist notion of labelling to theories of legitimation, which attempt to link the process of media amplification to the wider workings of the capitalist state in an era of crisis.

Over the last decade or so in Britain, this critical perspective has become a major focus of research and theorizing, and has largely displaced interactionist perspectives from the centre of sociological debate. The same period, however, has also seen a revival and strengthening of the behaviourist paradigm. This has taken place more or less simultaneously at the popular level through the moral crusading of Mrs Mary Whitehouse, and at the academic level through the militant advocacy of Hans Eysenck and the research efforts of William Belson and others (see Eysenck and Nias 1978; Belson 1978), and it is to this counter-current that I want to turn first.

MANIFEST CONTENT, EVIDENT EFFECTS

Although arguments about the links between media imagery and social violence have a history stretching back to the beginning of the modern industrial era, the most sustained debate, and most of the academic research, has focused on the effects of television, for two reasons. First, television appeared as a uniquely powerful medium, combining as it does the visual impact of the movies with the domestic penetration of comic books and the popular press. As a result, it attracted and intensified all the fears that surrounded these older media. Second, the fact that television's emergence as the dominant popular medium coincided with the final arrival of adolescence as a universal social category linked it securely with growing worries about 'the problem of youth'.

From the beginning of the postwar period, adolescents appeared as an ambiguous phenomenon. On the one hand, the landscape of teenage leisure offered a powerful and positive image of the new consumer capitalism, with its promises of affluence, mobility and opportunity for all. But on the other, this vision was soured by the feeling that change was happening too fast, destroying the old social and moral anchor points in the process. And as juvenile crime rates rose sharply on both sides of the Atlantic, this sense of unease coalesced around the image of the teenage tearaway. Accounting for delinquency presented a problem, however. Given the almost universal belief that the new capitalism was abolishing poverty, narrowing class differentials and increasing opportunity, explanations in terms of inequality and disadvantage seemed less and less convincing. This led to a revival of interest in individual-istic explanations, and further strengthened the hold of behaviourism within academic research. It also provoked a search for some powerful new 'X' factor in the modern environment that could account for the timing of the juvenile crime wave, and commercial television and the rock and roll industry were obvious candidates. Both had attracted massive audiences among working-class youth, and both had taken off at the same time as the jump in the delinquency statistics. Although the music industry penetrated most deeply into teenage experience, for the reasons just outlined, it was television that took the lion's share of concern. Debate was dominated by the question of whether or not watching televised violence caused teenagers to behave more aggressively, and in the search for answers behaviourist approaches had several advantages. Their underlying individualism fitted easily with the dominant ideology of the time, and their insistence on controlled experiments promised to deliver what the politicians and moral crusaders demanded: clear-cut evidence backed by the imprimatur of science.

There is no space here to do justice to the complexities and contradictions of the experimental literature. That will have to wait for another occasion. For the present, I simply want to highlight some of the general limits of this kind of work.

First, there is the familiar problem of sampling. Along with experimental psychology in general, laboratory work in this area has tended to rely on 'captive' subjects, such as the children of faculty staff, students and the inmates of institutions. Male college students have figured particularly prominently, while working-class subjects and women have been under-represented (see McCormack 1978). To hard-line behaviourists this is not a particularly relevant criticism, since they assume that aggressiveness is a universal and constant potentiality of human nature which is relatively unaffected by social and cultural conditions. The sociological evidence, however, persistently challenges this assumption by showing that aggressive behaviour varies very considerably in style and frequency between different social groups. This caveat raises the wider problem of how far the results of laboratory work can be generalized to everyday life.

The problem is that behaviourism simplifies the encounter between artefacts and audiences at every level. In the first place, it works with a radically reduced notion of the meanings carried by popular films and television programmes. As critics have repeatedly pointed out, the violent incidents in Westerns, thrillers and police series are embedded within explicit visions of justice and social order and cannot be understood apart from them. But behaviourists deliberately ignore the dimensions of connotation and ideology and concentrate solely on the level of manifest content.

Nor, apart from making crude distinctions between realistic and
fantasy material, do they deal with the subtle but powerful ways in
which meaning is organized by specific styles and forms of
presentation. But these dimensions of connotation, ideology and
form are not optional extras: on the contrary, it is only by grasping
the layered nature of media artefacts in all their complexity that we
can arrive at anything approaching an adequate formulation of
their effectiveness. Behaviourists, however, settle for a one-
dimensional definition.

This reductionist view of meaning goes along with a correspond-
ingly limited approach to the viewing experience in an attempt to
match manifest content to evident effects. In pursuit of this goal,
experiments de-contextualize viewing twice over. First, the clips
that act as stimuli are detached from the flow of images that usually
surround them, and inflect their meaning in crucial ways. And
second, subjects are removed from their normal social relations and
offered encounters with strangers. The aim is to create a sanitized
space, free from the contaminations of everyday life. However, this
does not mean that experiments are totally context-free. They
suspend 'normal' relations only to replace them with the specific
interactions of the laboratory situation itself, which raises the
possibility that the findings may be due, in part at least, to the
subjects' desire to satisfy the researchers. This is particularly likely
in experiments with students who are paid or given course credits
for taking part. Consequently, the results may well be measuring
compliance with authority or eagerness to please as much as reactions to the stimuli. Moreover, experiments differ significantly
from everyday life in that people are given a licence to behave
aggressively. There are no sanctions, no likelihood of retaliation,
and no unpleasant repercussions. Indeed, in many cases subjects
are rewarded for their anti-social behaviour.

However, even if we are prepared to accept that these studies are
measuring what they say they are, the interpretation of the results
is still complicated by the presence of conditions that *intervene*
between the visual stimuli and the behavioural response. The
leading experimentalists in this field, such as Leonard Berkowitz
and Albert Bandura, have always been more interested in uncover-
ing the general dynamics of aggression than in answering the
question of whether or not watching televised violence makes
viewers more aggressive. Consequently, they are less concerned

with demonstrating a direct link between imagery and behaviour than with *specifying the conditions* under which observing violence is likely to increase viewers' aggression. In Berkowitz's often quoted experiments, for example, subjects not only watched a film clip of a violent boxing match but were systematically insulted by one of his associates beforehand. This proved crucial to their subsequent aggressiveness, and where they were not insulted there was some evidence that exposure to filmed violence actually produced a mild 'catharsis' effect (see Kaplan and Singer 1976: 47). The key results in Bandura's famous 'Bobo Doll' experiments also depend on a mediating factor: in this case, the systematic frustrating of subjects after viewing filmed violence. Once again, there is evidence to suggest that this is crucial to the observed response, and that without it the imitation effect does not occur (see Hanratty *et al.* 1972).

On balance, then, the experimental evidence for a direct and powerful link between violent imagery and violent behaviour is rather less clear-cut than some of its supporters are apt to claim (see for example Anderson 1977; Geen 1976). Not only are some of the central findings dependent on conditions other than exposure to violent imagery, but the de-contextualization of the experimental situation considerably reduces generalizability of the results to everyday situations. In an effort to close this credibility gap, some behaviourists have stepped outside the laboratory and tried to establish a direct link between normal television viewing and real-life aggression. The two most important recent studies in this genre are Leftkowitz *et al.*'s (1977) longitudinal study of American adolescents and William Belson's (1978) interview survey of London schoolboys.

Leftkowitz *et al.*'s work produced a positive correlation ($r=0.3$) between childhood preferences for violent television shows and aggressive behaviour at the age of 19, which has been widely cited as clear-cut evidence of a direct link between television viewing and teenage violence. However, closer inspection of his key measures reveals serious problems. The crucial index of exposure to televised violence for example, is based on mothers' reports of their children's favourite shows. Consequently, it is quite likely to be incomplete or inaccurate, either because the mothers may not know for sure what their children's favourites are, or because they may misremember or misrepresent them in an effort to create a favourable image with the interviewers. Inaccuracies are also likely in the other key variable, the aggression rating, since this is based on ex-classmates' recollections of how people *used* to behave when they were at school together, even though they may hardly have known them. But even if the ratings are accurate, they still relate to past actions and cannot be used as an index of current behaviour. There are problems too with Lefkowitz's analysis, most notably the fact that he fails to test for the so-called 'reverse hypothesis'; that already aggressive youngsters are drawn to violent television shows because they reflect their existing dispositions and pre-occupations. In these cases, television may reinforce aggressive-ness but it cannot be said to cause it (see Armor 1976).

Belson also claims to have demonstrated a firm causal link between childhood exposure to televised violence and adolescent aggression while managing to avoid the more obvious errors of the Lefkowitz work. He derives his key indicators from lengthy inter-views with the boys themselves. He is careful to test for the 'reverse' hypothesis, and he attempts to control for the possible confounding influence of class location, educational situation and so on. Even so, his measures and procedures remain open to a number of important criticisms. As I have argued elsewhere, there are problems with the accuracy of the boys' accounts of their television viewing and involvement in violence, and with the way their answers are coded and analysed (see Murdock and McCron 1979). But the real difficulties are conceptual rather than pro-cedural, and stem from the behaviourist paradigm that underpins the study. Because he is interested only in proving a direct causal link between exposure to televised violence and violent behaviour, he makes no attempt to demonstrate television's *relative* importance *vis-à-vis* the other factors that are known to correlate with aggressiveness. Where this has been attempted, however, the results suggest that variations in violent behaviour have compari-tively little to do with television viewing and rather more to do with social and cultural location (see Hartnagel *et al.* 1975). Belson's behaviourist project prevents him from exploring these connec-tions, however, despite the fact that they are strongly supported by his own findings. Among other things, these clearly show that, whereas exposure to televised violence is relatively stable across the major class groups, involvement in violence is heavily skewed towards boys from working-class backgrounds (see Belson 1978:

358, 411). Moreover, he further undermines his central argument by showing that the most violent boys in his sample were not the ones who had seen the most violence on television. He explains this anomaly by suggesting that they were 'too "satiated" with television, and their time too much taken up by it, to have the energy or the time for very much violence of the serious kind' (Belson, 1978: 393). An alternative explanation is that they lacked the opportunities, since high exposure to television is indicative of a mainly home-centred leisure pattern. Conversely, moderate viewing (which was strongly correlated with violent behaviour) indicates a leisure style based on the local streets, and suggests that it is this milieu and the meanings that underpin it that provide the major key to understanding aggression among working-class boys. And it is precisely this assumption that provides the starting point for subcultural studies.

THE LIMITS OF SUBCULTURAL ANALYSIS

The postwar period has seen two main waves of subcultural work. The first was sparked off by the publication of Albert Cohen's *Delinquent Boys* in 1955 and lasted until the late 1960s, while the second gathered momentum in the aftermath of 1968 and continued through the 1970s. Since this history is ably reviewed by David Downes in chapter 3 above, I shall confine myself to raising some general criticisms of the dominant tendencies in recent work as they affect the analysis of media consumption.

As Stan Cohen has pointed out (1980), there are strong continuities between these two waves of subcultural analysis: both are grounded in an account of class inequalities; both rely on ethnographies for the major part of their evidence; and both focus predominantly on working-class boys. However, there are also significant shifts of emphasis between the two, including their approach to the mass media.

Where earlier work treated teenage media involvements as a peripheral phenomenon, second-wave studies took them as a central topic of investigation. Partly this was a response to changing conditions. Fuelled by the beat boom of the mid-1960s, Britain's teenage entertainment industry experienced a spectacular growth. And as the commodities and facilities it offered became more and more central to adolescent leisure, so they also became more central to research on youth. But there was another, more polemical, reason for this focus. One of the major aims of the new subcultural work was to discredit the dominant notion of youth culture and to shift the sociology of youth towards a more thoroughgoing class analysis. Consequently, a good deal of effort went in to showing that, far from creating a classless culture of youth (as many media and academic commentators had supposed), the teenage leisure industry was actually reproducing and cementing class divisions. By pointing up the links between sub-cultural styles and class locations, it was hoped to expose the idea of youth culture as a myth, an ideological manoeuvre designed to obscure the continuing resilience of class inequalities. As a result the behavioural styles of the successive working-class subcultures (including their violence) were presented as coded expressions of a negotiated settlement with the structures of class society. While this perspective marks a distinct advance over the simplicities of youth culture theory, it is now clear that it has important limitations.

At root, the whole enterprise rested on a curious paradox. Its main project was to demystify the prevailing media images of deviant youth by erecting counter-accounts grounded in radical class theory. To achieve this, however, researchers were obliged to take these images as their starting point, thereby *replicating* the structure of attention established by the media coverage. As a result, the new sociology of youth has tended to follow the news media in focusing on the more spectacular working-class styles – the Teds, Mods, bike boys, football hooligans and so on – so that, far from challenging news values, it has actually ended up reinforcing their emphases and exclusions.

This skew of attention is further compounded by the theoretical stress on class and the consequent neglect of ethnic and gender divisions. Recent work has begun to redress these imbalances to a certain extent, although here again there is a curious symbiotic relation between media imagery and critical research, with recent ethnographies of black youth tending to follow the news media's focus on deviant groups, notably the Rastas, and work on girls tending to reproduce the media's preoccupation with female sexuality. As a result, we still have very few studies of girls' delinquency to set against those of boys, and almost no studies of female violence (although Anne Campbell's work, which appears in chapter 9 below, is a notable and welcome exception). But even in its own terms, as an account of the links between behavioural style and social location among working-class boys, the new subcultural literature presents problems.

To some extent these can be laid at the door of its preferred methodology. As I have argued elsewhere (Murdock and McCron 1976), taking groups who are already committed to a particular subcultural style and then working backwards to uncover their social situation leads researchers to draw too tight a relation between style and class and to ignore alternative ways of negotiating the same basic situation. The studies are also restricted by their focus on behaviour in school and out on the streets and their relative neglect of family relations; though here again there is a curious paradox, since the family is presented as the primary transmission agency for the class-based meaning systems that supposedly play the key role in structuring adolescents' media involvements and leisure styles. Indeed, in the stronger versions of the theory, youth subcultures are explicitly seen as dramatizing the problems and possibilities of the parental culture (see S. Cohen 1972). And yet, second-wave studies have not bothered to explore how these connections are reproduced in and through the dynamics of family interaction. As well as seriously weakening their approach theoretically, this exclusion produces an important empirical gap. There is now a good deal of evidence from studies of child abuse, wife-battering and sexual assault to suggest that the family is a prime site of interpersonal violence in our society, particularly for women and girls. However, because it ignores these 'domesticated' forms of aggression and concentrates on public displays, the subcultural literature can offer only a partial account of social violence.

This by-passing of the domestic milieu goes along with a marked neglect of television and its potential influence. As a result we are currently in the peculiar position of having two substantial research literatures on adolescent aggression, one that scarcely ever mentions television while the other hardly ever mentions anything else. Subcultural theorists are partly to blame for this, since, rather than challenging the behaviourist paradigm at its centre, and offering an alternative account of television's potential impact, they have tended to view the issue as something of a pseudo-problem. This is a mistake for two reasons. First, it is at odds with the other central

stand in the critical approach, which assigns television a key role in
the process of legitimation. Acknowledging that television's effects
may be contradictory does not require two contradictory accounts
of its influence. Second, despite the counter-attractions of the
teenage leisure environment, television viewing still occupies a
sizeable slice of adolescents' free time, especially among girls.
Consequently, the possible links between television involvement
and patterns of consciousness and actions (including violent
behaviour), while they are certainly not central, cannot be entirely
ignored. At the same time, the issues cannot adequately be
addressed from within the behaviourist project with its single-
minded search for direct causal links. The important connections
work differently, more complexly, and in unexpected ways. What,
for example, is the link between working-class violence and the
frustrations generated by television's constant parading of spectacular consumption in a situation of mass unemployment, falling
real incomes and restricted opportunities? (See Halloran 1978: 821.)
And how do television's dominant images of masculinity connect
with cultural norms that legitimate violence among males? In order
to formulate these sorts of questions, however, we need to break
once and for all with the behaviourist paradigm and to consider the
possible impact of the whole range of television programming,
including those forms that are usually thought of as non-
problematic (see Murdock and McCron 1978). This is not to say that
images of violence are irrelevant, or that their effects are always
weak and indeterminate, but it is to insist that they be considered as
one factor among a number of others whose secondary role cannot
be assumed *a priori*. As well as extending the range of television
programming considered relevant, however, future work will also
need to broaden its conception of violence.

The new subcultural work adopts a problem-solving orientation in
which particular behavioural styles are seen as ways of negotiating
the limits and contradictions of specific class locations. As a
consequence, violence is presented mainly in instrumental terms,
as a means of pursuing some other goal such as creating excitement
or defending threatened identities. The intention is to demonstrate
the essential rationality and meaningfulness of acts that are
habitually described in the popular media as senseless and animal-
istic. In stressing the instrumentality of juvenile violence, however,
subcultural accounts tend to play down the role of the impulsive or

angry violence that is the main concern to experimentalists like Berkowitz; and a full account of violence needs to take account of both forms. Ironically, the subjects of subcultural ethnographies often have a better grasp of this than researchers. They frequently make distinctions between violence that is justified by the circumstances and the actions of 'nutters' or 'head cases', who engage in unprovoked acts of aggression, or who 'go over the top' and use unnecessary violence on their victims.

These specific deficiencies, although damaging, are not in the end disastrous for the critical approach. They can be remedied by letting go of the restrictive notion of subculture and undertaking studies that explore the links between media involvements and situational action in a more open-ended way and across the range of social locations. In the process, however, this work will need to confront and work its way through the theoretical divisions that critical research has taken over from Marxism.

The emphasis on the transformative power of human action within Marxism has always sat somewhat uneasily alongside the equal and parallel stress on structural constraints. But in recent years this duality has been further underlined by the events of 1968 and their aftermath, which provided the context within which the present wave of critical work was formed. From the outset, the 'lessons' of 1968 were contradictory. On the one hand, the student movement and the counter-culture appeared to signal the onset of a legitimation crisis, and ever since commentators have been quick to read every movement of struggle and dissent, from the ecology movement to gay rights, as a further sign that the ideological centre cannot hold. On the other hand, the way that these initiatives have been contained and accommodated has led to a renewed stress on the processes of coercion and incorporation, and to a revival of theoretical interest in Gramsci's work on hegemony and Althusser's essay on *Ideological State Apparatuses* (both of which appeared in readily available English translations early in 1971). Within critical research, however, these two strands have tended to separate out, with subcultural studies drawing mainly on the first and work legitimation relying heavily on the second.

Hence subcultural researchers have consistently interpreted working-class youth cultures as symptoms of ideological refusal and have emphasized the way in which the styles and commodities promoted by the mass media are taken over and invested with new potentially subversive meanings. 'By repositioning and recontext-ualizing commodities, by subverting their conventional uses and inventing new ones', so the argument goes, 'the subcultural stylist gives the lie to what Althusser has called the "false obviousness of everyday practice" and opens up the worlds of objects to new and covertly oppositional readings' (Hebdige 1979: 102). However, as Stan Cohen correctly points out, this 'constant impulse to decode the style in terms *only* of opposition and resistance' has led sub-cultural analysts to underestimate the ideological power of the media and to gloss over the many instances 'when style is not reworked or reassembled but taken over intact from dominant commercial culture' (Cohen 1980: xii). It also slips around the awkward fact that available evidence clearly shows that most working-class adolescents are deeply conservative, and that their radicalism, where it exists, is more likely to be of the right-wing variety than left-wing. According to recent opinion studies, for example, 89 per cent of 15–21-year-olds agreed that 'vandals and hooligans should be dealt with more severely', and 85 per cent of 15–25-year-olds said that 'the state should act more effectively against terrorists and violent criminals (see NOP 1978: 22, and McCann-Erickson International 1978: 18). Although these findings pose some problems for the subcultural approach as it stands, they are entirely consistent with the other main current of critical research, and it is to this that I want to turn now.

FROM LABELLING TO LEGITIMATION

From the mid-1950s onwards, the activities of young people in general, and delinquent youth in particular, became the focus of a continual barrage of media coverage offering identikit images of teenage delinquents and ready-made explanations of their be-haviour. These images helped to mobilize public concern and condemnation and to legitimate the escalation of control activity. This produced increased arrests and stiffer sentences, which in turn confirmed the seriousness of the threat and the validity of the original stereotype. The broad contours of this amplification process had been outlined by Leslie Wilkins (1964: ch. 4), but it was left to the generation who graduated in the early 1960s to trace the way it worked on the ground. The resulting research laid the essential base for later critical studies.

The first systematic empirical study of media amplification in Britain was Stan Cohen's research on the Mods and Rockers panic, which he began in the spring of 1964 (S. Cohen 1972). Following the traditional leisure pattern of working-class Londoners, contingents from both groups arrived in the seaside resort of Clacton for the Easter bank holiday. The weather was particularly bad and the amusement facilities inadequate, and fights broke out. These were given front-page treatment in the national press the next day and presented as confrontations between rival gangs on the model of *West Side Story*. This act of labelling, Cohen argues, had several important consequences. First, it sparked off a moral panic, which obliged the police to step up their surveillance of the two groups while providing them with readily identifiable stereotypes with which to work. The result was more frequent arrests, which further confirmed the initial panic. Second, by focusing on the stylistic divisions and emphasizing the antagonism between the groups, the publicity given to the Mods and Rockers encouraged adolescents to think of themselves in these terms. This, together with the group solidarity created by common subjection to police harassment, increasingly polarized the two groups, thereby cementing the original image. These processes combined to produce more clashes between the two groups, most notably at various holiday resorts on successive bank holidays. These in turn attracted renewed news coverage and increased control activity and further moral panic. Using a novel combination of naturalistic observation, content analysis and documentary evidence, Cohen succeeded in tracing the course of this amplification cycle through its various phases. Moreover, he developed an explanation of its dynamics that went well beyond anything else then available. The result was a pioneering work that opened up a whole series of novel questions for research and theorizing. Some of these were pursued in Jock Young's parallel work on images of drug-takers (1971) and in the research on media presentations of deviance conducted by members of the National Deviancy Conference (see for example, Cohen and Young 1973).

As accounts of labelling and amplification processes, however, these studies were weak at several crucial points. As Stuart Hall has argued, an adequate analysis needs to deal with 'the process by which ideologies are reproduced' and with 'the social praxis through which they renew themselves at the heart of social life'

(Hall 1971: 35). But it was exactly this concrete analysis of reproduction that was missing from studies of media amplification.

The question of reception was particularly problematic, since in
order to argue convincingly that the media sustain generalized
moral panics it is necessary to show that the dominant media
images do structure the definitions of the situation held by the
general public. In fact, there were very few attempts to demonstrate these links empirically. Instead, researchers tended to
concentrate on mapping the inferential structures of media coverage and assumed that these provided the organizing categories for
audience perceptions. There was a similar lack of empirical work on
the process of image production. There were no accounts of the
nuts and bolts of news-making, no exploration of the complex web
of relations binding journalists to their sources within the control
agencies and elite groups, and no examination of the ways in which
news production is shaped and constrained by the routine practices and assumptions of newsmen and by the pressures of market
competition. As a result, the question of where dominant ideas
about deviance come from and how exactly they are relayed and
reproduced never received a satisfactory answer.

Work on these questions was however beginning independently
within the small but growing field of media sociology in Britain,
which began to gather momentum in the second half of the 1960s.
This period produced Jeremy Tunstall's (1971) study of specialist
newspaper journalists (including crime reporters), and the
Leicester Centre's observational study of the way the news media
covered the anti-Vietnam War demonstration in London in the
autumn of 1968 (Halloran *et al.* 1970). Although conceived entirely
independently, the Leicester study clearly connected with the
central concerns of labelling and amplification theory while at the
same time shifting the emphasis somewhat. The fact that it focused
on political deviance raised the whole question of legitimation and
of the relations between ideology and coercion as modes of social
control in late capitalist states, although it was only after the study
was published that these themes were broached (see Murdock
1973).

Subsequent research on news, such as Steve Chibnall's (1977)
study of crime reporters and Philip Schlesinger's (1978) work on
news production in the BBC, have filled out the picture considerably. And, together with parallel American studies of news-

making (e.g. Epstein 1974; Tuchman 1978; Gans 1979) and the press construction of crime waves (Fishman 1978, 1980), this work provides a fairly full account of the forces shaping the presentation of violence in the news media. Nevertheless, conceptual difficulties still remain, notably the problem of understanding the relationship between the constraints that stem from the organization of news production and the competitive situation of news organizations, and the limit points imposed by the state – both directly, through legal restrictions on reporting, and indirectly, through the control of information flows from police and army sources. In their eagerness to get away from simplistic models of manipulation and bias, it is arguable that researchers have 'bent the stick' too far and discounted the role of interventions from above almost completely. The English media's organized myopia on the situation in Northern Ireland, however, has put this question firmly back on the agenda.

While the growth of research and debate on news-making represents a decided gain, there has so far been very little comparable work on the construction of television fiction and entertainment shows, although these are arguably the most potent sources of popular imagery of crime and violence. As a result, the production studies sit somewhat uneasily alongside recent work on reception. Attempts have been made to trace the connections between news presentations and popular perceptions of crime (e.g. Graber 1980), but the best work in this field has focused on other areas of social life, notably race and industrial relations (see Hartmann and Husband 1974; Hartmann 1976). On violence, however, the most comprehensive work so far is undoubtedly George Gerbner's research on the impact of television fiction.

For over a decade now, Gerbner and his team at the University of Pennsylvania have been monitoring the imagery of American prime-time television fiction and mapping the vision of social and moral order that it presents. Their analysis demonstrates beyond doubt that violence is absolutely central to popular drama's demonstration of 'the rules of the game of power' (Gerbner and Gross 1976a: 183). For Gerbner, then, messages about social violence are also always messages about social power, and as such they carry different lessons for different groups of viewers:

These may include lessons of victimization and ways to avoid

82   *Graham Murdock*

as well as to commit violence; caution and prudence as well as
pugnacity; a calculus of one's risks as well as the opportunities
to be gained from violence; a tendency to acquiesce to the use of
violence by others, as well as to imitate violence; and a sense of
fear and need for protection as well as of aggression. [Gerbner,
Gross *et al.* 1978: 184]

It is these last two effects – the heightened sense of fear and
increased demands for security and protection – that Gerbner has
been particularly interested in exploring in his audience studies.
His basic procedure is to divide his samples into 'high' and 'low'
television viewers (usually defined as those who watch four or
more hours a day and those who watch less than two) and to
compare their perceptions on a range of dimensions. The result of
this 'cultivation' analysis (as he calls it) appear to show consistent
differences between the two groups, with avid viewers tending to
overestimate their chances of being involved in violence and
expressing more fear about being out alone at night (see Gerbner
and Gross 1976a,b). This accentuated sense of risk and insecurity,
Gerbner argues, increases people's dependence upon established
authority, legitimizes the increased use of force by control
agencies, and mobilizes opinion behind demands for tougher law
and order policies. By insisting that the general ideological and
political 'effects' of violent imagery are more significant than their
role in stimulating individual acts of aggression, this argument
marks a decisive break with the behaviourist paradigm and a con-
certed attempt to shift the focus of debate. As such it makes a
welcome advance. However, it is not without its problems.

To begin with, Gerbner's demonstration of the link between high
television viewing and fear of violence is not as secure as it first
appears. Although he is careful to control for the confounding
effects of age, sex and educational level, his early audience surveys
ignore the role of race and other factors in shaping people's fear of
victimization. Other studies, for example, have shown that differences in direct knowledge of street violence stemming from
variations in neighbourhood crime rates are particularly important
in structuring people's attitudes (see Yin 1980). Moreover, as a
recent re-analysis of Gerbner's data shows, when these factors are
taken into account the key relationship between high television
viewing and fear of walking alone at night collapses (see Hughes

1980). These findings do not mean that media involvements are unimportant in forming perceptions, but they do suggest that the interaction between 'situated' and 'mediated' knowledge may be rather more complex and variable than Gerbner's early analyses suggested, a fact that he recognizes in his most recent work (see Gerbner, Gross *et al.* 1980). Nor can it be assumed that habitual viewing of televised violence will necessarily fuel demands for greater policing and tougher measures to combat crime: It may equally well confirm popular distrust and opposition to the police. Certainly there is evidence that media presentations play an important role cementing adverse views of police practice, especially among young people (see Belson 1975: 69). Gerbner recognizes these problems at a programmatic level but fails to follow them through in his empirical work. His data are too crude to sustain the argument he wants to make. The public opinion poll questions he uses cannot catch the layers and contradictions of common sense, and an analysis based on simple demographic 'variables' cannot provide an adequate map of the social locations that generate differences in popular consciousness and action.

In addition to these methodological difficulties, however, Gerbner's analysis is theoretically weak at key points. Throughout his work he justifies his focus on television on the grounds that it has displaced organized religion as the key agency of legitimation in advanced Western societies. Having raised the issue of legitimation, however, he has surprisingly little to say about who controls the process and how. At certain points he seems to endorse the Marxist formulation of a 'ruling class' (Gerbner and Gross 1976b: 89), while at others he avoids the question of control altogether by describing television as 'an agency of the established order' (Gerbner and Gross 1976a: 175). This moving between terms is indicative of a double failure on Gerbner's part. Not only does he provide no account of the location and operation of ideological power; he also fails to explore the *relations between* the institutions of ideological transmission (including television) and the coercive apparatuses centred on the institutions of law and order, despite the fact that these connections are central to a full account of the way that television operates as an agency of legitimation and control. Critical research, in contrast, has taken these linkages as a central focus of investigation.

The main theoretical impetus behind this thrust in Britain came from the growing interest in Gramsci and Althusser's work on 'the relations of unity and difference between the ideological institutions of "indirect hegomony" and the state institutions of "direct domination" ' (Hall 1971: 40). This line of analysis has been pursued most forcefully by Stuart Hall and his collaborators, and finds its fullest expression in their study of the 'mugging' panic of the early 1970s (Hall *et al.* 1978). They show how the news media, working with images from the New York ghetto, defined the increasing incidence of street robberies by adolescents as an outbreak of a new and dangerous kind of violent crime – 'mugging'. They trace the way that this definition was employed to justify punitive sentencing, and they show how it reinforced the gathering moral panic about the breakdown of law and order and helped to legitimate the movement towards more coercive forms of social control. At one level, then, the study provides a detailed account of another panic about juvenile crime to set alongside Stan Cohen's work. At the same time, it transcends his interactionist framework and links the 'mugging' panic to the economic crisis of British capitalism and the emerging control strategies of the state. Both the 'muggings' themselves and the responses to them are placed firmly in the context of deteriorating material conditions in the inner cities, worsening race relations, the fracturing of the political consensus, and the development of a 'law and order' state. Reactions to 'mugging' are therefore seen not simply as an illustration of another amplification spiral in action, but as a key component in the overall strategy through which the dominant class alliance sought to manage a social system in crisis. They are presented as part of the general process of persuading the public to accept control measures that were already being prepared to cope with the social unrest that the deepening recession was expected to produce.

The manufacture of moral panics therefore appears as one of the major means by 'which a "silent majority" is won over to the support of increasingly coercive measures on the part of the state, and lends its legitimacy to a "more than usual" exercise of control' (Hall *et al.* 1978: 221). It is a provocative thesis, which opens up a number of important but neglected questions about the links between media imagery, public opinion and social control, and as such it marks a decisive advance. Even so, the argument remains underdeveloped at certain critical points.

Although the study explicitly focuses on the links between the mass media system and the institutions of coercion, the analysis of these relations is somewhat sketchy and abstract. Hall does not provide a sustained account of the policy-making process, nor does he explore the detailed connections between the news media, the political institutions and the control agencies that feed and sustain it. Once these links are examined, however, a more complex picture begins to emerge. With the single exception of the BBC, all the major British mass media are commercial enterprises. Consequently, their relations to the various state apparatuses are subject to all the general contradictions of capital–state relations, plus the specific contradictions that stem from the fact that the state has consistently challenged the news media's definition of themselves as an independent Fourth Estate, by increasingly curbing the circulation of official information. These latent antagonisms work unevenly, however. Because of the pressures and routines of news production, they are likely to be at their least visible in the daily news coverage that Hall concentrates on. Conversely, they will be most in evidence in weekly and documentary journalism, where reporters are licensed to look for trouble and to pick up on divisions within the political and state agencies as they struggle to cope with the effects of crisis. This split, in turn, is mapped on to the division between 'vertical' communication from the top downwards and 'horizontal' communication within the dominant groups. Legitimation is a double process, which requires not only the consent of the governed but also the cohesion of the various power blocs and state apparatuses (see Therborn 1980: ch. 5). Consequently, any analysis of the mass media's role in this process must address this duality and explore the way in which the elite media construct a consensus of the powerful as well as the way the popular media help to engineer the consent of the powerless. Examining the relations between different levels of the mass media and the process of policy formation will be an important task for future work if the critical approach is to provide a comprehensive and convincing account of the links between the circulation of ideologies and the legitimation of social order.

The other major gap in Hall's argument opens up around the familiar question of reception, since he offers very little direct evidence of the way the interpretative frames offered by the media actually structured popular consciousness and helped mobilize opinion in favour of increased support for law and order policies. Opinion poll results certainly show a steady escalation in concern about violent crime through the 1970s and increased support for tougher measures (see *New Society* 1980: 220). But this kind of evidence is insufficient. By using 'violence' as a catch-all term it disguises the important variations in public perceptions of different kinds of violence. As three of Britain's leading critical criminologists pointed out some time ago, 'The time is clearly ripe for investigation of the extent of consensus or dissensus over crime amongst members of different social classes' (Taylor, Walton and Young 1975: 43). Surveys of public attitudes towards crime have been conducted but have tended to employ class as a stratifying variable rather than a theoretical construct. Consequently, they have not explored the ways in which attitudes to deviance and violence are embedded in class-based meaning systems which support negotiated or oppositional readings of dominant imagery and ideology.

Over and above its specific gaps, however, Hall's work on 'mugging' highlights certain general weaknesses in the critical approach as it currently stands. Despite its obvious debts to social historians such as Edward Thompson, the study is curiously ahistorical. Its major aim is to elucidate the specific 'conjuncture' within which the 'mugging' panic took place and to trace its roots in the postwar era. This relatively foreshortened perspective leads Hall to argue that the early 1970s saw the emergence of a new and exceptional form of the British state, which he dubs the 'law and order state'. Recent historical research raises a query against this conclusion, however. Despite the century that separates them, for example, the 'garotting' panic of 1862 is in many ways very similar to the 'mugging' panic of 1972, both in the form of the crime itself (street robbery) and in the responses it generated (see Davis 1979). There are also important differences, but to specify their nature and significance we need to go back to the formation of the modern British state in the second half of the nineteenth century. For it was then that the institutions of law and order assumed their present form and entered into a complex set of relations with a mature capitalist economy, with a political system based on the mass franchise, and with a mass media system centred around the commercial distribution of news and entertainment. What forms these relations took, how they have shifted since, and the extent of their resilience and inertia are matters for detailed empirical study. A start has been made on this in the last few years, however, as critical sociologists have increasingly turned to historical research and social historians have become more interested in the areas of crime, law, social policy and the popular media. This coincidence of interests offers one of the most promising growth points for future work and provides one of the basic preconditions for breaking away from the restrictive terms of the current media–violence debate.

In addition to an adequate historical perspective, future work will also require more and better comparative studies. Although British critical research has drawn heavily on continental Marxism for its theoretical underpinnings, its empirical concerns have remained surprisingly parochial and firmly fixed on 'the condition of England' question. This isolationism needs to be broken down for two reasons. First, a comparative perspective will enable us to specify much more precisely what is unique about the British situation as against parallel developments in other advanced capitalist societies such as West Germany and Italy. And second, a critical perspective worthy of the name needs to address itself to the current crisis of socialist formations as well as to the crisis of capitalism, and to explore the mass media's role in the countries of the Third World, paying particular attention to periods of insurrection and counter-revolution.

Now it could be argued that these suggestions move us rather a long way from current discussions of the possible links between mass communications and social violence, perhaps too far. My answer is yes, the movement is considerable, but it is also necessary; for without it, critical research will never break out of the research agenda set by individualism and interactionism and develop a comprehensive and convincing alternative. It is not enough to provide different answers to the dominant questions; we also need to ask other kinds of questions, and to work our way towards plausible answers. This then is the task and the promise facing future research.

REFERENCES

Anderson, F. Scott 1977: 'TV violence and viewer aggression: a cumulation of study results 1956–1976', *Public Opinion Quarterly*, 41: 314–31.

Armor, D.J. 1976: *Measuring the Effects of Television on Aggressive Behaviour*, Santa Monica: Rand Corporation.

Belson, William A. 1975: *The Police and the Public*, London: Harper & Row.

Belson, William A. 1978: *Television Violence and the Adolescent Boy*, Farnborough: Saxon House.

Blumer, Herbert and Hauser, Philip M. 1933: *Movies, Delinquency and Crime*, New York: Macmillan.

Chibnall, Steve 1977: *Law-and-Order News: An Analysis of Crime Reporting in the British Press*, London: Tavistock.

Cohen, Phil 1972: 'Subcultural conflict and working-class community', *Working Papers in Cultural Studies*, no 2: 5–51.

Cohen, Stanley 1972: *Folk Devils and Moral Panics: The Creation of the Mods and Rockers*, London: MacGibbon & Kee.

Cohen, Stanley 1980: 'Symbols of trouble', Introduction to the new edition of *Folk Devils and Moral Panics*, Oxford: Martin Robertson, i–xxxiv.

Cohen, Stanley and Young, Jock 1973: *The Manufacture of News: Deviance, Social Problems and the Mass Media*, London: Constable.

Davis, Jennifer 1979: 'The London garotting panic of 1862', in *Crime and Law: The Social History of Crime in Western Europe since 1500*, ed. V.A.C. Gatrell *et al.* London: Europa.

Epstein, Edward Jay 1974: *News From Nowhere: Television and the News*, New York: Vintage Books.

Eysenck, H.J. and Nias, D.K.B. 1978: *Sex, Violence and the Media*, London: Maurice Temple Smith.

Fishman, Mark 1978: 'Crime waves as ideology', *Social Problems*, 25 (5): 531–43.

Fishman, Mark 1980: *Manufacturing the News*, Austin: University of Texas Press.

Gans, Herbert 1979: *Deciding What's News*, New York: Pantheon.

Geen, Russell, G. 1976: 'Observing violence in the mass media: implications of basic research' in *Perspectives on Aggression*, ed. Russell Geen, New York: Academic Press, 193–234.

Gerbner, George and Gross, Larry 1976a: 'Living with television: the violence profile', *Journal of Communication*, 26: 173–99.

Gerbner, George and Gross, Larry 1976b: 'The scary world of TV's heavy viewer', *Psychology Today*, 9: 41–5, 89.

Gerbner, George, Gross, Larry, *et al.* 1978: 'Cultural indicators: violence profile no. 9', *Journal of Communication*, 28: 176–207.

Gerbner, George, Gross, Larry *et al.* 1979: 'The demonstration of power: violence profile no. 10', *Journal of Communication*, 29: 177–96.

Gerbner, George, Gross, Larry *et al.* 1980: 'the "mainstreaming" of America: violence profile no. 11', *Journal of Communication*, 30: 10–29.

Graber, Doris A. 1980: *Crime News and the Public*, New York: Praeger.

Hall, Stuart 1971: 'Deviancy, politics and the media', paper presented to

the British Sociological Association Annual Conference.
Hall, Stuart *et al.* 1978: *Policing the Crisis: Mugging, the State, and Law and Order*, London: Macmillan.
Halloran, James D. 1978: 'Mass communications: symptom or cause of violence?' *International Social Science Journal*, 30(4): 816–33.
Halloran, James D., Elliott, Philip and Murdock, Graham 1970: *Demonstrations and Communication: A Case Study*, Harmondsworth: Penguin.
Hanratty, M.A. *et al.* 1972: 'Effects of frustration upon imitation of aggression', *Journal of Personality and Social Psychology*, 21: 30–4.
Hartmann, Paul 1976: *The Media and Industrial Relations*, Final Report to the Leverhulme Trust.
Hartmann, Paul and Husband, Charles 1974: *Racism and the Mass Media*, London: Davis-Poynter.
Hartnagel, Timothy F. *et al.* 1975: 'TV violence and violent behaviour', *Social Forces*, 54(2): 341–51.
Hebdige, Dick 1979: *Subculture: The Meaning of Style*, London: Methuen.
Hughes, Michael 1980: 'The fruits of cultivation analysis: a re-examination of some effects of television watching', *Public Opinion Quarterly*, 44(3): 287–302.
Kaplan, Robert M. and Singer, Robert, D. 1976: 'Television violence and viewer aggression: a re-examination of the evidence', *Journal of Social Issues*, 32(4): 35–70.
Lefkowitz, M.M., Eron, L.D., Walder, L.O. and Halesman, L.R. 1977: *Growing Up to be Violent: A Longitudinal Study of the Development of Aggression*, New York: Pergamon Press.
McCann-Erickson International 1978: *Youth in Europe: A Study of the Young People of Eleven Countries*, London: McCann-Erickson International.
McCormack, Thelma 1978: 'Machismo in media research: a critical review of research on violence and pornography', *Social Problems*, 25(5): 544–55.
Murdock, Graham 1973: 'Political deviance: the press presentation of a militant mass demonstration', in Cohen and Young, 156–75.
Murdock, Graham 1979: *Adolescent Culture and the Mass Media*, Final Report to the Social Science Research Council.
Murdock, Graham and McCron, Robin 1976: 'Consciousness of class and consciousness of generation', in *Resistance Through Rituals*, ed. Stuart Hall and Tony Jefferson, London: Hutchinson, 192–207.
Murdock, Graham and McCron, Robin 1978: 'Teenagers and television violence', *New Society*, 14(845): 632–3.
Murdock, Graham and McCron, Robin 1979: 'The television and delinquency debate', *Screen Education*, no. 30: 51–67.
New Society 1980: 'The law'n order vote', *New Society*, no. 917: p. 12 June, 220.
National Opinion Poll 1978: 'Young people', *NOP Political, Social, Economic Review*, no. 17: 13–26.

Schlesinger, Philip 1978: *Putting 'Reality' Together: BBC News*, London: Constable.

Taylor, Ian, Walton, Paul and Young, Jock 1975: 'Critical criminology in Britain: review and prospects', in *Critical Criminology* ed. Ian Taylor, Paul Walton and Jock Young, London: Routledge & Kegan Paul, 6–57.

Therborn, Göran 1980: *The Ideology of Power and the Power of Ideology*, London: Verso.

Thompson, E.P. 1968: *The Making of the English Working Class*, Harmondsworth: Penguin.

Tuchman, Gaye 1978: *Making News: A Study in the Construction of Reality*, New York: Free Press.

Tunstall, Jeremy 1971: *Journalists at Work*, London: Constable.

Wilkins, Leslie T. 1964: *Social Deviance*, London: Tavistock.

Yin, Peter P. 1980: 'Fear of crime among the elderly: some issues and suggestions', *Social Problems*, 27(4): 492–504.

Young, Jock 1971: *The Drug Takers*, London: MacGibbon and Kee.

CHAPTER 6

Violence and Rule-Following Behaviour

Leonard Berkowitz

In their attempt to make sense out of human behaviour, some analysts have emphasized the individual's proclivity to follow rules. For these writers one of the central qualities differentiating the human being from other animals is his capacity to establish and recognize social standards, norms that define particular actions as appropriate or good and other behaviours as inappropriate or bad. The person employs these standards or rules in imparting meaning to the conduct he witnesses, and even uses them to control the major part of his own actions. Marsh, Rosser and Harré (1978) adopted this perspective when they argued that much of the violence at times exhibited by fans at soccer matches or by students in classrooms is actually governed by social rules. In their words, 'To assert that conduct is orderly is, from our point of view, to imply that it is directed by a sense of social propriety – that not only is it nonrandom but that it is both generated and limited by pre-scriptions and the possibility of sanction, in particular the sanction of expressed disapproval' (p. 16). This statement seems to imply that virtually every action – or at least those behaviours that are not 'random' – is in large part an attempt to adhere to some social rule, with the rule being a prescription for conduct. Practically every-thing the person does it presumably governed by his anticipations of the rewards he might obtain by following the appropriate social standard and the punishments he would receive if he deviated from this rule.

Criminal violence is frequently interpreted in very similar terms. Here, too, it is often held that a good deal of aggression is rule-following behaviour. Many aggressors supposedly strike their victim because they believe such an action is required by the norms of their particular social group. Wolfgang (1959) summarized this thesis in his discussion of how subcultural norms might produce ethnic and racial differences in rates of violent crimes: 'Quick resort to phyical combat as a measure of daring, courage, or defense of status appears to be a cultural expectation, especially for lower socioeconomic class males of both races'. Thus, the men living in a 'subculture of violence' theoretically attack others mainly because they believe they are expected to do so. If they have been provoked, the only way they can receive the respect and approval they desire from the bystanders is to lash out at their opponent. A failure to strike is a deviation from the group's rules and could therefore bring punishment in the form of a decline in the onlookers' regard for them. As Wolfgang and Ferracuti (1967) put it, 'The juvenile who fails to live up to the conflict gang's requirements is pushed outside the group. The adult male who does not defend his honor or his female companion will be socially emasculated. The "coward" is forced to move out of the territory, to find new friends and make new alliances'.

This type of analysis is widely accepted by students of social deviance (e.g. Clinard 1974; Gibbons 1973; Schur 1969). It is now quite common for social scientists to attribute the criminal assaults committed by low-SES men to the values and expectations these people acquired in their subculture of violence and to their striving for the social rewards that violence would presumably bring them. Such a conception implicitly maintains that many violent offenders are basically not very different from those who behave less aggressively. All of us govern our conduct by the social rules we have learned. Highly aggressive persons are supposedly merely living up to a different set of rules from those operating in middle-class society.

However, as popular as this formulation is in the social sciences, there are growing doubts as to whether it can serve as a general theory of aggressive behaviour. For one thing, it is now increasingly recognized, as Wolfgang and Ferracuti (1967) had acknowledged, that much of the reasoning is quite circular. The proponents explain group differences in violence by positing subcultural values, and then use the same differences in aggressive behaviour as evidence that the groups do have different values. As a matter of fact, when researchers explicitly ask about these attitudes and values, they do not find the expected group differences in the glorification of aggression (Baker and Ball 1969; Erlanger 1974a,b). Furthermore, even violent offenders frequently do not subscribe to the values of toughness and machismo as the subculture notion contends (Ball-Rokeach 1973).

There is another problem with which I have been particularly concerned. The conception of aggression as rule-governed be-haviour essentially views most aggressive actions as being basically alike; if all of these violent behaviours are largely governed by social rules, they must all operate in very similar ways, conceptually speaking. Such an analysis fails to recognize the different types of aggression. It especially neglects the important distinction between instrumental and hostile (or angry) aggression (Feshbach 1964). Most psychologists, it is fair to say, define aggression as the intentional injury of another. However, in the case of instrumental aggression the aggressor wants more than to hurt his victim. He strikes someone because he believes this behaviour will bring him another and more important goal, such as money or social status. Those arguments that envision aggression as rule-following con-duct basically assume that this behaviour is instrumental aggression; the assault is carried out presumably because the aggressor thinks he will thereby attain approval, acceptance or social status, or at least will avoid rejection. But all aggression is not instrumental behaviour. As more and more psychologists are coming to recognize, quite a few attacks should be regarded as hostile (or angry) aggression, in which the aggressor's major aim is the injury of his victim. This type of action is governed chiefly by anticipations of the act's injurious outcomes, and is reinforced when the attacker learns that he has inflicted what he regards as an appropriate level of pain (Swart and Berkowitz 1976).

I have now participated in two separate investigations of violent incidents and am currently in the midst of a third study, all in the United Kingdom, which have highlighted the limited utility of the rule conception of violence. Without denying that some aggressive acts are governed by particular social norms, these investigations suggest that a good many criminal assaults are far more impulsive and much less calculating than the rule idea would have us believe.

Quite frequently, they are instances of angry aggression and are chiefly aimed at the injury or even destruction of the victim.

The first study involved interviews with 65 British men who had each been convicted of assaulting another man and were now in prisons in or around East Anglia. Most of the offenders were in their late twenties or younger; the great majority had been convicted of another crime before the offence for which they were now in gaol; and in two-thirds of the cases at least one of the prior convictions was for violence. Typically, they were persistent troublemakers with a history of extreme aggression. By design, however, none of the assaults in our sample was committed in the course of a robbery.

All of the respondents were asked detailed questions about the encounter that had led up to their present conviction. According to their reports, the incident typically began with an argument or some other kind of quarrel which usually increased in intensity fairly rapidly until the fight broke out. The second most frequent cause was a friend's need for assistance. When the men were queried about what they had sought to accomplish when they hit their opponent, most indicated that they had had one of two principal aims: either they had wanted to hurt their opponent or, somewhat less frequently, they had tried to protect themselves or ward off some danger. None of the offenders reported wanting to protect or enhance their reputation or to gain other people's approval.

A clear theme emerged in the descriptions given by those who had sought chiefly to injure their opponent. The precipitating event, whatever it was, infuriated them, and their anger (or, better, their rage) propelled the attack. Again and again, these men indicated their assault was driven by the internal excitation within them, and a number of them described themselves as having gone beserk.

All this is not to say that the offenders were totally indifferent to what other people thought of them. About a third of the men indicated during the interview that they had at least some desire to appear tough and strong. But even these cases did not explode into violence mainly because they had wanted to gain respect or look tough. One of the respondents, a 30-year-old man with quite a few convictions for assaults (including the use of weapons), reported having a reputation for fighting and admitted that he tried to live up to his public image. Yet even he said he often got into fights without thinking of his reputation at all. 'At the time I'm not thinking that at all. It's afterwards I think this all out, but at the time I don't stop to think. At the time it seems the natural thing to do or the right thing to do.'

Another one of our sample who also spoke about not wanting to be disgraced in front of his mates described one of his violent outbursts, an attempted murder, in similar terms. When the interviewer asked him whether he had attacked his opponent because he thought he would look bad if he did not do anything, he answered, 'No, I didn't think nothing like that. Just done it on the spur of the moment'.

These cases are instructive, especially the first one. We have a suggestion here that the men thought up reasons for their behaviour after they had acted, perhaps in order to make sense out of what they had done. The first man I just quoted said he hadn't considered his reputation (or other possible consequences) until 'afterwards'. 'It's afterwards I think this all out, but at the time I don't stop to think'. Could it be that many of the accounts people offer to explain some highly emotional action are after-the-fact interpretations? When they say they hit their opponent in an angry outburst because they wanted respect or because others would expect them to act that way, they might actually be voicing an explanation they can understand but which does not give sufficient weight to the actual determinants of their explosive attack. The internal stimulation within them might have impelled the impulsive aggression, and not anticipation of the social benefits they might gain by hitting their victim.

At any rate, I can summarize the picture I developed from these interviews in this manner. The men seemed to have very fragile egos, and were quick to define another person's behaviour as an insult or a challenge threatening their self-esteem. This threat tended to infuriate them. Unless there was an obvious reason for them to restrain themselves (such as their opponent being clearly dangerous), in many instances they did not inhibit the aggressive inclinations that built up quickly inside them. Their internal controls were weak, partly because of the great amounts of alcohol so many of them had recently imbibed but also because they had not learned how to contain their violent urges. And so, they struck out at their antagonist in rage, wanting more than anything else to hurt him and not thinking of other possible outcomes. They exhibited hostile and not instrumental aggression.

Another study with which I have been associated also points to the necessity of distinguishing among different kinds of violent incidents. This investigation is a re-analysis of fights described by the boys participating in the Cambridge Study of Juvenile Development (West 1969; West and Farrington 1973; West and Farrington 1977). Starting out with a sample of 411 eight-year-old males, largely Caucasian, from a working-class area in London, the researchers have followed these youths for the past 17 years. When the participants were between 18 and 19 years of age, about 95 per cent of them were re-interviewed and were asked, among other things, about any fights they had in the previous three years. Fights were defined as incidents in which at least one blow was deliberately aimed at and connected with another individual. The youths were also questioned about the 'most vicious' fight they had during this period. One-third of the 389 boys did not report any fights, and my present summary is thus based on the 257 youngsters who did describe their most vicious fights.

David Farrington, Donald West and I were mainly interested in the differences between group and individual encounters. A boy joined with a group of peers might have very different motives from those impelling a youngster engaged in solitary battle. Very conscious of his mates nearby, the group fighter could be more intent on doing what his peers expect of him in order to gain their approval. He might not even be angry with his opponents at the time: group traditions, group considerations and the social influence exerted by the dominant members of his group might have prompted the incident. All in all, there is a pretty good chance that the group battle is instrumental aggression. The youth involved in single conflict, on the other hand, is more likely to be fighting because he is angry rather than because of the social pressures operating on him at that moment, and so he is more apt to be exhibiting hostile aggression.

On comparing the individual fights (54 per cent of the sample) with the group encounters, we found impressive differences between these two kinds of incidents very much along the lines I've just indicated. As we would expect, those who said they were alone at the time of their most vicious fight were far more likely to have only one opponent; 80 per cent of them reported only a single foe as against only 12 per cent of the group fighters doing so. Much more important, the two kinds of fights did not arise in the same way. The individual fighters typically maintained that the battle started because the other person had provoked or insulted either them or their girl friends or had stared at them (75 per cent saying this as against 42 per cent of the group fighters), whereas those who were in a group when they had their most vicious fight were more apt to claim the fight began when they were waylaid or when they came to the assistance of a friend (46 per cent as compared with only 10 per cent of the individual fighters). As we would also expect, the individual aggression was more likely to have been stimulated by angry feelings. Forty-five per cent of the individual fighters but only 19 per cent of the group fighters said they themselves had started the fight. In keeping with this difference, even though they were not explicitly asked about their emotional state at the time, 17 per cent of the individual fighters spontaneously reported being angry as compared with only 3 per cent of the group fighters. In sum, if the youth had been alone, the fight started because he had been provoked in some way; he became angry and hit out first. If he was in a group, however, he became involved in the fight because he went to the aid of a friend or was attacked.

In contrast with the individual fights, the group fights come closer to the popular conception of youthful gang battles. If the 'most vicious' fight had been a group rather than individual encounter, it was more likely to have taken place in a pub or in the street, was much more apt to have involved weapons (40 as against 15 per cent) produced injuries (54 compared with 32 per cent), and led to police intervention (24 against 4 per cent).

We also have a picture of very different kinds of youths being involved in these two types of incidents. The boys who had their most vicious battle in a group were more apt to be the product of a socially deviant way of life and perhaps even of a subculture of violence. For one thing, they reported having had many more fights in the previous three years. (For example, 71 per cent of the group fighters but only 41 per cent of the individual fighters said they had been involved in three or more fights during this period.) They also liked fighting more and had more positive attitudes towards aggression. When all of the boys were asked questions assessing their aggressive attitudes, a greater proportion of the group fighters agreed that they enjoyed a 'punch up', that anyone insulting them was asking for a fight, that they sometimes hit someone without being angry with him, and that it did not take much for them to lose their temper. Equally important, at least some of these youngsters not only fought in groups but also tended to commit other anti-social acts in groups as well. Farrington and West identified a subsample of 81 youths who engaged in group violence or group vandalism relatively frequently. These boys were more than twice as likely to be group rather than individual fighters in our present sense (43 per cent of the 81 were in our present 'group fight' category as compared with only 19 per cent of them being individual fighters).

However much of their group fighting might have been dictated by the rules of their group or subculture, their aggression also seems to be part of a broader pattern of social deviance. Thus, we also find that a higher proportion of group than individual fighters reported engaging in such delinquent acts as vandalism and burglary at age 18–19; more of them were convicted of illegal actions between 17 and 21 years of age; they were more prone to have an unstable job record; and a greater proportion of them admitted to heavy drinking. Their parents evidently contributed to this delinquent pattern: more of the group fighters than individual fighters had parents with criminal records by the time their children were 10 years of age.

All of these observations taken together, it seems to me, question the notion that anti-social aggression can be generally understood as rule-following behaviour. We have seen that in a good many instances people strike out at an antagonist in anger, wanting only to hurt their opponent and not thinking of other persons' expectations. The rule-following conception exaggerates the extent to which angry aggression is controlled by a conscious awareness of social standards and unduly minimizes the degree to which this kind of aggression is driven by inner rage.

I am sure there are numerous reasons why so many social scientists subscribe to the subcultural theory of violence or explain criminal violence almost exclusively in terms of group norms. While we cannot go into all of these reasons here, two are worth mentioning, one political and the other conceptual. In the former instance, I suspect at least some social scientists have adopted the rule-following perspective out of sympathy with the low-socio-economic-status men who comprise so much of the population of violent offenders. As I noted at the start of this paper, we can make the offenders' behaviour seem less 'wrong' by attributing it to group norms that society as a whole fails to comprehend. These persons are no different from you or me, the argument essentially goes; they are just living up to different rules. In fact, there is also the implication that the middle-class public is substantially at fault for not understanding, acknowledging and even tolerating the operation of these non-middle-class standards of conduct. Without debating the complexities of this thesis, it seems to me that this line of thought fails to grasp the extent to which many aggressive actions are deviant behaviours in the working-class as well as the middle-class sections of society. Consider the case of American blacks. Although blacks have the highest rate of violent crimes in the USA, opinion surveys indicate that the black residents of the crime-ridden areas of our cities as a group are strongly opposed to violent behaviour (Erlanger 1974a,b). This behaviour may be relatively common, but it is still disapproved. In the Cambridge research, as another example, the group fighters tended to display a good deal of aggression, but this conduct was clearly part of a general pattern of social deviance that injured others from their own walk of life as well as from the middle class.

I have just alluded to the second problem in the rule-following thesis. As I see it, some proponents of this line of thought have confused frequent behaviour with approved behaviour. Just because a particular mode of conduct is fairly common in some groups doesn't necessarily mean the members of these groups regard that action as desirable or proper. Socially deprived segments of society may have high rates of violent crimes because of the hardships in their lives and the ways they have learned to define other people rather than because they possess rules prescribing aggression in particular situations. Again returning to the gang fighters in the Cambridge study, these youths may be prone to violence largely as a result of the inadequate parenting and social and economic frustrations they suffered in the course of growing up, together with the aggressive models immediately around them, more than because their groups call on them to attack others.

This is not to say that social rules and subcultural learning do not contribute to the group differences in violent crimes. People can become angry when their rules of proper behaviour are violated. The members of some groups may believe one ought to stare at someone else, and may become furious when someone violates this standard and stares at them. Their subculture may also teach them it is important to gain other persons' respect as a tough man, so that they are readily angered when another individual seems to be questioning their toughness or virility. Whatever the specific rule, they are quickly and intensely infuriated when the rule is broken, partly because of their life experiences. They also have weak controls against aggression, because of their past learning and the alcohol they have drunk, and so they fail to restrain their aggressive inclinations. They might then lash out at the offending party as a result of their rage, and not because they believe they will gain approval from their peers.

James Patrick (1973) has given us a good example of just this kind of process in his well-known book, *A Glasgow Gang Observed*. Soon after Patrick started participating in the activities of the 'Young Team', a gang of Glaswegian teenagers, one of the gang members became involved in a fight when they were all in a pub on a Saturday night. According to Patrick, a labourer had accidentally nudged this boy in the back while reaching across the bar for his drink. This enraged the youth – he evidently thought his dignity had suffered – and he immediately challenged the offending man and his mate, both hefty six-footers, to a fight. Words quickly led to blows. The other boys leaped in and the two labourers were knocked to the floor. Now, parts of this incident were rule-governed. The other gang members followed a rule in coming to the aid of their friend, and this boy might have believed a rule was violated when the labourer accidentally nudged him. But his violent reaction apparently had not been dictated by the group's social code. Right after the fight, Patrick tells us, the youngster 'criticized himself for having started the fight, "Ah should hiv' ma heid examined" ' (p. 31). The boy was already in trouble with the law and was scheduled for a court appearance in a few days. There was little to be gained and much to be lost in starting the fight. His aggression was prompted by his feelings rather than by his head.

Simply put, the conception of aggression as rule-governed behaviour minimizes the importance of these feelings and gives too much weight to the role of the head in emotional behaviour.

REFERENCES

Baker, R.K. and Ball, S.J. 1969: 'The actual world of violence', in *Violence and the Media*, vol. 9. *Staff Report to the National Commission on the Causes and Prevention of Violence*. Washington, DC: US Government Printing Office, 341–62.

Ball-Rokeach, S.J. 1973: 'Values and violence: a test of the subculture of violence thesis', *American Sociological Review*, 38: 736–49.

Clinard, M.B. 1974: *Sociology of Deviant Behavior*, 4th edn, New York: Holt, Rinehart & Winston.

Erlanger, H.S. 1974a: 'Social class and corporal punishment in child rearing: a reassessment', *American Sociological Review*, 39: 68–85.

Erlanger, H.S. 1974b: 'Violence by blacks and low income whites: some new evidence on the subculture of violence thesis', Madison: University of Wisconsin Institute for Research on Poverty, Discussion Paper 208–74.

Feshbach, S. 1964: 'The function of aggression and the regulation of aggressive drive', *Psychological Review*, 71: 257–72.

Gibbons, D.C. 1973: *Society, Crime and Criminal Careers*, 2nd edn, Englewood Cliffs, NJ: Prentice-Hall.

Marsh, P., Rosser, E. and Harré, R. 1978: *The Rules of Disorder*, London: Routledge & Kegan Paul.

Patrick, J. 1973: *A Glasgow Gang Observed*, London: Eyre Methuen.

Schur, E.M. 1969: *Our Criminal Society*, Englewood Cliffs, NJ: Prentice-Hall.

Swart, C. and Berkowitz, L. 1976: 'The effect of a stimulus associated with a victim's pain on later aggression', *Journal of Personality and Social Psychology*, 33: 623–31.

West, D.J. 1969: *Present Conduct and Future Delinquency*, London: Heinemann.

West, D.J. and Farrington, D.P. 1973: *Who Becomes Delinquent?* London: Heinemann.

West, D.J. and Farrington, D.P. 1977: *The Delinquent Way of Life*. London: Heinemann.

Wolfgang, M.E. 1959: *Patterns in Criminal Homicide*, Philadelphia: University Pennsylvania Press.

Wolfgang, M.E. and Ferracuti, F. 1967: *The Subculture of Violence: Towards Integrated Theory in Criminology*, London: Social Science Paperbacks.

CHAPTER 7

Rhetorics of Violence

Peter Marsh

Ten years ago *The Explanation of Social Behaviour* by Rom Harré and Paul Secord was published. It was a timely book, in that its appearance coincided with a peak of dissatisfaction with the traditional methodologies of social psychology. The 'experiment' had failed to produce the fruits promised by those eager to be classed as true scientists. Indeed, some of us had come to feel that not only was social psychological inquiry in danger of becoming a sterile and mechanical ritual; it was also suffering from its own arrogance, and at times bordered on the morally objectionable.

The arguments put forward by Harré and Secord were not, in themselves, wholly original. Nor did they provide a fully articulated and coherent alternative approach. What they succeeded in doing, however, was to crystallize an alternative standpoint, one that had its roots in phenomenologically oriented philosophy. Central to this standpoint was the idea that, if you wanted to understand why people did the things they did, you should ask them. You should, as a practising social scientist, collect the accounts that folk offered in connection with their actions. Social action was meaningful, and the best arbiter of the meaning was the actor himself. Contained within the justifications and reasons offered for the action was the *explanation* of that action. One didn't discover the *causes* of that action, nor did one discover the *truth*: one obtained a perspective. And the value of that perspective rested on one's faith in the essentially rational and understanding fashion with which the person *qua* person conducts his social existence.

I raise this issue, very briefly, by way of a prelude to an autobiographical note. For it was shortly after the heated debate over *The Explanation of Social Behaviour* had died down a little that I began research work on aggression in young people, and in football fans in particular. Ron Harré was one of my supervisors in Oxford, and it was therefore only natural that I should make use of the sketchy accounts methodology and the ethogenic approach in an attempt to illuminate a fairly opaque and enigmatic social phenomenon. The work on football fans was eventually written up in the *Rules of Disorder* and elsewhere (see Marsh 1978a,b,c) and, within limits, illustrated the utility of the research approach that was adopted. At the same time, however, a very serious issue emerged which necessitated a fairly radical reshaping of the analytic schema to which accounts were subjected. The collection of accounts was straightforward: the major dilemma was what to do with them once they had been collected. How is a coherent perspective to be isolated from a collection of often opaque rhetorics? What is the relationship between that perspective and the actions on which it focuses?

The major point I wish to argue here is that accounts, on their own, can rarely be used to 'fix' a standpoint regarding social behaviour of even the most routine nature. When one is concerned with activities that have significant moral implications, the problem is magnified. This, of course, is hardly a novel conclusion. The same problem has been discussed extensively but not resolved, by Deutscher (1973) and many others. Despite this, the few developments in accounts methodology that have taken place in the last few years have primarily been concerned with increased sophistication in statistical treatment rather than with the adequacy of the data base itself. Work by David Canter and his colleagues at the University of Surrey exemplifies the pitfalls inherent in this approach. The fundamental problem of gaining access to action via talk remains. But in research that focuses on aggression and violence, there is rarely an alternative to methods that rely heavily on participants' own reports, ideas, conclusions and rhetorics. Violence is rare and fleeting. It is not the kind of behaviour that is conveniently repeated for the benefit of inquisitive social scientists. It is a covert activity, rarely seen but talked about endlessly.

I am not suggesting that talk about violence is valueless – quite the contrary. The rhetorics people use in talking about such acts are a vital means to their understanding. But understanding is possible only when one has some kind of model or theoretical framework which illuminates the relationship between the social nature of the rhetoric and the social nature of the action. Essential ingredients of such a framework will be the motivations for offering a particular type of account and sets of isolated social rules governing both action and how action should be spoken of. Without such an analysis, not only are the data one is dealing with – the text – liable to be very ambiguous, but one is likely to draw quite the wrong conclusions from them. One will, in fact, fall into the many traps that beset those who conduct what used to be known as 'self-report' research.

A classic example of misguided self-report work is to be found in Belson's book *Television Violence and the Adolescent Boy* (1978). This is a very lengthy tome, but in essence Belson claims a substantial correlation between the amount of violence watched on television and the frequency and severity of acts of violence that boys say they have committed. When, however, one looks at the self-reports of violent behaviour, one finds some rather surprising data. We are asked to believe that one in eight (12 per cent) of a random sample of 1,500 London schoolboys engages in acts of violence of a serious nature at a frequency of more than 20 such acts per year. Included in this category of acts were: 'I attacked someone in the street with an iron bar'; 'I tried to force a girl to have sexual intercourse with me'; 'While my mates held him down, I burned a boy on the chest with a cigarette'; 'I deliberately cut a boy's face with a penknife'; etc.

The claim being made is extreme and hardly compatible with the findings of other researchers concerning levels of violent behaviour among a 'normal' teenage population. Belson's fundamental mistake is to assume that his data base is unproblematic – that there are no difficulties with interpretation of the ascription of meaning and that it can all be taken at face value. In his study Belson used a fairly standard card-sort technique, in which the above acts were printed on to cards and subjects asked to sort them into piles of those that they had committed and those that they had not. And yet, even the most inexperienced researcher is aware that material collected in such a manner can be given little credence without some further means of assessing its validity. A significant feature of such validation must be the establishment of terms of reference, and how such terms might be at variance with those assumed from the outside standpoint of the researcher.

This problem, so prominently highlighted in Belson's work, cannot be glossed over by the inclusion of suitable apologia in research reports. Some way must be found of making sense of questions that are posed, otherwise one might argue there is no point asking the questions in the first place. Consider this short extract from a conversation with two football fans:

Question:	What do you do when you 'put the boot in'?
Fan A:	Well, you kicks 'em in the 'ead don't you – heavy boots with metal toe-caps an' that.
Q:	What happens then?
	(*puzzled look from fans*)
Fan A:	He's dead.
Fan B:	Nah! He's alright – usually anyway.

That illustrates the kind of opacity that can be a result of asking a question that, on the surface, seems appropriate and straightforward. As data, the replies, as they stand, are completely useless. How can a victim be both 'dead' and 'alright'?

The example, of course, is a little extreme, and luckily not all accounts are quite so enigmatic. But present in many accounts are distinctive types of exaggeration and distortion which, if unrecognized, can lead to the kinds of error made by Belson, and perhaps also the confusions inherent in Len Berkowitz's chapter in this volume (chapter 6). Having recognized patterns of distortion, it is however possible to devise a means of dealing with them, particularly when the individuals offering accounts are members of an indentifiable micro-society or subcultural group. In such cases it is practical to assume that both the form and the content of the account will be shaped by certain conventions and rules extant within that cultural framework. Such rules will embrace conventionalized terms of reference, descriptive categories and acceptable 'glosses' of action. And underlying this framework will be motivations directed by the fact that certain actions (and hence talk of such actions) are held in esteem and confer value and reputation on those who commit them or can 'carry off' talk about them.

These considerations, while applying most markedly to patterns of aggression and violence among, say, football fans, Skinheads, Teddy Boys, Punks, etc., also apply, but in a somewhat less dramatic sense, to the study of teenage male behaviour in general. Subcultural mores do not emerge out of thin air – they tend to reflect significant features of the overarching cultural frameworks in which they are embedded. And while a radical reshaping of traditional values may take place within a subculture, such innovatory aspects are intelligible only given an understanding of the contrasts that are eventually created.

One of the primary functions of a subculture is the provision of alternative arenas for demonstrations of personal worth and the achievement of identity. While the emergence of a particular subcultural phenomenon may be explained in socio-political terms (see for example Ian Taylor, 1969), its immediate value in social–psychological terms can be seen in terms of the sense of belonging and prestige experienced by individual members. The manner in which self may be enhanced is, of course, clearly prescribed by the tacitly held sense of propriety existing within a particular subcultural context. The social requirements attached to membership may vary from group to group and include prescriptions for dress, musical interest, broad social attitudes and more specific day-to-day habits and styles. Pervading much of working-class youth culture, however, is a requirement that within-group bonds be reinforced by outwardly directed displays of aggression. In some cases legitimate targets may be identified by their membership of a rival subcultural group, while in others 'enemies' can be selected from a much wider class of outsiders.

All of this may seem quite straightforward, and a large amount of European sociological research has been directed towards an understanding of the genesis and structure of the rather fluid youth 'problems' that have characterized postwar society. Of particular interest here, however, is the manner in which aggression directed towards out-groups is enacted and managed, and the precise manner in which associated self-enhancement is achieved.

Given a social context that is conducive to aggressive acts, one might assume that status would be achieved via the commission of such acts. A football fan of one team who commits violence against a fan of a rival team might be expected to be afforded a degree of respect and deference as a result. A problem arises, however, when the tacit rule frameworks and conventionalized routines mitigate against the commission of such acts to the extent that the frequency of their occurrence is very low. It is at this point that rhetorics become far more important in social terms than actions.

This is not the place to enter into a long treatise on the ways in which rules and rituals channel aggression into symbolic and relatively non-injurious displays. It should be sufficient to assert that aggression is rarely enacted in a random or gratuitous fashion, and that, within male youth-cultural settings in particular, acts of violence are highly constrained by well understood conventions. The availability and routine use of symbolic substitutes for violence, plus the potential for meeting out of social sanctions, often render (perhaps ironically) the perpetrator of injurious violence a deviant within his own peer group. [1]

To some extent one can view the existence of these aggression management systems as reflecting traditional codes of behaviour which have a long history in European societies. Ideas of honour, fair fighting and socially appropriate means of issuing and accepting challenges, coupled with opportunities for achieving dominance without fatal bloodshed, recur often in contemporary accounts of social life throughout the ages. It should come as no surprise to find that these same values are present among today's youth. The media would have us believe that a large sector of the teenage population has suddenly been transformed into an anarchic and demonic mob and that the streets of our major cities lack the safety they once had in times past. But newspapers rarely provide a reliable source of data for social scientists.

While symbolic substitutes emerge partially to replace injurious violence, they do not themselves provide for much self-enhancement. A confident swagger, a piercing stare, well tested verbal insults, certain facial expressions – all these might serve to induce submission in a rival. At the same time, just engaging in such displays will rarely be the topic of subsequent social talk. In order to win prestige, the actions have to be rendered less mundane and more worthy of comment. Thus, certain distortions of a specific nature will be introduced. In particular, references to physical injury will be included. While the rule frameworks serve to limit the occurrence of injury, conventionalized social talk restores this ingredient and conversations will be conducted as if the rules did not exist. So long as the distortions are not too excessive (for this

[1] There are of course significant cross-sex and cross-cultural differences in the extent to which tacit rule frameworks exert a constraining influence on violence. These aspects are considered, to some degree, in Marsh (1978b and forthcoming, a).

exaggeration process is itself highly rule-governed) the rhetorics offered by participants will rarely be challenged. Only when distortions are introduced which are unacceptable to these terms will the individual be liable to sanction.[2]

The distortion and exaggeration process is so much an everyday feature of life in these contexts that it is taken for granted and becomes part of the unquestioned backdrop of social life. It is possible to view the whole process as a kind of social conspiracy. But it is not an active or conscious conspiracy. The rhetorics are based on routine ways of describing events. A mundane piece of conflict becomes a 'good kicking' or a 'punch-up'. Daily existence is rendered remarkable, and in this way subcultural life can be built up as an exciting and gratifying alternative to regular and unproductive life in school, work or the family.

The effect of these routine transformations of daily life on accounts offered by participants to those engaged in research is extremely marked. However one chooses to elicit them, one's data will inescapably reflect the 'transformed' reality rather than any other perspective. It will also contain the kind of inconsistencies I illustrated earlier. While social rules are rarely articulated in everyday life, they can be brought to the surface by the researcher who poses appropriate questions and who is able to render routine activities problematic to the informant. But while an informant may show clear evidence of a tacit understanding of existing social rules that govern or direct his behaviour, and this may be evident in the justificatory accounts he offers, it will be hard for him to escape from his routine terms of reference for describing conflicts and aggressive encounters. Only in such terms do events have meaning to the individual, and only then do they have reality. The problem is quite insurmountable given a phenomenologically oriented method of research. However, certain pragmatic steps can sometimes be taken to relieve the dilemma.

First, the isolation of this transformation process is evident only when one has some other perspective on the events to which a rhetoric relates. It is possible to spend time with informants, watch closely what they do and listen carefully to how they speak about what they do. This is no guarantee of understanding, but at least it

---

[2] Examples of unaccepted distortions are published elsewhere, e.g. Marsh (1978c and forthcoming, b).

offers some anchor points. Given some insight into the relationship between just a few pieces of social talk and the actions and events to which they relate, it is possible to build up a primitive schema for the interpretation of other rhetorics. In addition, one can pay particular attention to the occasions on which individuals are sanctioned by their peers for 'bullshitting'. At these points the distortions introduced lie outside of the rules governing transformation, and thus the limits of acceptable distortion can be isolated.

Isolation of 'bullshit' points can also be gained through cross-negotiation of accounts. The account offered by one member is made the subject for further accounting by another. If done systematically, and given some knowledge about the pattern of relationships among informants, a more adequate appreciation of the terms of reference being employed can be gained. One still requires that extra perspective gained through observation and association. But in work on violence and aggression that is often very hard to achieve.

This dilemma is aptly highlighted by current research being conducted at Oxford Polytechnic with my colleague Amanda Brookes on violence and aggression among girls, work that follows on from some of the pioneering studies of Anne Campbell (see chapter 9 below). Female violence tends to be more covert than that among males. There are fewer social arenas for the expression of aggression and its visibility is therefore very limited. There is little opportunity of obtaining an observational perspective to contrast against the highly charged rhetorics that some girls offer concerning their 'bloody' activities. The accounts in themselves are fascinating documents. They raise many important issues and open up new directions for research. And quite clearly, elements of a transformation process are apparent in what the girls have to say. Consider the following extracts.

Elaine: About three months ago I had a fight with this girl called Michele. . . . We was up [pub] one time, my sister was there and she was giving my sister dirty looks and my sister said 'What's that half-caste dog looking at?' and she said it was me that called it her, and one time I went to L——— to this dance and she came and called me up and said 'You called me a half-caste dog'. I said 'No, I did not'. She said 'Yes you did - you're only saying that'. I said 'My sister called you a half-caste dog'. She said 'You are trying to say that was your sister but it was you', and then the next morning I was coming to school, I heard from one of my friends that she has been spreading it round to other people that I was supposed to be jealous of her, because she can flirt around with this other man and I can't, so I went up to her, I goes 'What do I hear about what you have been telling other people?' and she dropped her bag to fight me so we started fighting. . . . I used by fists and I give her a black eye and some scratches. And then the second time, she used a weapon and stabbed me in my face that's why I have got a scar. . . she used a stick or a twig or something, I don't know. . . . That was the only way she could get me back because she couldn't use her hand or her fist or anything.

Contrast with:

Des (*male*): I broke a kid's nose before. . . . I kicked her in the face. 'I am going to a football match'. 'Oh, no you're not'. Chuung, chuung. . . .

Debbie: Well, I've been in quite a few fights, you know and I've seen, well, I've seen about three, I've seen one and I've heard about a few and most of the girls end up with scratches all over their faces – especially coloured girls because. . . .

Des: Massive, they are. This girl. . . .
Deb: They use them for scratching. . . .
Dawn: Yeah.
Des: Her nails are out here somewhere. . . .
Deb: They are nearly curling over, aren't they?
Des: She has got really long nails. . . .
PM: What about weapons?
Dawn: Elaine got dug in the face with a dagger, didn't she?
Deb: Yeah, Elaine did.
Des: No, who was that girl? She hit a girl. . . .
Deb: That was Michele. . . .
Dawn: She had a fight with a dagger and she dug a dagger in her face.

Some form of distortion/transformation process is clearly evident. But whether it parallels the typical male process in both structure and function must remain an open question until sufficient knowledge concerning the motor patterns of aggression enactment, utilization of effective symbolic displays, etc., is gathered. And that looks like a lengthy business.

Certain less direct, and therefore less conclusive but still valuable, strategies remain open in this kind of research, which is primarily concerned with sex differences. Of particular interest is the way in which boys and girls differ in their attributions of socially appropriate action in a variety of relevant and salient conflict situations. The situations themselves can be presented in story or cartoon form and involve male and female characters. Using male and female subjects generates a four-cell table in which a number of useful contrasts can be made in a systematic fashion. These are shown by the solid lines in figure 7.1.

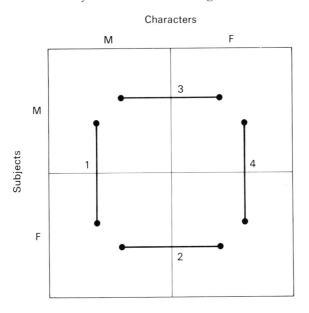

Figure 7.1 Male and female subjects' attribution of socially appropriate action.

The first comparison to be made is between male and female subjects' attribution of socially appropriate action by male characters. Given that previous research has revealed the existence of tacit rules which guide their enactment of aggression, one can compare the data for males and females across situations to reveal the extent to which such rules are evident in these cases and, more significantly, whether they are also understood by females (line no. 1).

Following this, one can proceed to examine the extent to which males and females differ in their expectations of both male and female characters (line nos. 2 and 3). Previous research has shown (*en passant*) that males have very clear ideas of what is appropriate (and therefore expected) action in a wide range of conflict situations but that they rarely expect females to adhere to such conventions. Accounts from female informants indicate that, not only do they attribute less rule directedness to male behaviour, but they also see less differences in the expectations of action between males and females than do males. This can be clarified by further contrasting lines 2 and 3 with each other.

Finally, comparison line 4 is made for the sake of completeness, but is unlikely to be very illuminating without the others. From the girls' accounts one would anticipate that females would expect a higher frequency of 'male'-type behaviour (e.g. 'punching', 'putting the boot in', etc.) on the part of females than would males (who would expect more stereotypically 'female' behaviour, such as scratching, pulling hair and crying). The comparisons are necessarily complex; but taken in this stepwise progression, they can perhaps illuminate some aspects of the female account. Starting with an understanding of the relationship between male rhetoric and male action, given female rhetoric, given contrasts between male and female expectations of the actions of both males and females, one can gain some insights into the underlying generation of the female rhetoric with reference to those features that underline social talk about violence in males. At that stage one can make more informed speculation concerning the likely patterns of aggression enactment in females.

The main purpose of this essay, however, is not to enter into a detailed discussion of methodology. Rather, it is to point out that what people, young males in particular, say about their own violent activities cannot simply be recast, through various statistical procedures, as a statement about what is actually going on in our society. I have tried to show that an accounts methodology, while an essential feature (in one form or another) of field research, cannot provide, in this context, an adequate foundation on its own, nor can its limitations be offset by subsequent coding and number crunching. Certain opaque features of accounts can be removed by careful cross-negotiation and the use of techniques that allow specific comparisons to be made. But the assumption that at the end of this process an explanation of social behaviour can be achieved is one that, in the light of experience, must seriously be questioned.

A further theoretical problem associated with accounts has recently been raised by John Shotter (personal comment) in relation to recent work being done in the field of collective representations (see for example Herzlich 1972 and Moscovici 1963). He suggests that accounts tap a rather superficial level of justification and rationalization of action. Because of its immediacy, I would add, it is therefore likely to be encapsulated by the routinized rhetorical frames I mentioned earlier. A guide to the reasons responsible for social action, however, is not likely to be found in such rationalizations, since these are, as Shotter says, embodied. They are individual internalizations of a *représentation sociale*, which are manifest in social activities of a broad nature, and rather less in accounts.

In many ways this is an important point. If these deep-seated, diffuse generations of social action are not amenable to being tapped through the elicitation of accounts, it means that we are obliged to use other strategies for their discovery – ones that might allow for a more realistic expression of whatever it is that is embodied. A number of candidates present themselves – role-playing being one.

Hanney *et al.*'s (1973) classic study has aptly shown the power of this particular approach (see also Ginsberg 1978). One must ask, of course, whether a role-play gives any clearer indication of real-life action than a rhetoric or an account. The problems involved in setting up role-plays of aggressive encounters are considerable, as some of us have found out to our cost! But such extra perspectives are precisely what is required to make an ethogenic approach to understanding violence and aggression a truly viable one.

Although Harré (1979) urges that research be focused on the 'expressive order' (as opposed to the practical order), a concern with a wider range of expression is urgently required – expressions that are rather more reflective of individual embodiment or self. Even ephemera such as pop songs may reflect more about the values, attitudes and patterns of social activity within the subcultures in which they originate than accounts offered in response to direct prompting. (I am concerned here not with purely commercial products thrust upon a subculture from the outside, but with those that have grass-roots credentials.) Take for example this rather different kind of rhetoric from a girl called Honey Bane of the 'Fatal Microbes', a girl with a background of removing herself from youth treatment centres and seeking a more exhilarating time in the punk world:

While you are getting kicked to death in a London pedestrian subway,
Don't think passers-by will help, they will just look the other way,
They have seen too much, they don't want to know, they don't want to
  know.
Violence grows, violence grows, violence grows, violence grows.

People travel on the bus but they don't pay their way,
It's so easy to say push off when the conductor asks you to pay,
Now the conductor keeps it shut, because the conductor knows,
Violence grows, violence grows, violence grows, violence grows.

Children at home just come and go, their parents can't say 'No',
Now they know what's best, now they know violence grows,
This generation's changing fast, this generation glorifies violence,
Violence grows, violence grows, violence grows, [etc.]

People travel on the bus they don't pay their way.
It's so easy to say push off when the conductor asks you to pay.
Now the conductor keeps it shut, because the conductor knows.
Everybody keeps it shut because everybody knows,
Violence grows, violence grows, violence grows, [etc.]
['Violence Grows', Xntrix records].

   Encapsulated within this particular rhetoric is a formulation which is rather different from an immediate rationalization. It is an 'insider's' view, and it illuminates values, sentiments and beliefs existing within a social order and relating to wider societal concerns. They are taken for granted by members but can be virtually invisible to outsiders. In other words, the 'keys' for rendering accounts intelligible may be sought in the various products of social worlds, which may be viewed as reflecting in-corporated, rarely negotiated, social meanings to do with aggression and conflict and the routine manner of their enactment. There is no reason to suppose, of course, that there will be a simple relationship between these products and overt social behaviour. But it is reasonable to conclude that the social forces that give rise to the products are also instrumental in shaping and constraining action.

The intention here is to press for a wider approach to the serious issue of how violence and aggression can be understood – what should we be examining, and how can an explanatory framework be constructed? Accepting that the collection of accounts is an essential feature of any realistic inquiry, the crucial stage involves the isolation of conceptual tools for the translation of accounts into a form that tells us something about what is happening *in action* and the reasons for that action. This is fundamentally a qualitative and interpretative process, and the validity of the end product is necessarily open to challenge.

In many ways this overall approach is not at all unlike the principles of triangulation regularly employed in some areas of sociology. Here, however, the concern is with individual action in specific social contexts, which means that a further level of analysis concerned with the individual's perception of the context and setting, his/her immediate motivations, ambitions and self-enhancement strategies, is required.

At a practical level, there is no substitute for the general strategy of listening to individuals talk, witnessing them in action and examining the day-to-day features of the social worlds they inhabit. An explanation of violence and aggression that does not rest on material derived in this way is very unlikely to have salience or applicability to individuals in specific groups or social settings. In fact, it is only *after* such a strategy has been pursued – one that, following C. Wright Mills, we might see as 'intellectual craftsmanship' – that social science is possible. Only then can we develop the more elaborate scientific paraphernalia that traditionally has been used prematurely. Tools such as repertory grids, role-play scenarios – even questionnaires and experiments – necessarily require an already established corpus of knowledge and insight before their use is rational or meaningful. We need to know what it is that needs to be explained.

This is really a crucial point, because it seems that a number of current theories about violence are attempting to explain that which is inexplicable by virtue of its non-existence. One finds, for example, rather loosely assembled explanations of 'the frightening rise in violent crime', or of women 'turning' to violence, or the sudden increase of assaults on schoolteachers. Such 'explanations' often assume that crime statistics or other notoriously unreliable data define the problem and proceed from there. But if the data base is unreliable, then the explanation is invalid in direct proportion. An explanation of wife-beating, for example, that assumes that this is a fairly novel type of activity since the crime figures have risen dramatically in the last few years, is unlikely to be terribly illuminating. The crime figures have gone up because the social climate now enables wives to *report* such acts to the police and seek refuge away from their husbands. But wife-beating is a very old type of activity, and explanations must necessarily take into account such a heritage.

A few years ago I tried to counter this tendency of assuming that there is a lot of violence about (violence in general, not wife-beating in particular) and that it is getting worse, by proposing the 'It never quite happens' theory. This approach also reflected my own research experience of looking for acts of violence and not finding very many. As a theory it didn't have a great deal going for it, and clearly violence *does* happen sometimes. But it can provide a fairly rational way of approaching the subject. What does happen a great deal is that people *talk* about violence. There is certainly more talk than there is action. Thus, one could argue, it is the talk that requires the explanation. And once we have separated out the talk, we might find that there is less action to be explained.

Rhetorics of violence become of special relevance in this context not because they can necessarily illuminate action but because they might very well serve in place of it. As I pointed out earlier, the distortions and transformations that are carried through rhetorics serve to enhance personal prestige and worth, particularly when 'embodied' constraints against violence seem to mitigate against that possibility. Once we view the rhetorics as transformations, and see that further insights into the nature of such transformations are required before explanation of either talk or action is possible, we can begin to avoid some of the traps inevitable in a simplistic account collection procedure. We can also avoid the truly absurd conclusions of people like Belson, whose mistake is to erect a complex statistical castle on the shifting sands of misunderstood self-reports.

REFERENCES

Belson, W.A. 1978: *Television Violence and the Adolescent Boy*, Farnborough: Saxon House.
Deutscher, I. 1973: *What We Say/What We Do*, Glenview, Ill.: Scott, Foresman.
Ginsberg, G.P. 1978: 'Role-playing and role performance in social psychological research', in *Social Context of Method*, ed. M. Brenner, P. Marsh and M. Brenner, London: Croom Helm.
Hanney, C., Banks, W.C. and Zimbardo, P.G. 1973: 'Interpersonal dynamics in a simulated prison', *International Journal of Criminology and Psychology*, 1: 69–97.
Harré, R. 1979: *Social Being*, Oxford: Basil Blackwell.
Harré, R. and Secord, P. 1972: *The Explanation of Social Behaviour*, Oxford: Basil Blackwell.
Herzlich, C. 1972: 'La représentation sociale', ch. 9 in *Introduction á la Psychologie Sociale*, ed. S. Moscovici, vol. 1. Paris: Librarie Larousse.
Marsh, P. 1978a: *The Rules of Disorder*, London: Routledge & Kegan Paul.
Marsh, P. 1978b: *Aggro: The Illusion of Violence*, London: Dent.
Marsh, P. 1978c: 'Life and careers on the soccer terraces', in *Football Hooliganism – The Wider Context*, ed. R. Ingham, Inter-action Reprint.
Marsh, P. forthcoming, a: *The Rites of Anger*, Oxford: Basil Blackwell.
Marsh, P. forthcoming, b: 'Rules in the organization of action: empirical studies', in *The Analysis of Action: Some Recent Empirical and Theoretical Advances*, ed. R. Harré and M. von Cranach, Cambridge: University Press.
Moscovici, S. 1963: 'Attitudes and opinions', in *Annual Review of Psychology*, 231–60.
Taylor, I. 1969: 'Hooligans: soccer's resistance movement', *New Society*, 7 August.

CHAPTER 8

Aggression in Primate Social Groups

Hormonal Correlates

Rachel Meller

INTRODUCTION

Great care must always be taken when attempting to extrapolate
from studies on animal behaviour to the behaviour of man. This is
particularly important when the behaviour under consideration is
as ill-defined as that which we call aggression. In everyday
language, the term 'aggressiveness' is used in a number of ways: it
can be applied as easily to actions that cause physical damage to
others as to that assertiveness or drive that was once considered
primarily a masculine attribute. This problem of definition has been
discussed by others in detail elsewhere (see for example Hinde
1974: ch. 16). The present chapter will consider aggression in
groups of non-human primates; this will be discussed in terms not
only of obvious behaviours, such as attacks and threats, but also of
more subtle responses which reflect the social structure of the
group. The aim here is not to attempt an explanation of the causes
of human aggression or violence. Instead, this chapter will look at
studies of primate behaviour with respect to an aspect of aggressive
interactions that cannot be investigated readily in man – that is, the
physiological side of aggression, or, specifically, the relationship
between hormones and aggressive behaviour.

Hormones are the so-called 'chemical messengers' secreted by
the endocrine glands of both monkeys and men to be carried via the
bloodstream to their target organs. Perhaps the most familiar are

the sex hormones, oestrogen (produced by the ovaries in the female) and testosterone (produced by the testes of the male). In non-primate species, these hormones have long been known to affect not only the reproductive state, but also the behaviour of the individual – including his or her propensity to show aggression (Guhl 1961). A question of some importance to primatologists is whether hormones can similarly influence the behaviour of these 'higher' mammals – so-called owing to their having evolved on extremely large neocortex, that part of the brain thought to be concerned with reasoning and cognition. As Beach proposed (1947), the development of this feature suggests that the behaviour of monkeys and apes is more emancipated from hormonal control than is that of smaller-brained animals, with stronger influences coming instead from factors related to learned – especially social – experiences.

Nearly all primates – and here man is the example *par excellence* – live in highly organized social groups. This fact is fundamental to any consideration of the behaviour of human or non-human primates. While our own societies are of an order of magnitude more complex than those of other primates, since we have verbal language with which to impose laws and establish institutions (see Hinde 1978), nevertheless, the existence of the common principle of social rules or conventions governing the behaviour of the individual makes the study of non-human primates of real interest. The following questions will be considered below with respect to aggression as a factor constraining the behaviour of primates within a social framework: Is aggression a natural part of primate societies? Are there hormonal causes or consequences of aggression? Can any principles be derived from studies of non-human primates that are of relevance to man?

THE CONCEPT OF DOMINANCE

Over the last 15 years or so there has been some debate concerning the use of the term 'social dominance' in studies of primate behaviour. The idea that aggressive interactions in groups of animals are hierarchically organized was first introduced by Schjelderup-Ebbe in 1913, with reference to the near-linear pecking order of domestic fowl (Schjelderup-Ebbe 1935). Following this, the concept of dominance hierarchies was rapidly adopted and applied to a wide variety of vertebrate societies. In particular, it came to be considered a fundamental principle underlying primate behaviour (e.g. Zuckerman 1932; Maslow 1936), despite the fact that no clear definition of dominance ever appeared. Instead, dominance was viewed as a qualitative state, shown to varying degrees by different individuals and measured in terms of bullying, cringeing, style of walking or posture, and access to desiderata (see for example Maslow 1936). The weakness of this view is underlined by Maslow's statement (referring to the type of measures just mentioned) that 'whenever dominance is fairly marked, these characteristics make its diagnosis very easy' (1936: 266).

It is perhaps not surprising then that in the 1960s, when both an increase in the number of primate field studies and a more scientific approach to the study of animal behaviour in general were seen, a number of writers seriously criticized the early concept of dominance (e.g. Gartlan 1964, 1968; Rowell 1966). Among their criticisms was the fact that attempts at assessing an individual's rank by using the various putative indices of dominance often failed to give good correlations – indeed, contradictory scores occurred (Gartlan 1964). This either argues against the unitary nature of dominance, or indicates the use of inappropriate measures. Even more fundamental was the criticism that while caged groups of primates generally show a pronounced aggressive hierarchy, this was far less obvious in many species in the wild, where the frequency of aggression was much lower. Dominance was thus considered to be an artefact of captivity. This second objection loses much of its meaning on closer consideration. While the conditions of caging may well increase the number of aggressive interactions between individuals (who have no means of escape and limited space), the low level of overt aggression among feral primates is no proof that dominance relationships do not exist. Indeed, an alternative – and arguably more productive – interpretation is that hierarchical organization within a society actually serves to reduce intra-group aggression (see for example Collias 1944 and p. 121 below).

The criticism concerning the definition of dominance is more valid. It is unlikely that social status in such large-brained animals as primates would be an inflexible quality, measured as simply as tooth size. Thus coalitions and dependent rank are both situations where dominance status can change according to which other individuals may be present. However, in terms of the interaction between any two individuals, the concept of dominance can be useful if it can enable predictions to be made concerning their behaviour. It is very often the case that, in a pair of individuals, the behaviour of one is generally constrained or limited by the presence of the other – or, simply, A consistently bosses B (see Hinde 1978). This interaction may be the result of overt or merely potential aggression – in the latter case, aggression has probably occurred in the past and resulted in the learned relative status. Here lies the essence of the argument for a reduction in actual aggression being the consequence of an established hierarchy: once status is settled, fighting is unnecessary on each occasion that competition arises. The common observation that aggression is at its highest level during the formation of a new group supports this argument. Once relationships have been established, physical aggression may be minimal, with threats sufficing to maintain the *status quo*. It is only when the social structure is disturbed (e.g. by the death of established members or the addition of new ones) that aggression may increase again.

The terms 'dominant' and 'subordinate', then, can be used validly if defined strictly in terms of the direction of aggression between individuals, a use that has real significance since this relationship imposes constraints on many aspects of behaviour. Unidirectionality of aggression has long been observed in many primate groups (e.g. Sade 1967; Marsden 1968). It is the chronic effect of such a social hierarchy in established groups that will be considered in this chapter. While overt aggression may be low, the learned status of individuals is a real phenomenon which may be picked up by the observer using non-aggressive measures such as visual monitoring of other group members and utilization of social space (Keverne *et al.*, 1978b). To return to one of the measures used by the early primatologists, even the general bearing of different animals can communicate their status when aggression is no longer present (figure 8.1). It must be emphasized that dominance should not be equated with aggressiveness: it is the patterning, not the amount of aggression, that is important, and the highest ranking individual is often one of the least aggressive.

A final general point should be made concerning the principle that a hierarchy results from aggressive behaviour during the formation of a group. This has in fact been observed in the case of

Figure 8.1 Typical postures of subordinate (above) and dominant (below) male rhesus monkeys.
(Drawings by Priscilla Edwards, from R.A. Hinde *Biological Bases of Human Social Behaviour,* copyright © 1974 McGraw-Hill Inc., New York. Used with the permission of McGraw-Hill Book Company.)

human interactions. From a 35-day study of young boys in a summer camp, Savin-Williams (1977) was able to rank the six individuals in a linear dominance hierarchy. Status was determined from a number of indices of 'domination', such as verbal or physical aggression, and commands given or obeyed. It is of significance that 25 per cent of these assertive interactions occurred in the first three days of the camp, after which time status was apparently established.

SITUATIONS ASSOCIATED WITH AGGRESSION IN
PRIMATE GROUPS

While the social hierarchy minimizes aggression in established groups of primates, a number of situations exist that are predictably associated with an increase in aggression. Much information concerning the causes of aggression in social groups of monkeys has been derived by Southwick and his colleagues, who studied the reaction of rhesus macaques in North India to a number of social or environmental manipulations (Southwick *et al.* 1974). Reductions in food supply had negligible effects on aggression, while decreasing the available space tended to increase agonistic interactions. However, the most effective stimulus in eliciting aggression involved the alteration of the existing social structure by introducing a new animal to the group. This caused a violent mobbing response from the other group members if the stranger was adult; on the other hand, if it was an infant, then the aggressive reaction was replaced by one of great interest, and the newcomer was adopted into the group. An aggressive response to strange adults has also been seen in laboratory studies (e.g. Scruton and Herbert 1972).

Another stimulus seen to elicit aggression in an established group is the maturation of young males. In many primate species puberty in the male is associated with the development of secondary sexual characteristics, such as changes in musculature, coloration and tooth size. Simultaneously, not only does the male's own aggressiveness increase, but so may that of other males in the group towards him. Thus Hall and Mayer (1967) described how on showing such changes a formerly tolerated male patas monkey was violently attacked by the other male present. While this occurred in captivity, it supports the suggestion that maturing male patas are naturally driven out of their one-male reproductive units by the altered aggressiveness of the sexually active male (Gartlan 1975). Such behaviour is common in other terrestrial species, e.g. baboons and macaques, where the presence of many sexually mature males in the large social groups leads to competition for females. This is probably one of the reasons for the aggressive nature of these species, in which dominance relationships are more clearly observed than in, for example, arboreal monogamous primates like the gibbon. Inter-male competition is reflected by marked sexual dimorphism, also absent in the gibbon.

The relationship between aggressive and sexual motivation has been recognized classically, and cannot be over-emphasized here. It underlies the final situation to be mentioned in this section: the onset of the mating season in social groups. Feral primates tend to show annual peaks of mating activity (Lancaster and Lee 1965), and the ensuing competition for females is associated with the highest annual levels of aggression (Wilson and Boelkins 1970). This can also be demonstrated experimentally in the laboratory by inducing a 'mating season', by administration of oestrogen to ovariectomized females. In the case of the talapoin monkey, this leads to the swelling of the female's sexual skin and to her becoming attractive to the male. This manipulation in a social group of talapoins (four males and four females) led not only to an increase in the males' sexual interest in the females, but also to a change in their aggressive behaviour (Keverne *et al.* 1978a). Before the females were made attractive, the most dominant male (defined in terms of the direction of aggression) was one of the least aggressive ones; after this, however, he significantly increased his attacks and threats on other males and became the most aggressive of the four (figure 8.2). The others in fact decreased their own aggression at this time. Thus the pattern, rather than simply the overall level, of aggressive interactions changed in the presence of attractive females.

HORMONAL CAUSES OF AGGRESSION

The relationship between sexual and aggressive activity in the male primate suggests the possibility of a hormonal basis for aggression. Many people have supposed that the changes in both behaviours during the mating period are related to the action of the male 'sex hormone', testosterone. A number of observations have lent sup-

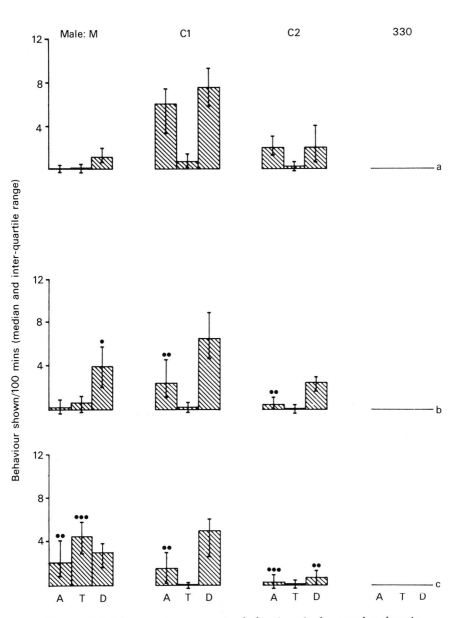

Figure 8.2 Changes in aggressive behaviour in four male talapoin monkeys after ovariectomized females in the group treated with oestrogen. a: baseline; b and c: transient and established phases of oestrogen treatment; ., . . and . . . = $p < 0.05$, 0.02 and 0.002 comparing b and c with a. Male rank decreases from left to right. A: attacks; T: threats; D: displaces. (Taken from Meller 1978.)

port to this supposition. First, the male's aggressiveness increases at puberty, when testosterone is also rising (see review by Rose *et al.* 1971). Second, adult males tend to be more aggressive than adult females, who have negligible testosterone levels (Rose *et al.* 1971). Finally, as discussed above, the male is often most aggressive during the mating season, when testosterone secretion is also at its peak (Gordon *et al.* 1976). While this evidence is merely correlative, and is no proof of causality, it has led to the implicit assumption that testosterone is responsible for aggressiveness in male primates. Support came from the experimental finding of Rose and Bernstein and colleagues (Rose *et al.* 1971), which positively correlated aggressiveness and plasma testosterone in rhesus monkeys (here rank was also correlated with aggressiveness). Rose obtained similar data from a group of violent criminals: those individuals who had shown aggression at the earliest ages were also those with the highest testosterone levels at the time of the study (Kreuz and Rose 1972). However, no relationship could be found between current scores of aggressiveness and plasma hormone levels, and this has been the case in other human studies (e.g. Doering *et al.* 1975). Furthermore, subsequent reports on non-human primates have failed to show a positive correlation between rank and testosterone titres (e.g. Eaton and Resko 1974; Gordon *et al.* 1976); however, the literature is often confused because of the failure to distinguish between dominance and aggressiveness.

To test the assumption that the male sex hormone is in some way causally related to the aggressiveness or assertiveness that leads to high social rank, the effects of experimental manipulation of testosterone must be determined. A number of studies have investigated this. In laboratory groups of squirrel monkeys, castration of the most dominant male had no effect on his status (Green *et al.* 1972). In social groups of talapoins, a castrated male was seen to dominate intact males; further, administration of large doses of testosterone to subordinate males failed to elevate their position in the hierarchy (Dixson and Herbert 1977). Evidence also shows that the rank of males cannot be predicted on the basis of their testosterone levels before entering a social group.

In the light of these findings there appears little support for the suggested causal relationship between testosterone and dominance or aggression. What then, if any, is the significance of the

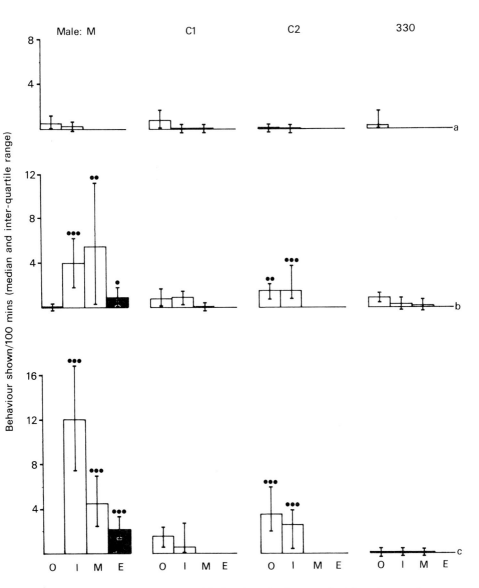

Figure 8.3 Changes in sexual behaviour in four male talapoin monkeys after ovariectomized females treated with oestrogen; layout and significance values as in figure 8.2. O: masturbation; I: inspections of females' sexual skin swellings; M: mounts; E: ejaculatory mounts.
(Taken from Meller 1978.)

reported correlation between social rank and testosterone – is
another variable involved? The answer may be found with respect
to another behaviour which (as has been alluded to above) is often
correlated with high rank in primates: sexual activity. The positive
relationship between male rank and sexual behaviour or reproductive success has been shown to varying degrees in both the field
and the laboratory. In the latter case, a clear example is the talapoin
monkey. Figure 8.3 shows the sexual activity of males in a group
before and after the ovariectomized females were treated with
oestrogen. Before treatment, this was negligible. After the females
were made attractive, only the highest-ranking male mounted
frequently and ejaculated with females, despite the high interest of
the subordinates. Although this laboratory situation is an extreme
one, it is important in indicating a trend that might be seen in the
wild. Field studies on primates have long linked male rank and
reproductive success (e.g. Carpenter 1942; Hall and DeVore 1965);
more recently, Duvall *et al.* (1976) used blood tests to determine the
paternity of infants born in a semi-wild rhesus group. They found
that the four high- and middle-ranking males (of eight in the
group) fathered 80 per cent of the infants born over two years.
While the correlation is clearly not absolute, it is very suggestive of
the trend.

  With respect to the relationship between testosterone and
aggression, the above data are significant because sexual activity
itself can lead to an elevation in the male sex hormone. This has
been shown in a study on talapoin monkeys, in which males were
introduced individually from single cages (where aggressive interactions are clearly negligible) to a group of attractive females
(where, in the absence of other males, aggression remained low).
Under these conditions, each male now mated, and each showed a
significant elevation in plasma testosterone (Keverne 1979). Such
evidence of course provides a possible indirect link between rank
and testosterone, with sexual behaviour complicating the relationship. This leads to an important general consideration: rather than
hormones influencing behaviour, can behavioural events affect
hormonal state? For example, can giving or receiving aggression
alter testosterone in the male?

HORMONAL CONSEQUENCES OF AGGRESSION

Rose and his co-workers continued their studies on semi-free-ranging rhesus monkeys by investigating the hormonal consequences of manipulating the structure of the social group. They introduced four adult males into a large, well-established breeding group, with the result that the four were seriously attacked and defeated by the resident males (Rose *et al.* 1975). The introduced animals each showed a profound decrease in testosterone levels, which persisted for weeks after the initial violence had subsided (figure 8.4). Evidence from captive talapoin monkeys also shows that the receipt of aggression can suppress testosterone secretion in males, leading to a tendency for subordinates to have lower levels of this hormone than dominant (Eberhart *et al.* 1980). This difference is further enhanced by the elevation of testosterone seen in sexually active dominant males (see above), but there does not seem to be a similar effect resulting from the actual giving of aggression (Eberhart *et al.* 1980). In the case of man, the stress of severe military training has also been shown to suppress testosterone levels (Kreuz *et al.* 1972), which suggests that psychological pressures or constraints (analogous to social subordination in non-human primates?) may be sufficient stimulus to alter hormone secretion.

To summarize, it seems that the influence of behavioural events on hormonal state in the primate may be of more significance than vice versa. Thus in the male, sexual activity is associated with an increase, and the receipt of aggression with a decrease, in plasma testosterone. The latter effect may be important with respect to the male's reproductive potential, since reduced androgen has been associated with lowered spermatogenesis. Such a consequence of the social hierarchy – i.e. altered fertility – may be even more obvious in the case of the female: this will be considered below.

The experience of chronic subordination is associated with the constant threat of potential aggression, even in the absence of actual fighting. It might be expected therefore to affect the production of the body's so-called 'stress' hormones. These include cortisol and prolactin (produced respectively by the adrenal cortex and the pituitary gland), hormones that are secreted in response to stress in many species. In captive talapoin monkeys there is a tendency for both cortisol and prolactin to be elevated in subor-

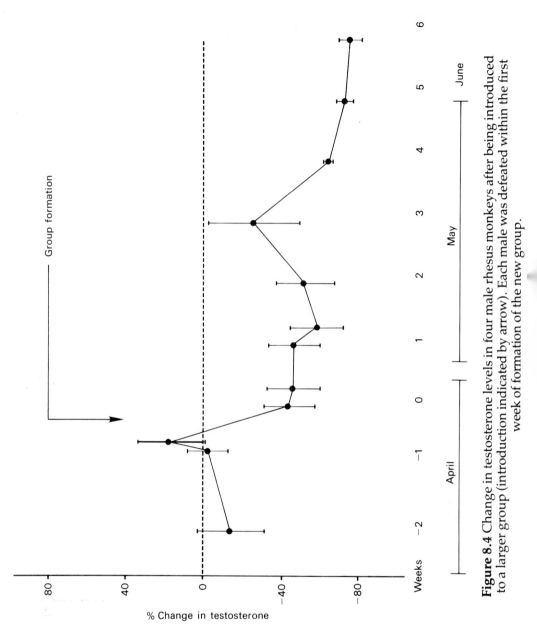

Figure 8.4 Change in testosterone levels in four male rhesus monkeys after being introduced to a larger group (introduction indicated by arrow). Each male was defeated within the first week of formation of the new group.

dinate as compared with high-ranking individuals, an effect most pronounced in the case of prolactin in females (Keverne 1979). This takes some weeks to occur and hence appears to be a response to chronic rather than acute social stress. Such an alteration in endocrine state could be particularly significant in terms of the female's reproductive potential, since in women abnormally high levels of prolactin are associated with loss of menstrual cycles and hence with inability to conceive (see, e.g., Thorner *et al.* 1975). Evidence from studies on the female talapoin monkey suggests the possibility of socially induced infertility. Normally in the primate menstrual cycle, rising levels of the hormone oestrogen at midcycle lead to a rapid surge in the pituitary's secretion of luteinizing hormone (LH). This LH surge results in ovulation. While ovulation clearly cannot be studied directly in ovariectomized female monkeys, the mechanism that brings it about can be investigated indirectly by challenging the system to see if the pituitary can respond to rising oestrogen with an LH surge. Is this ability affected by social rank?

To test this, Keverne and co-workers carried out an experiment in which the response of females at the bottom of the dominance hierarchy – who had elevated prolactin – was compared with that of dominant females – who showed low titres of prolactin (Bowman *et al.* 1978). Both females were administered a pulse of oestrogen. In response to this, however, only the dominant female responded with a surge of LH (figure 8.5). The hormone remained low in the subordinate female: in other words, her neuroendocrine system was effectively infertile. Furthermore, it was found that it was actually the elevated prolactin that was responsible for this 'infertility'. Thus, when prolactin was lowered pharmacologically in the subordinate, she was now able to show an LH surge in response to oestrogen. In addition, the converse was also true, with the LH surge being blocked in the dominant female following the pharmacological elevation of the prolactin. Most convincing, perhaps, in terms of relating the receipt of aggression to a change in endocrine responsiveness is the finding that removal of the lowest-ranking female from the social group, i.e. away from her aggressors, to a single cage led after some weeks to her ability also to show an LH surge. These results are of particular clinical interest, since they point to the possibility of a stressful social environment being responsible for that infertility which is associ-

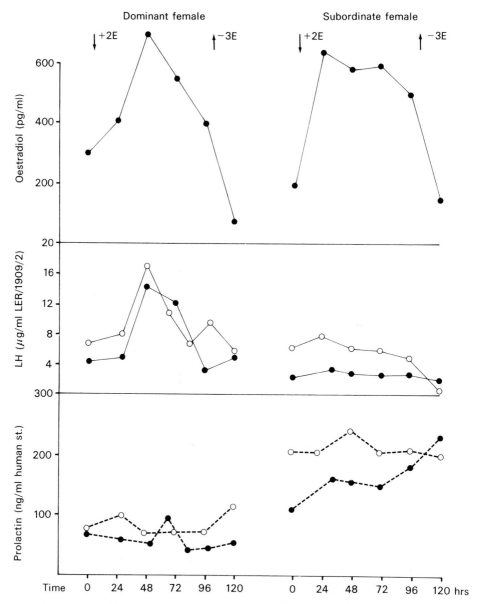

Figure 8.5 Effect on LH levels of giving an oestrogen pulse to dominant and subordinate female talapoin monkeys. Raising oestrogen (upper panel) leads to a surge in LH in the dominant but not the subordinate female (middle panel: experiment repeated). Prolactin is markedly higher in subordinate than in dominant individual (lower panel).

ated with hyperprolactinaemia and which responds to drugs that lower this hormone. They also suggest a possible mechanism that explains the finding that subordinate female gelada baboons are less fertile than their more dominant companions (Dunbar and Dunbar 1977).

CONCLUSION

Overall, then, it can now be seen that studies on social groups of primates have shown that an individual's position in the dominance hierarchy can have profound effects on both behavioural and hormonal responses. The following statements can be made concerning aggression and its hormonal correlates in primate societies.

In primate social groups aggression initially occurs, with the result that some form of dominance hierarchy is established and social stability ensues.

Subsequently, overt aggression may be rare: however, position in the hierarchy leads to real predictable effects on both hormones and behaviour.

In some individuals, chronic subordination may be associated with maladaptive neuroendocrine changes.

From these points – and particularly from the last one – it is possible to derive a principle that may be of importance and relevance to man. The phenomena described in this chapter have not been concerned with the acute consequences of aggression, such as might occur during the formation of a group. Instead, the subsequent effects of the hierarchical society on the animal's activity and endocrine state have been considered. In an established group, the individual's behaviour and attitudes are modified not by constant overt aggression, but rather by learned social rules or pressures which may be reinforced by means of ritualized, non-physical aggression such as threats. In some cases these constraints lead to marked physiological, as well as behavioural, changes which can affect the reproductive capacity of the individual. Our own society is surely at least as constrained by social rules as is that of the non-human primate – again, usually in the absence of overt aggression. Would it not therefore be of significant value when considering the aetiology of human health problems and endocrine disturbance to look much more closely at social factors and constraints than is the case at present?

REFERENCES

Beach, F.A. 1947: 'Evolutionary changes in the physiological control of mating behaviour in mammals', *Psychology Review* 54: 404–6.

Bernstein, I.S. 1964: 'The integration of rhesus monkeys introduced to a group', *Folia primatologica* 2: 50–64.

Bowman, L.A., Dilley, S.R. and Keverne, E.B. 1978: 'Suppression of oestrogen-induced LH surges by social subordination in talapoin monkeys', *Nature* 275: 56–8.

Carpenter, C.R. 1942: 'Sexual behaviour of free-ranging rhesus monkeys', *Journal of Comparative Psychology* 33: 113–62.

Collias, N.E. 1944: 'Aggressive behaviour among vertebrate animals', *Physiology and Zoology* 17: 83–123.

Dixson, A.F. and Herbert, J. 1977: 'Gonadal hormones and sexual behaviour in groups of adult talapoin monkeys (*Miopithicus talapoin*)', *Hormones and Behaviour* 8: 141–45.

Doering, C.H., Brodie, K.H., Kraemer, H.C., Moos, R.H., Becker, H.B. and Hamburg, D.A. 1975: 'Negative affect and plasma testosterone: a longitudinal human study', *Psychosomatic Medicine* 37: 484–91.

Dunbar, R.I.M. and Dunbar, E.P. 1977: 'Dominance and reproductive success among female gelada baboons', *Nature* 266: 351–2.

Duvall, S.W., Bernstein, I.S. and Gordon, T.P. 1976: 'Paternity and status in a rhesus monkey group', *Journal of Reproduction and Fertility* 47: 25–31.

Eaton, G.G. and Resko, J.A. 1974: 'Plasma testosterone and male dominance in a Japanese macaque (*Macaca fuscata*) troop compared with repeated measures of testosterone in laboratory males', *Hormones and Behaviour* 5: 251–9.

Eberhart, J.A., Keverne, E.B. and Meller, R.E. 1980: 'Social influences on plasma testosterone levels in male talapoin monkeys', *Hormones and Behaviour* 14: 247–66.

Gartlan, J.S. 1964: 'Dominance in East African monkeys', *Proceedings of the East African Academy* 2: 75–9.

Gartlan, J.S. 1968: 'Structure and function in primate society', *Folia primatologica* 8: 89–120.

Gartlan, J.S. 1975: 'Adaptive aspects of social structure in *Erythrocebus patas*', in *Symposium of the 5th Congress of the International Primatology Society*, ed. S. Kondo, M. Kawai, A. Ehara and S. Kawamura, Tokyo: Japan Science Press, 161–71.

Gordon, T.P., Rose, R.M. and Bernstein, I.S. 1976: 'Seasonal rhythm in plasma testosterone levels in the rhesus monkey (*Macaca mulatta*): a three-year study', *Hormones and Behaviour* 7: 229–43.

Green, R., Whalen, R.E., Rutley, B. and Battie, C. 1972: 'Dominance hierarchy in squirrel monkeys (*Saimiri sciureus*). Role of the gonads and androgen on genital display and feeding order', *Folia primatologica* 18: 185–95.

Guhl, A.M. 1961: 'Gonadal hormones and social behaviour in infra-human vertebrates', in *Sex and Internal Secretions*, ed. W.C. Young and G.W. Corner, Baltimore: Williams and Wilkins, 1240–67.

Hall, K.R.L. and DeVore, I. 1965: 'Baboon social behaviour', in *Primate Behaviour*, ed. I. DeVore, New York: Holt, Rinehart & Winston, 53–110.

Hall, K.R.L. and Mayer, R. 1967: 'Social interactions in a group of captive patas monkeys (*Erythrocebus patas*)', *Folia primatologica* 5: 213–36.

Hinde, R.A. 1974: *The Biological Bases of Human Social Behaviour*, Maidenhead: McGraw-Hill.

Hinde, R.A. 1978: 'Dominance and role – two concepts with dual meanings', *Journal of Social and Biological Structure* 1: 27–38.

Keverne, E.B. 1979: 'Sexual and aggressive behaviour in social groups of talapoin monkeys', in *Sex, Hormones and Behaviour, Ciba Foundation Symposium* 62 (Excerpta Medica): 271–86.

Keverne, E.B., Meller, R.E. and Martinez-Arias, A. 1978a: 'Dominance, aggression and sexual behaviour in social groups of talapoin monkeys', in *Recent Advances in Primatology*, ed. D.J. Chivers and J. Herbert, London & New York: Academic Press, 533–48.

Keverne, E.B., Leonard, R.A., Scruton, D.M. and Young, S.K. 1978b: 'Visual monitoring in social groups of talapoin monkeys', *Animal Behaviour* 26: 933–944.

Kreuz, L.E. and Rose, R.M. 1972: 'Assessment of aggressive behaviour and plasma testosterone in a young criminal population', *Psychosomatic Medicine* 34: 321–32.

Kreuz, L.E., Rose, R.M. and Jennings, J.R. 1972: 'Suppression of plasma testosterone levels and psychological stress', *Archives of General Psychiatry* 26: 479–82.

Lancaster, J.B. and Lee, R.B. 1965: 'The annual reproductive cycle in monkeys and apes', in *Primate Behaviour*, ed. I. DeVore, New York: Holt, Rinehart & Winston, 486–513.

Marsden, H.M. 1968: 'Agonistic behaviour of young rhesus monkeys after changes induced in social rank of their mothers', *Animal Behaviour* 16: 38–44.

Maslow, A.H. 1936: 'The role of dominance in the social and sexual behaviour of infra-human primates', *Journal of Genetic Psychology* 48: 261–338.

Meller, R.E. 1978: 'Sexual and aggressive behaviour in talapoin monkeys', PhD thesis, University of Cambridge.

Rose, R.M, Bernstein, I.S. and Gordon, T.P. 1975: 'Consequences of social conflict on plasma testosterone levels in rhesus monkeys', *Psychosomatic Medicine* 37: 50–61.

Rose, R.M., Bernstein, I.S., Gordon, T.P. and Catlin, S.F. 1974: 'Androgens and aggression: a review and recent findings in primates', in *Primate Aggression, Territoriality and Xenophobia*, ed. R.L. Holloway, New York and London: Academic Press, 275–304.

Rose, R.M., Holaday, J.W. and Bernstein, I.S. 1971: 'Plasma testosterone, dominance rank and aggressive behaviour in male rhesus monkeys', *Nature* 231: 366–8.

Rowell, T.E. 1966: 'Hierarchy in the organization of a captive baboon group', *Animal Behaviour* 14: 430–43.

Sade, D.S. 1967: 'Determinants of dominance in a group of free-ranging monkeys', in *Social Communication among Primates*, ed. S.A. Altmann, Chicago: University Press, 99–114.

Savin-Williams, R.C. 1977: 'Dominance in a human adolescent group', *Animal Behaviour* 25: 400–6.

Schjelderup-Ebbe, T. 1935: 'Social behaviour of birds' (first published in 1913), in *A Handbook of Social Psychology*, ed. C. Murchison, Worcester, Mass.: Clark University Press, 947–73.

Scruton, D.M. and Herbert, J. 1972: 'The reaction of captive talapoin monkeys to the introduction of male and female strangers of the same species', *Animal Behaviour* 20: 463–73.

Southwick, C.H., Siddiqi, M.F., Farooqui, M.Y. and Pal, B.C. 1974: 'Xenophobia among free-ranging rhesus groups in India', in *Primate Aggression, Territoriality and Xenophobia*, ed. R.L. Holloway, New York and London: Academic Press, 185–209.

Thorner, M.O., Besser, G.M., Jones, A., Dacie, J. and Jones, A.E. 1975: 'Bromocriptine therapy of female infertility – a report of thirteen pregnancies', *British Medical Journal* 4: 694–7.

Wilson, A.P. and Boelkins, R.C. 1970: 'Evidence for seasonal variation in aggressive behaviour by *Macaca mulatta*', *Animal Behaviour* 18: 719–24.

Zuckerman, S. 1932: *The Social Life of Monkeys and Apes*, London: Kegan Paul, Trench and Trubner.

CHAPTER 9

Female Aggression

Anne Campbell

Of the small quantity of available work on female aggression, the bulk of it takes the form of a footnote to research primarily directed at males. There are two possible reasons for this. First, common sense suggests that aggression is relatively rare among females; and second, academic research has been a traditionally male-dominated area, and this has been reflected in the choice of subject matter. Both have probably played some part in the paucity of work on aggression in girls.

Physiologists have considered the role of genetics and hormones in aggressive behaviour. The incidence of XXY genetic make-up in female criminals and delinquents has been found to be non-existent or low (Kaplan; cited in Ferdon 1971). Hormonal studies in animals have reported that an excess of androgens administered to a neonate female will result in more 'masculinized' social behaviour in adulthood (Gray and Drewett 1977). Money and Erhardt (1972) have shown that females suffering from progestin-induced hermaphroditism and adreno-genital syndrome (which masculinize genital structure and hormones, respectively) show greater levels of rough-and-tumble play and male interests than a control group. In this study, however, there were no significant differences with respect to the amount of fighting by the two groups. In many cross-cultural studies, fighting had such a low rate of occurrence that rough play was taken as an alternative measure of aggression. In nearly all the studies, play aggression was found to be higher among males than among females (see Maccoby and Jacklin 1974 for a review). Studies such as these do not of them-

selves require any genetic explanation. Social structure may
determine socialization differences in children, and social structure
need not be related to physical aggression. Experimental studies
have looked at subjects' willingness to deliver what they believed
to be high-intensity electric shocks to victims in a laboratory
'learning' situation. The majority of studies found that males were
willing to give higher-frequency and longer-duration shocks than
were women. Knott and Drost (1970) even found that 'masculine'
women gave more intense and lengthy shocks than more 'femi-
nine' women. Most psychologists do not accept this as a valid
measure of *aggression*. It is more likely to reflect compliance to the
experimental demands of the situation and lacks any of the affective components of aggression. Other studies have looked at the
role of learning in aggression by reinforcement and observation.
Although girls do not display as high levels of aggressive behaviour
as do boys in these situations, they can match the boys' performance when offered incentives to do so (Bandura, Ross and Ross
1961). Criminological studies have tended to focus on more spectacular instances of female violence, where death or serious injury
has been the result (see for example Rosenblatt and Greenland
1974, Ward, Jackson and Ward 1968, Cole, Fisher and Cole 1968).

There has been a virtual absence of studies concerned with the
natural expression of aggression by girls, particularly at the
developmental period of adolescence when acts of aggression are
at their height for boys and girls. Findings of guilt in magistrates'
courts in 1978 for wounding showed that 45 per cent of males and
50 per cent of females were aged between 10 and 21 years of age.
Ethnographic studies of male youth groups have offered rich
accounts of the boys' attitudes, values and norms concerning
aggression (see Miller 1958; Whyte 1943; Marsh 1978; Parker 1974).
From these 'insider's' accounts it is possible to view fighting as
having a meaningful place in maintaining social structure, aiding
male sex role development and creating in-group loyalty. Without
it, we are in danger of viewing fighting as a random or chaotic
activity reflecting individual pathology or inadequate (middle-
class) socialization. The findings reported here represent a
preliminary and incomplete step towards gaining such information
for females.

In this area of research, a distinction has been made between
instrumental and hostile or expressive aggression. In the first, the

aim of the behaviour is to gain rewards other than the victim's suffering. Hilgard *et al.* (1979) include in this category fighting in self-defence, assault during a robbery, fighting to prove one's power or dominance, or defending the rights of an underdog. In fact, the two categories are far from mutually exclusive. It is clear that fighting can encompass aspects of both, and indeed in some cases must do. For example, the achievement of dominance very often requires some suffering on the part of the opponent. On the other hand, expressive aggression (such as hitting a child in anger) may have instrumental effects in terms of modifying the child's future behaviour. The particular aspect of aggression to be considered here relates to interpersonal disputes. The goal of the behaviour is the resolution of the dispute, whether it be in terms of regaining self-respect or deterring the victim from repeating the actions that gave rise to the conflict. Instrumental aggression, in terms of coercion to obtain money, goods or sex, will not be considered.

Yet another distinction has been made between normative and expressive aggression. Berkowitz (chapter 6 above) suggests that some men become involved in fights because it is expected of them by their peers. However, since these fights do not occur at random but are the result of what is clearly perceived as a provocation on the part of the opponent, they are very likely to contain elements of expressive aggression (i.e. anger and other appropriate affective states). This study attempted to consider normative influences on the expression of aggression in terms of the peer group's conceptualization of legitimate provocation and their social rules of fight management. The affective component was all too evident in the responses given by the girls themselves.

The girls who took part in the study were 16 years old and were in their last year of compulsory school attendance. The schools selected were all in working-class areas of large towns. Although the girls were not asked for information on their fathers' occupation, those familiar with the areas would certainly recognize them as primarily working-class. This was in order to make their data compatible with that of males, which has been mostly gathered from working-class youth. Two hundred and fifty-one girls completed the questionnaire. They were drawn from Kelvinside (Glasgow), Drumchapel (Glasgow), Liverpool, Marston (Oxford) and Elephant and Castle (London). After completing the questionnaires (which was done in a classroom situation but without any teachers present), subsets of girls were chosen at random for further discussion. This was done in groups of about eight to ten girls at a time. Quotations that are used in the text are taken from these discussion sessions.

Every one of the schoolgirls had seen a fight, and 89 per cent had been in at least one themselves. The majority (58 per cent) had begun fighting in childhood, that is when they were aged ten or less, and 43 per cent had been involved in at least one fight in the preceding year. Fights were not as frequent as they might appear, however. Only 26 per cent had been in more than six fights in their life. Of all the girls, only 6 per cent had ever had the police involved in one of their fights, and only 1 per cent had been prosecuted as a result of fighting. In their spare time, the girls were split evenly between going round with mixed-sex groups and associating with exclusively female groups. Only 3 per cent claimed to spend their leisure time only with boys. Interestingly, girls in mixed-sex groups were significantly more likely to admit to having had a number of fights than those in all-female peer groups. The reason for this is open to speculation. Perhaps these girls learned to fight from male friends, or they may have joined mixed-sex groups because they enjoyed characteristically 'male' activities. My impression was that it was the more socially mature girls who were in these heterosexual groups, and both personality and age may have a mediating effect on fighting.

With respect to the fights themselves, girls were asked to remember one typical fight in detail and were asked specific questions about it. From such data we can gain some idea of a 'modal' fight experience. Such a picture may not correspond to any one fight described, and is indicative only of the general circumstances surrounding female fighting.

The majority of fights took place in the street (47 per cent) or at school (29 per cent). In 88 per cent of cases the girl was with her friends at the time of the fight. Seventy-five per cent fought only one opponent – that is, it was a one-on-one or 'fair' fight. In 74 per cent of cases the opponent was another girl. The circumstances are clearly similar to those among boys, with the possible exception of the location of the fight. Fox (1977) and Marsh (1978) have suggested that certain public events provide an 'arena' for male aggression. Fox notes the dance hall, while Marsh picks out the football stand. Many of these fights may spill out on to the streets, however. Fox describes how the Tory Island men continued the fight outside the hall accompanied by a crowd of spectators, and Marsh has noted that the ritual domination of the opposing team may build up before the match on the streets and be continued after it as the opposition is 'escorted' back to the railway station. McClintock (1963) found that 28 per cent of the crimes of violence that he studied happened on the street. Nine per cent of the girls in this study had fought in discos or public houses, compared with 20 per cent in the McClintock study. The lower age of the present sample probably accounts for the preponderance of school fights, and a study of similar aged males might well reveal a similar pattern.

The reason for the fight was broken down into eight categories for the purpose of coding. The majority of responses indicated issues of personal integrity. This category included all instances of perceived attacks on the girl's private or public self-concept. Failure to retaliate in such a situation would have inevitably meant a loss of face. Such provocations included false accusations against the girl, gossip behind her back and any pejorative remark about her sexual morality, delinquency, courage or intelligence. Thirty five per cent of fights were the result of such reasons. The second highest category was loyalty. Loyalty was defined as any contravention of self-concept directed at a relative or friend who was not present or able to defend herself. This constituted a further 10 per cent of all fights. Nine per cent arose over issues of jealousy, and a further 9 per cent over minor frustrations (being in a bad mood, being irritated by another girl's stupidity, events that 'got on her nerves'); 6 per cent were over disputed ownership of property and 3 per cent had happened as a result of an unintended physical injury or play fighting that got out of hand. Only 2 per cent were about race, and 1 per cent were instrumental acts to obtain money.

The girls were asked to indicate the 'triggering' remark (whether made by themselves or the other girl) that provoked the first blow to be struck. Many refused to answer the question – perhaps for fear of offending the researcher's delicate sensibility. Those who did most commonly cited insults to their sexual reputation (such as 'slag', 'tart' or 'scrubber') or remarks directly related to the subject of the dispute (e.g. 'You nicked my boyfriend' or 'You told her I was a liar'). Each category accounted for 18 per cent of responses. In

12 per cent of cases, there was a straightforward piece of abuse ('Fuck you', 'sod off'), and in another 10 per cent a direct challenge to fight ('Make me', 'Go on then, hit me'). Racial insults were so low as to be negligible.

In spite of the folklore pre-eminence of jealousy as a motive, the data show that self-respect and social status are very important among girls. One brief passage sums up very nicely the similarities and differences of male and female fights:

AC: What do girls fight about?
—   Boys.
—   Ripping up one another's clothes and calling each other names.
—   Jealousy.
—   Breaking up best friends.
AC: What sort of names?
—   'Slag', things like that.
AC: What do boys fight about?
—   Girls.
—   Who's better than who.
—   'I've seen you with her.'
—   Chickening out – they say 'Oh, you chickened out of that' and fight about it to show they're tough.
AC: Does machismo work for girls too?
—   Yeah, yeah.
—   It does.
—   There's always some girl you say 'I wouldn't have a fight with her', but when it comes to it you do.
AC: So do boys and girls fight about the same things or not?
—   Boils down to the same thing really, 'cos girls fight over boys, boys fight over girls. Fight for their pride, things like that, and boys fight about the same things.
—   A girl that's been called a slag is the same as a boy that's been called a chicken.
—   But they [boys] never fight when they're by themselves. They've always got to have a big crowd.
—   Groups of boys will fight for the sake of just being groups.
—   Girls don't do that do they?
—   I don't think girls just go round in a group and fight another girl group.
—   You get some – it's usually individuals talking to another group – fighting and then they'll all join in, but it's not like that with boys.

One of the most important differences, as the girls perceive it, is the group nature of boys' fights. Boys will fight merely by virtue of being an established group. This is most clearly exemplified in football supporters but can also be seen in various branches of youth subculture. In the Mods and Rockers disturbances on the south coast in the 1960s, Cohen notes:

> The groups were merely loose collectivities or crowds, within which there was occasionally some more structured grouping based on territorial loyalty, e.g. 'The Walthamstow Boys', 'The Lot from Eltham'. Constant repetition of the gang image made these collectivities see themselves as gangs and behave in a gang fashion. [Cohen 1972: 282]

This territorial loyalty has also been described by White (1971) in Birmingham and in London by Daniel and McGuire (1972). It is best exemplified in the United States in the fighting gangs of the 1950s, whose defence of their 'turf' has become legendary. In general, the girls suggested that, while female fighting is a group activity, it does not occur *by virtue of* being a group. Interpersonal disputes between individual girls will usually be settled between themselves, with the group present to provide an audience and to break things up if they go too far. Occasionally it may even spread into an inter-group fight, but the initial impetus is a particular individual grievance rather than a desire to demonstrate one group's superiority.

However the schoolgirls, at least in Glasgow and London, were convinced that girl gangs did exist. In Glasgow, male gangs have a long history (see Patrick 1973). Some of the girls admitted their participation in gang fights. While not playing a central part, they would be prepared to enter a fight to support their male friends from their home area.

AC: Do you mean a real gang with a proper name or just a group of people?
— No, real gang.
— In the town you've got The Cowards, The Cumby, The Tongs. . . .
— Hundreds of them.
— Blue Angels.
— Its more or less the names of the places they come from.
— Drummie team.
— There's a lot of people from Drumchapel. Then you've got lots of people from Posel.

—   The Carlton Tongs and all that.
—   They don't fight or anything. It's just 'Right, that crowd comes from Carlton, call them Carlton Tongs'. It doesn't mean they're going to go out and start trouble. It's just to separate them out.
AC: Do you consider yourself part of the team?
—   No.
—   But say we were up the town and there was a crowd of guys and there was a crowd of lassies jumping in. Just say Drumchapel were fighting Carlton and then the lassies jumped in. I think it would be really necessary to jump in. But I wouldn't consider us part of the team.
—   If someone came up and said 'We need you, you've got to help us out', then we'd jump in.
AC: Would they do it for you?
—   Aye, they've done it many a time.
AC: Would you bring a bloke to help you fight a girl?
—   No. But see there's a lot of lassies that'll say. . . If I say 'Right, I'll see you outside', they'll not know whether I'm going to go and get a team. I mean, one night somebody was fighting me, there was this big team waiting for me. It was someone I knew and there was this big team of guys and lassies standing there, and I took a couple of pals and this lassie who'd a big team felt dead stupid 'cos we just toddled out ourselves. It was funny.
AC: What happens if you change areas, do you change teams?
—   No.
—   Depends what age you're at.
—   Say if someone gets a doing or they're jumped or something like that – our team will help out. Then you get one team fighting another.

In London, the girls suggested that they knew of all-girl gangs. There was little indication of formal structure, and their chief activity seemed to be petty theft and extortion from their school-mates. However, the leader won her position by toughness and physical strangth.

AC: Are there girl gangs in London?
—   Yeah, Drapsey.
AC: What do they do?
—   Take your jewellery or just frighten you, take your money, things like that.
AC: Just on the street?
—   Yeah.
AC: Has this happened to you round here, round South London?
—   Most of it is South London. This side and Lambeth, East End, Poplar way.

—   My cousin went to a club and all these girls come up and said 'Oh, that's a nice ring can I see it?' So my cousin just showed them and they said 'We're not going to give it to you now.' So my cousin called over all her friends and they said 'You'd better give her back that ring.' And they gave it her back. [Laughter]

AC: But they were going to take it were they?

—   If you're going to school, you know, everyone's got sovereigns and gate bracelets these days. You never come home with them if you get in a gang. That's the sort of thing they do.

AC: Do you think some girls have got reputations for fighting – they're known as really tough girls?

—   Coxwell Manor – they think they have. Always going round fighting. Until they get beaten, then they shut up.

—   But girls with reputations usually go round in gangs.

—   Yeah.

—   Then there's the gang leader. The one with the best reputation is the gang leader.

AC: How does someone get to be leader?

—   Being toughest, having the most fights.

—   They probably usually go round picking fights just to be leader.

—   Standing up to teachers and things like that in school.

—   Cheeking teachers, that's meant to be big.

It should be remembered that such groups as these are far from typical. While girls hang round in groups, they do not fight for position within them and do not seek out fights for the sake of it. Rather, fights are seen as a necessary means of regaining self-respect just as they are with males.

In terms of verbal provocation, one girl remarked that 'A girl that's been called a slag is the same as a boy that's been called a chicken'. Certainly, references to promiscuous sex still have a very potent effect in provoking aggression. In spite of predominantly middle-class efforts to end the dual sexual morality, little has changed among working-class girls. A study by Wilson (1978) showed that 85 per cent of the teenage girls interviewed who admitted to having had sex had done so only with one partner. A study in the United States found similar results: 62 per cent of all teenage girls who were non-virgins were 'serial monogamists' (Sorenson 1973). Wilson notes that any deviation from the 'repressive triangle' of love, sexuality and marriage was severely sanctioned by the girls themselves, as well as the boys. Boys maintained the girls' commitment to love as a precondition for sex by passing round the names of 'easy' girls and thereby 'cheapening' their reputation. Girls endorsed this by group exclusion, often fearing that by associating with such a girl their own reputation was in danger. While sex before marriage has become acceptable for a girl, sex with many partners has not. This may be related as much to the males' attitudes as to the economic advantages accruing to the girl who saves herself for a good marriage. Girls who dispense sexual favours too freely lower the market rate for sex and thus harm their contemporaries. 'Cheapness' carries its old stigma.

Sexual insults among males do not take the form of accusations of promiscuity. They are more likely to suggest that the boy is homosexual ('poof', 'bender' 'queer') or sexually inadequate or immature ('wanker'). By desexualizing the boy, his courage and bravery are challenged (see Marsh 1978). By hyper-sexualizing the girl, her femininity is challenged. Nice girls do not want sex too often.

Both Fox (1977) and Marsh (1978) have noted that male fights rarely lead to severe injury. Marsh has argued that males adhere to tacit rules of conduct in fights that militate against anybody being badly hurt. These rules culturally duplicate the rituals used by animals in agonistic encounters within groups. In humans, they take the form of prohibiting a number of people fighting a single combatant and the use of weapons. They encourage blows to be directed to relatively robust parts of the anatomy and ensure that combatants will stop the fight as soon as dominance has been achieved, rather than waiting for severe injury or death to decide the winner. The girls were asked, as part of the questionnaire, to indicate which behaviours would be considered legitimate in the course of a fight. In this way it was hoped that social rules governing the fight might be discovered. In a perfectly rule-governed world, one would anticipate 100 per cent consensus on the existence of rules. In fact, this is rarely achieved. Some peripheral group members may be unaware of the rules, or the rules themselves may be in a state of transition or development of which only some members are aware. Some rules are conditional; they state that X may not be done unless Y. Inadequate specification of the circumstantial conditions may then cause disagreement. No quantitative analysis has been made of male fighting rules. In the present material, a rule was said to exist if it received endorsement from at least 75 per cent of the population sampled. Such a criterion is particularly strict since the girls were drawn from five distinct geographical locations.

Proscriptive rules (those that state what *must not* be done) were more common than prescriptive rules (which state what *should be* done). Eleven proscriptive rules emerged, of which seven showed the required degree of consensus. Five of these were related to the social setting and 'stage management' of fights; you should not take on more than one opponent at a time, ask your friends to join in, get your friends to call the police or report it yourself to the police or school. These rules clearly have the effect of withholding access to agents of the adult world and of limiting the fight to a fair 'one-on-one' situation. The other two proscriptive rules were the prohibition of the use of bottles or knives in the fight, thus limiting the extent of possible damage. The two significant prescriptive rules that emerged were the legitimacy of punching and slapping. Kicking very nearly achieved the 75 per cent criterion.

Some of the girls disagreed with their peers in rejecting some of the generally accepted rules. By performing chi-square tests across the most universally endorsed rules, it was possible to investigate the clustering of such 'deviant' individuals. Two groups clearly emerged. Girls who believe it is permissible to tell the school about the fight are also likely to break other proscriptives rules by telling police and parents and by getting friends to stop the fight or call the police. A second type of girl, who believe it is legitimate to use a knife in a fight, is also likely to endorse taking on more than one opponent, using abusive names, biting, using a weapon and carrying on with the fight even when the opponent is on the ground. The clusterings seem to correspond well with the common notion of 'cissies' and 'toughs' – both untypical of the general population.

The rules seemed to succeed in limiting the extent of damage within the fight. Most of the girls said that their opponent had come out worst. The most common injuries were bruises (46 per cent), cuts (25 per cent) and scratches (21 per cent). With respect to themselves, the girls admitted to sustaining bruises (41 per cent) and scratches (22 per cent) but 26 per cent said they had received no injuries at all.

The final part of the questionnaire asked girls to indicate who had won the fight and how the winner was established. The answers were surprising. Fifty-two per cent did not know who had won the fight and 55 per cent had no idea how to tell who had won. Among males, the point of fighting has been taken to be the establishment of dominance. What can the function be among girls who do not seem to interpret the fight in terms of winning and losing? It seemed from the discussion that fighting was an end in itself. The fight demonstrated that both parties had the required degree of courage and determination to enter it without backing off. To be involved in a fight, even if the girl lost, earned her some level of status. But status was different from reputation. Among girls who regularly engaged in fights, reputation came to depend on winning. It was often a reputation that began more by chance than design. Once a fight had been won against a tougher or older girl, the victor inherited the loser's tough reputation which in turn involved her in more fights either to help out underdogs or to answer the challenge of the aspiring fighters in the school.

In conclusion, the present data are no more than a first step in understanding the full picture of female adolescent fighting. It is based solely on self-reported material, and the tendencies both to concealment and exaggeration cannot be fully known. Work on the validity of self-reported delinquency has indicated that respondents are surprisingly honest (Farrington 1973, Hardt and Peterson-Hardt 1977). Without further behavioural data, which would require observational methods, the conclusions must be tentative. In the past, studies have often looked at levels of male and female aggression in a theoretical vacuum. It is time for an analysis that encompasses both the function and form of aggression. Girls as well as boys need to establish and maintain a positive public self-concept. In the face of an assault on their personal integrity, steps must be taken to regain the *status quo*.

We have often derived our ideas of female aggression from a stereotypically middle-class perspective. We see girls as devious, cunning and conspiratorial – ganging up together in silent coalitions to ostracize enemies. Among working-class girls this is no longer the case (if it ever was). The capacity to stand up for one's self and to take pride in that fact is very evident in the talk of working-class girls. It is no virtue to suffer in martyred silence. To this extent it approximates closely to the male experience. Sex role may still exercise its effect in determining what constitutes a challenge to self-concept. It may even determine how and where that challenge is answered. But the need to prove one's worth may well turn out to be much more a *human* quality than a male one.

REFERENCES

Bandura, A., Ross, D. and Ross, S.A. 1961: 'Transmission of aggression through imitation of aggressive models', *Journal of Abnormal and Social Psychology* 63: 575–82.

Cohen, S. 1972: *Folk Devils and Moral Panics,* London: MacGibbon & Kee.

Cole, K.E., Fisher, G. and Cole, S.S. 1968: 'Women who kill: a socio-psychological study', *Archives of General Psychiatry* 19: 1–8.

Daniel, S. and McGuire, P. (eds) 1972: *The Paint House,* Harmondsworth: Penguin.

Farrington, D.P. 1973: 'Self-reports of deviant behaviour: predictive and stable?' *Journal of Criminal Law and Criminology* 64: 99–110.

Ferdon, N.M. 1971: 'Cromosomal abnormalities and antisocial behaviour', *Journal of Genetic Psychology* 118: 281–92.

Fox, R. 1977: 'The inherent rules of violence', in *Social Rules and Social Behaviour,* ed. P. Collett, Oxford: Basil Blackwell.

Gray, J.A. and Drewett, R.F. 1977: 'The genetics and development of sex differences', in *Handbook of Modern Personality Theory,* ed. R.B. Cattell and R.M. Dreger, Chichester: John Wiley.

Hardt, R.H. and Peterson-Hardt, S. 1977: 'On determining the quality of the delinquency self-report method', *Journal of Research in Crime and Delinquency* 14: 247–61.

Hilgard, E.R., Atkinson, R.L. and Atkinson, R.C. 1979: *Introduction to Psychology,* 7th edn, New York: Harcourt Brace Jovanovich.

Knott, P.D. and Drost, B.A. 1970: 'Sex role identification, interpersonal aggression and anger', *Psychological Reports* 27: 154.

Maccoby, E. and Jacklin, C.N. 1974: *The Psychology of Sex Differences,* Stanford: University Press.

McClintock, F.H. 1963: *Crimes of Violence,* London: Macmillan.

Marsh, P. 1978: *Aggro: The Illusion of Violence,* London: Dent.

Miller, W.B. 1958: 'Lower class culture as a generating milieu of gang delinquency', *Journal of Social Issues* 14: 5–19.

Money, J. and Erhardt, A.A. 1972: *Man and Woman, Boy and Girl,* Baltimore and London: Johns Hopkins University Press.

Parker, H. 1974: *The View from the Boys,* Newton Abbott, Devon: David & Charles.

Patrick, J. 1973: *A Glasgow Gang Observed,* Bristol: Eyre Methuen.

Rosenblatt, E. and Greenland, C. 1974: 'Female crimes of violence', *Canadian Journal of Criminology and Corrections* 16: 173–80.

Sorenson, R.C. 1973: *Adolescent Sexuality in Contemporary America,* New York: World Publishing.

Ward, D.J., Jackson, M. and Ward, R.E. 1968: 'Crimes of violence by women', in *Crimes of Violence,* vol. 13, ed. D.H. Mulvihill and M.M. Tumin, Washington, DC: US Government Printing Office.

White, D. 1971: 'Brum's mobs', *New Society* 18: 760–3.

Whyte, W.F. 1943: *Street Corner Society*, Chicago: University of Chicago Press.

Wilson, D. 1978: 'Sexual code and conduct: a study of teenage girls', in *Women, Sexuality and Social Control*, ed. C. Smart and B. Smart, London: Routledge & Kegan Paul.

CHAPTER 10

Children's Understanding of Aggression

Neil Frude and Hugh Gault

Aggression, like sex and eating, is a highly cultural, cognitive, strategic and even symbolic activity, and yet it is also a basic biological response. The integration of known facts about violence and aggression is a major challenge. Violence may be part of the natural order, but it also tends to occur more on Saturdays than on other days. Aggressive tendencies may be related to levels of brain catecholamines, but aggressive outbursts also sometimes reflect the film that happens to be showing in town. Aggression is difficult to define, difficult to measure and difficult to control. It is also something that we are all intimately familiar with; we see it from within and without.

Some people are more aggressive than other people, but also any individual is more aggressive at some times than at others. In addition, some types of situation give rise to aggression much more frequently than do others. With such formidable multiple sources of variability it is not surprising that the activities of those involved in 'understanding aggression' range widely, and include snipping rat brains, insulting psychology students, interviewing vandals, watching fighting fish and examining patterns in murder rate statistics. The mammoth task of integration seems to recede, rather than draw nearer, as more disparate facts are added to the pile. Perhaps the hope of a convergence is based upon an invalid and implicit premise about the uniformity of aggression as 'a phenomenon'. Maybe we need to 'unpack' the variable, to make fewer generalizations and more distinctions. A philosopher of science once said that a pretzel-shaped reality needs a pretzel-shaped theory (Kaplan 1964).

We've opted for a rather simple pretzel, and we've been using a very basic model of the aggression incident as the central focus for thinking about how the various social and biological aspects of aggression might be integrated (figure 10.1). Something similar to this is to be found in many elementary textbooks. In this simplest representation alternative exits and entrances at the various points are ignored, as are feedback loops. There are two pathways – this is based on that over-simple but very useful distinction between 'instrumental aggression' (i.e. aggression carried out for some primary purpose other than 'pure' hostility) and 'anger aggression' (Buss 1961). Our main concern here is with anger aggression.

Five stages are differentiated in the model. The first of these is the *situation*. Clearly, some situations in the world frequently give rise to aggression and some do not. Generally, people know how to arrange a situation to promote aggression, and one useful view of aggression is that of a reaction to a situation. Aggressive outbursts are almost never without some observable antecedent.

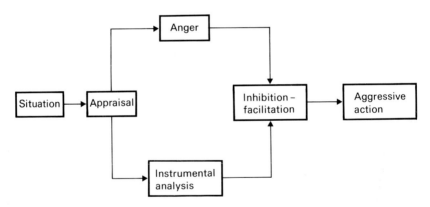

Figure 10.1 The aggression incident model.

However, the same objective situation may be judged in many different ways. A verbal jibe may be interpreted, for example, as a joke or as a real insult. The potential variation of interpretation, or *appraisal*, is especially great with social situations (for example, when we have to judge what the person *meant* by using a particular gesture), and the great majority of situations that provoke human aggression are precisely of this type (McKellar 1949). So the same situation can be interpreted, or appraised, differently by two individuals: one may see it as aggressive, the other may not. Also, some people may be in the *habit* of interpreting situations as aggressive. It may be their style to think the worst of all they see. As such, appraisal style – as well as the particular appraisal that results from this and other factors – clearly needs to be taken into account.

Yet even if a situation could be found that was appraised in the same way by everybody, this situation would still not provoke the same degree of emotional response, or *anger*, in every person. Nor indeed would it provoke the same amount of anger in the same person at different times. We have some idea of how the emotional response (with its affective, cognitive and physiological components) is amplified or attenuated by various environmental, physiological and pharmacological conditions.

Furthermore, some anger comes out as 'angry behaviour' and some does not. There are particular *inhibitions*, such as feelings of conscience, fear of physical punishment and fear of disapproval, which may prevent such behavioural expression. As well as internal factors, such as conscience, there may also be external inhibitions that prevent aggressive behaviour in a particular situation. These may be a product of our past, present or, indeed, of our expected future. There may also be facilitatory factors present in the situation which will increase the likelihood of aggressive behaviour. Whether anger is expressed as *aggression*, therefore, depends largely on the relative weights of the inhibitory and facilitatory factors in the aggression equation. Aggression is more likely to result if the facilitatory factors outweigh the inhibitory ones.

Finally, there is the *aggressive action* itself. Verbal or physical, symbolic or injurious, the precise nature of the action is shaped by habit and opportunity, by previously stated threats and by the judged appropriateness of the reaction.

Two important features of the approach that result from such a model are, first, that it focuses primarily on the *psychological* level rather than the physiological or sociological and, second, that it focuses on the *incident* of aggression rather than on, say, aggressiveness as a personality construct or group rules concerning legitimate expression of anger.

Each box can be 'unpacked' and related on the one hand to 'underlying' physiological concomitants in turn related to genetic influences and, on the other, to important context variables – cultural norms, early experiences of the individual, values and beliefs – which are also associated with processes occurring during the incident itself. The model is in the form of a basic equation in which the specific values change considerably, so that it permits certain generalizations, but also forms a framework within which *individual* cases and incidents may be described.

Models are not theories and do not have a truth value. They are tools, and the criterion for judging them is one of usefulness. Three relevant claims are made for the usefulness of this model:

1. that it is a useful tool for the examination of specific incidents and certain types of incident;
2. that it can provide a way of integrating the very disparate evidence from different kinds of study;
3. that it corresponds to a common-sense or lay view of aggression incidents.

This last point is not without importance. Because of our direct acquaintance with aggression a model that 'feels right' has passed some sort of preliminary test of usefulness.

The model has been employed and explored by us in a number of ways. One focus of interest has been family violence. There is now a large literature on this, based on clinical and research work, and by and large it makes no reference to aggression theory. We have been able to show that the available evidence can be integrated with the help of the model (Frude 1979). Abusing parents, for example, are faced with potential aggression situations more frequently than other parents, and some of them also have a tendency to judge the child's actions in unrealistic and harsh ways. Incidents involving injury often come when there has been a build-up of tension, resentment and anger. And abusive parents, on the whole, have fewer inhibitions about physical punishment and habitually treat the child more harshly. This analysis has involved evidence from whole population studies, but the model has also proved useful in describing and accounting for particular incidents of child abuse and marital violence (Frude and Roberts 1980). The model has also been employed as a framework in interviews with violent young offenders. This use of the model will be discussed in some detail later.

Another interest has been that of trying to integrate the diffuse evidence and theoretical formulations relating alcohol and violence. Various cultural and social effects are well documented, of course, but these must be considered alongside the known physiological effects. We have suggested that alcohol may be seen as involved in each stage of the model independently.

These analyses illustrate some of the ways in which the aggression incident model has been used as a means to explain incidents and integrate the available literature. A further interest has been that of the correspondence of the model to the layman's view of aggression. In the studies we are now going to describe we wanted to know specifically whether there is any evidence that *children* understand the hypothesized links between stages.

It has been claimed that by the age of five most children have witnessed hundreds of incidents of aggression or near-aggression (Bandura 1973). They have also, by that time, been exposed to the various socializing influences of parents, peers and media. By this time then they may have developed some model of their own about the nature of aggression incidents. It was not expected, of course, that they would be able to draw a freehand copy of the model, but we wanted to examine indirectly any implicit understanding of the relations between particular stages along the suggested pathway. We studied 160 children between the ages of three and ten years, testing each one individually in eight separate studies, of which two are reported here.

CHILDREN'S UNDERSTANDING OF INTER-STAGE
RELATIONSHIPS OF THE MODEL

The first of the two studies to be reported here involves children's awareness and understanding of the relations between the cognitions, emotions and behaviour that the stages of the model represent. Specifically, we were interested in finding out whether young children do appreciate that the stages are interrelated, and at what age such an appreciation is readily apparent. Our problem, therefore, was to devise a method that would allow us to draw conclusions to these questions.

Eight dolls were chosen from commercially available toys and were used in a ranking procedure to interrelate the different stages of the model (figure 10.2). During the individual testing of each

Figure 10.2 Dolls used as elements in the ranking procedure.

child, these eight dolls were set out in random order across the table. The child was then asked to select, for example, the 'happiest' doll. This doll was removed and the child was then told to choose the 'next happiest'. This one was then also taken away from the line-up and the child was asked for the 'next happiest', and so on. This procedure was repeated until all eight dolls had effectively been ranked according to the criterion of 'happiest'. The eight dolls were then all set out on the table again – in a different order – and the child was asked to apply the criterion of, say 'angriest' in the same way.

It was assumed that the criteria of 'happiest' and 'angriest' represented the extreme poles of the Anger stage of the model. The Situation, Appraisal and Inhibition stages were presented to the children using stories, composed on the basis of pilot work. For the Situation stage, for example, the following story was composed:

> One day the dolls were all given some money to go and buy some sweets from the shop. But, as they were going down the road, they all lost some of their money. Which one lost the *most* money?

At a more general level the question being asked here (i.e., 'Which of the dolls is most likely to find themselves in an anger-arousing, irritating situation?') is clearly related to the Situation stage of the model.

For the construct representing the Appraisal stage of the model, the following story was used:

> One day the dolls were all watching TV when suddenly they heard a loud crash behind them. They turned round and saw that the dog had knocked over a plate and smashed it. Some of them thought that it was an accident, but others thought that it was a naughty dog and must have done it on purpose. Which one *most of all* thought that it was a naughty dog and did it on purpose?

The general question implied here is 'Which of the dolls is most likely to see an event as provocative?' As in the Situation example, this represents the aggression-precipitating extreme of the appropriate stage of the model.

In the case of the Inhibition stage, however, the story that was used –

They all think that it's naughty to fight – that you must not fight – but which one *most of all* thinks that it's naughty to fight?

is allied to the construct of aggression-inhibition rather than aggression-facilitation. It might reasonably be expected, therefore, that there would be a negative relationship between the rankings of the dolls for the stages of Situation and Inhibition, and also for those of Appraisal and Inhibition.

In all, therefore, with two stories for the Aggression stage, one physical, one verbal ('Who fights the most?'; 'Who shouts at people most?'), the children were asked to rank the dolls according to seven criteria. By using stories that required the children to choose among the dolls in this way, it is possible to establish the relationships that each child implicitly understands to hold between the various stages of the model. The order in which the constructs were presented was, of course, random.

One focus of interest was the age at which children first show an understanding of the inter-stage relationships. Accordingly, the 160 children tested came from four equally-sized age groups: 3- and 4-year-olds, 5- and 6-year-olds, 7- and 8-year-olds, and 9- and 10-year-olds. In order to examine the data for possible sex differences, the results of the 20 boys and 20 girls in each age group were kept separate. For each inter-stage relationship, therefore, there were eight distinct group results – boys and girls in each of four age groups.

Hypotheses had already been formulated as to the nature of these relationships. To take as an example the relationship between the two poles of the Anger stage, it was expected that those dolls that were seen as being happiest would be *least* likely to be seen as angriest, and vice versa. In other words, it was hypothesized that there would be a negative relationship – a negative correlation on average – between the two constructs related to the Anger stage. It was also expected that this relationship would be stronger – that the average correlation would be more strongly negative – for the older groups of children.

Or, to take as a further example the relationship between the

Anger and physical Aggression stages, it was expected that those dolls that were chosen as the angriest ones would be the dolls most likely to be chosen as getting into lots of fights, and vice versa. In other words, a positive relationship was hypothesized between the Anger and Aggression stages of the model. And, again, it was expected that this relationship would be stronger – in this case that the average correlation would be more strongly positive – for the older groups of children.

Results

The results for the Happy–Angry relationship are illustrated in figure 10.3. This shows the average correlations for the eight groups, four groups of boys and four groups of girls. In the case of both sexes the four groups are, from left to right, 3- and 4-year-olds, 5- and 6-year-olds, 7- and 8-year-olds, and 9- and 10-year-olds. What this histogram demonstrates is that, on average, the children believed there to be a significant negative relationship

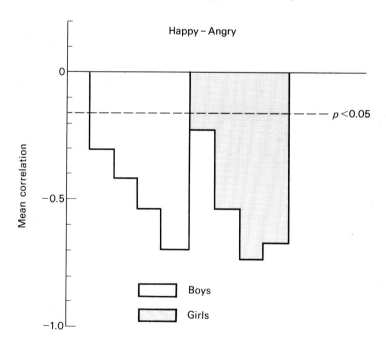

Figure 10.3 Mean correlations for relationship between 'happy' and 'angry' constructs.

between the states of happiness and anger – as was hypothesized. It also indicates that, with the exception of the oldest girls, this relationship becomes stronger, or more negative, on average, as the children get older. In other words, here is strong evidence for our hypotheses about the relationship between happiness and anger in children's understanding.

The results for the Anger–physical Aggression relationships are illustrated in figure 10.4. Here again, for most of the groups the relationship between these two stages was in the direction hypothesized. The exception this time was that of the youngest group of girls, for whom the average correlation did not differ significantly from zero. All of the other seven produced significant positive correlations, and six of these were at a level that would be expected to occur less than 1 in 1,000 times by chance. In the case of both boys and girls, the correlations were the more positive the older the group of children concerned.

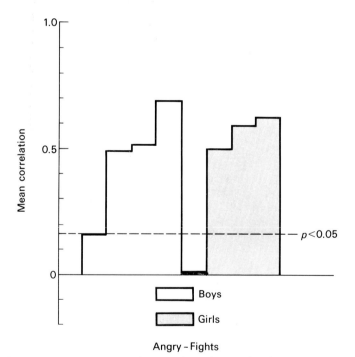

Figure 10.4 Mean correlations for relationship between 'angry' and 'fights' constructs.

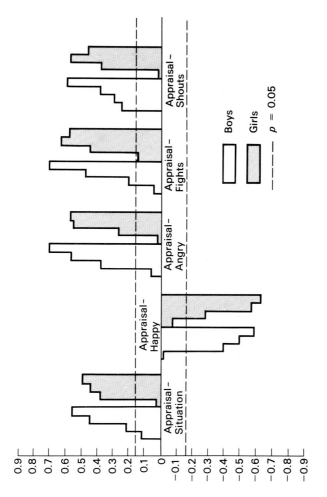

Figure 10.5 Mean correlations for the inter-construct relationships associated with 'appraisal' construct.

As a further example of children's understanding of the inter-stage relationships, the average correlations between the Appraisal stage and five of the other six constructs – the Inhibition stage has been omitted – can be seen in figure 10.5. In this histogram all the inter-stage relationships are in the appropriate directions – look, for example, at the mirror-images Appraisal–Happy and Appraisal–Angry – and the vast majority of them become increasingly significant with age. Incidentally, no significant sex differences were found for these or any other inter-stage relationships.

Histograms representing the relationships between the other constructs could be presented, but an overall picture of the data may be gained by means of two percentages. Out of a total of 168 average correlations – 21 correlations for each of the eight groups of children – 122, or 73 per cent (against a chance expectancy of 5 per cent), were significant and in the directions hypothesized. *All* of the inter-stage relationships that did not achieve significance were from the two age groups under seven years. In other words, for the children over seven years of age, every single one of the group average correlations significantly followed the hypothesized direction.

It was also predicted that the size of the average correlations would be significantly greater for the older children than for the younger ones. This was found to be the case in 48 per cent of consecutive age group comparisons (as against a chance expectancy of 5 per cent).

Conclusion

In conclusion, therefore, it can be stated that, by the age of seven or eight, children do exhibit an understanding of the relationships between certain constructs representing stages of the aggression incident model. These results imply a judged relationship between aggressive behaviour, the situations in which it is most likely to occur and the appraisals and emotions that are concomitant with it. Each stage related to the others in an expected and identifiable way.

Indeed, since most children have been in frequent social contact for a number of years by the time they reach the age of seven or eight, it would be surprising if they didn't build up implicit theories about the behaviours in which they participate and that they continually witness. In the case of aggression, these theories seem to be in line with the model that we have suggested as conforming to an adult viewpoint.

Sex Differences in Aggression

Most authorities would agree with the view that there are sex differences in levels and styles of aggressive response (Maccoby and Jacklin 1975). Evidence for this comes from sources as diverse as laboratory experiments and data on the sex ratio of murderers. There is less consensus, however, when we come to explain the differences. It is not difficult to point to certain 'pro-aggressive' values associated with maleness and masculinity, and to demonstrate differences in the socialization of boys and girls, but there are also those facts regarding the uniformity of male aggressiveness across many species and the literature linking sex hormone levels with aggressive behaviour.

Use of the Model

The model described earlier in this chapter can be used to look at the problem from a somewhat novel angle. We can ask whether there is differential exposure to aggression-provoking Situations for males and females; whether there are sex-linked styles of Appraisal and social judgement; whether there are sex differences in the Anger reaction to identical appraisals; whether there are sex differences in the levels of Inhibition against verbal and physical aggression; and, finally, whether there are habitual Aggression behaviours that differentiate the sexes. There could well be differences at each of these stages, and it might be anticipated that, whereas, say, sex hormone effects play a part at the anger stage, socialization influences broad appraisal styles more. It might be hypothesized that the differential 'training for aggression' received by boys and girls would affect the inhibition and aggression stages, and that the different social worlds that men and women inhabit would influence the frequency with which they are confronted with provocative situations.

Relevant direct studies of sex differences for each specific stage are not yet available, so these hypotheses remain as speculations.

They do seem to have some face validity, however, and this raises another interesting point – that of *sex stereotyping and aggression*. That there are strong sex stereotypes in this area is undeniable. Men are seen as more aggressive than women. But if those stereotypes are examined more closely, it might be discovered whether men are seen as less inhibited about being aggressive, for example, or as getting angry more often. Men may be seen as being faced with more situational threats and insults, or simply as being keener to fight.

Children's Aggression-related Sex Stereotypes

In the particular study to be reported, sex stereotyping in *children's* understanding of aggression was examined. The following questions were asked:
1. Is there evidence of sex stereotyping in children's understanding of aggression?
2. Can such sex-stereotyping be established for different stages of the aggression incident pathway?
3. At what age can such stereotyping first be demonstrated, and how does it change thereafter?
4. Is sex stereotyping related to the sex of the child?

Short stories were constructed, each of which illustrated as 'purely' as possible one of the five stages in the pathway. There were six stories relating to each stage, thus 30 stories in all. Each story introduced two characters by name – a boy and girl. It then described a situation, an event, a feeling or a reaction, and the child was asked a question about the story, to which the response was either the boy's name or the girl's name. A few examples will make the format clear.

Situation Story

S2

John and Karen both had money to buy sweets, but when they were going down the road, one of them dropped their money and that one couldn't buy sweets. Did John lose the money, or did Karen?

Appraisal Story 1

Ap4

Peter and Jane were helping in the garden and a dog came in

and ate one of the best flowers. One of them said, 'What a naughty dog', but the other one said 'It doesn't know that it's naughty to eat flowers.' Who thought that the dog *wasn't* naughty, was it Peter or was it Jane?

Appraisal Story 2

Ap5

Tom and Caroline left a big red balloon in the garden. When they came out after tea the balloon wasn't there. One of them thought that it had just blown away, but the other one thought that it had been stolen. Who thought that it had been stolen, was it Tom or was it Caroline?

Anger Story

A1

Lisa and Paul were both shouted at by their mummy. It made one of them very angry, but one didn't get angry. Who *didn't* get angry, was it Lisa or was it Paul?

Inhibition Story

16

Jane and Paul like watching television. One of them would never hit somebody even if they were very angry, because they think that it's naughty to hit. Which one thinks that it's naughty to hit, is it Jane or is it Paul?

Aggression Story

Ag1

Lisa and Michael share a pet rabbit called Claud. One of them sometimes pulls its ears. Which one is *never* cruel to the pet rabbit? It is Lisa or Michael who is *never* cruel?

Each story was constructed with a particular hypothesis regarding the 'pro-stereotype response'. In half the cases the 'pro-stereotype' response was the girl's name, and in half the cases it was the boy's. In half of the cases the pro-stereotype response was the second-named. In half of the cases the girl's name came first and in half the boy's. It was possible to show later that there was, overall, little bias in the children's responses towards either giving a particular sex as a response or giving a first- or second-named character as a response.

These stories were then presented orally to individual children – 160 in all – and, as before, they ranged in age from three to ten years old. Stories were written on cards and these were shuffled each time before being used.

Results

1. The first question asked was whether there was evidence of stereotyping. In our stories the children were presented with a choice – a 'heads or tails' choice – but we did not get a 50–50 breakdown of responses. In over half of these cases (17/30) the split was such as would occur less than 1 in 1,000 times by chance. All of these biases were in the direction of our prior hypotheses about sex stereotyping.

2. The results from individual stories were then grouped in terms of the 'stages', and it can be seen in figure 10.6 that the stereotyping was present independently at *each* stage. Thus, for each subset of stories it was possible to calculate for each child a 'pro-stereotype score' out of a possible 6, 3.00 being the theoretical average. Figure 10.6 represents the average of these scores for all 160 children, for each of the five stages. The distribution of responses is clearly well outside that which would be expected by chance alone and, considering the balances that were employed to eliminate other biases, then, as far as the stories really do apply 'purely' to the relevant stage, stereotyping appears to have been established independently for each stage.

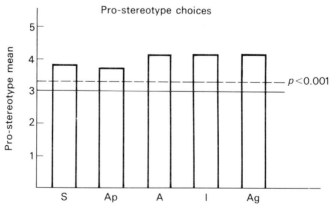

Figure 10.6 Mean stereotype choices for each stage.

3. The next question concerned the age at which this could first be demonstrated. How old did children have to be before we could show a significant stereotyping effect? The age-linked analysis for stereotyping at each of the stages is illustrated in Figure 10.7. This figure shows an increase in demonstrated stereotyping with age for all stages. In some cases the rise is more dramatic than in others. By the age of six significant stereotyping has occurred at all stages. Stereotyping in the very young children was not established except for Anger and Appraisal. It cannot of course be said that stereotyping is *not* present where we failed to demonstrate it, but it is important to be aware that it is not really possible to compare stages since the specific content material in each was different. It can, however, be said that there is increasing evidence of stereotyping with age, and that by the age of six significant stereotyping is present for all stages.

4. The final question asked was whether sex stereotyping was related to the sex of the child. There were *no* overall sex differences for any stage, and stereotyping was not demonstrated significantly earlier or later for boys than for girls. There were, however, just a few individual stories on which significant sex differences did emerge.

In one story a boy and girl were both told off by the mother and the child was asked which one had not become angry:

Lisa and Paul were both shouted at by their Mummy. It made one of them very angry, but one didn't get angry. Who *didn't* get angry, was it Lisa or was it Paul?

Whereas 48 out of the 80 boys thought that Paul didn't get angry, only 36 out of the 80 girls thought this. Boys tended to think that the boy didn't get angry and girls tended to think that the girl didn't get angry. The difference in the proportion of girls and boys opting for Paul and for Lisa was significant statistically at the 5 per cent level.

In another story the children were asked which had a nice teacher, a boy or a girl:

Emily and Matthew both went to school. One had a very nice teacher. Who had a nice teacher, was it Emily or was it Matthew?

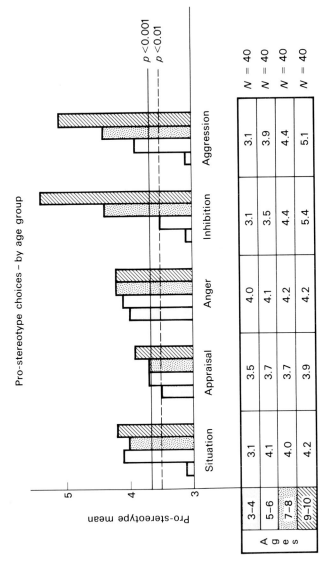

Figure 10.7 Mean stereotype choices for each stage and for each age group.

Here 33 of the boys and 56 of the girls felt that it was Emily, a distribution significantly different at the 1 in 1,000 (0.1 per cent) level.

Finally, there was a question about who had lost some money:

> John and Karen both had money to buy sweets, but when they were going down the road one of them dropped their money and that one couldn't buy sweets. Did John lose the money, or did Karen?

Here the boys tended to say that Karen had lost the money (46 out of 80) and the girls tended to say that John had lost the money (56 out of 80). Again this difference is significant at the 0.1 per cent level.

EMPIRICAL CONCLUSIONS

Several conclusions can be drawn from these studies. The study in which dolls were ranked in accordance with the constructs described provides strong evidence that, certainly by the age of nine and probably before then, children do have considerable understanding of the relationships that exist between the stages of the model. Every single group correlation for those above the age of seven followed the hypothesized direction, the majority of them with less than a 1 in 1,000 chance of occurring fortuitously.

The results of the study with stereotype stories provides clear evidence here of sex stereotyping for all stages of the model. By the age of six, both boys and girls believe that boys are more likely to be faced with irritating situations, are more likely than girls to see situations as provocative, to get angry, to be unable to restrain anger once it is aroused, and also to express anger as aggression.

Furthermore, as in the doll study there was evidence of greater consensus in these beliefs among the older children.

Overall, therefore, it seems apparent that children's beliefs about aggression do show some correspondence to the assumptions implicit in the simple theoretical model of the aggression incident.

There are a number of possible explanations for the lack of some significant results in the youngest children. It is possible that the relevant beliefs don't exist at the earlier ages, that the children are less reliable and consistent in their judgements, or that they find it difficult to understand or comply with the requirements of the experimental task.

Further Studies: Representational Level

Even remaining at the judgemental, or representational, level, there are clearly several studies that follow naturally from the present ones. It would be of interest to carry out similar work with adults. Sex differences might be found between men and women even though they weren't identified for boys and girls. There might be interesting differences between the inter-construct relationships of adults and children, and certain groups might be found that show important variations in belief structure.

Related questions could be asked about people's judgements of particular acts of violence. Some individuals may place emphasis on one of the stages, for example, while others concentrate on another. Thus some people might tend to judge an aggressive act in terms of the situation, while others attribute the occurrence of the same act to 'internal' factors – such as a lack of self-control.

Further Studies: In the Real World

However, there is no requirement to remain at the representational level; and, moving away from the theories that people have of the antecedents of aggressive acts, it is possible to look directly at the individual stages of the model as they occur in the real world. In a pilot study conducted at the same time as the doll and stereotype experiments, a first approximation to a study of appraisal styles in children was conducted. The children were asked to listen to a tape recording in which a mother told her son not to play with an unnamed object. This was followed by a loud crash – the sound of which appeared to be a plate smashing. The children were then asked what had happened. In other words, they were to recon-struct, on the basis of the limited sounds available to them, the nature of this event. In using this 'projective' technique the par-ticular interest was whether, in the children's accounts, the plate was seen as having been smashed accidentally or on purpose.

The attribution of intent is, of course, a major variable contri-buting to differences in the appraisal of situations: if I judge that you have stepped on my toe deliberately then I am likely to view your action in a very different light from a situation in which I judged that you did so accidentally – and my reactions will vary accordingly.

It was found in this projective tape study that, whereas the vast majority of the youngest age group said that the plate had been smashed on purpose, very few of the oldest group said that this was so. In other words, most of the oldest group said that it was an accident. These results suggest, therefore, that there may be differences in appraisal styles. Such differences suggest that some people come to adopt 'aggression-prone' styles. It could be that the aggressive person is not simply 'ready with his fists' or 'lacking inhibitions about physical violence', but that he actually 'sees' situations differently. It is known, for example, that among certain youth cultures there is a socialized 'reading' of cues. Looking at someone repeatedly or for more than a prescribed limit – what used in the days of skinheads to be called 'screwing' – can lead to considerable aggro. The lad under surveillance adopts the gang view that such a look is the threat that invites open confrontation. To ignore such an 'invitation' is to risk losing status in the gang. Furthermore, in social situations of dense machismo, such infringements may be so easy to commit that any casual behaviour may produce an explosive reaction.

Frude and Goss (1979) have conducted a population survey of the strategies that parents use to prevent themselves from being aggressive towards their children. Some parents seem to concentrate on maximizing their inhibitions against hitting, while others turn their attention to activities incompatible with abuse. Some try to appraise the child's behaviour sympathetically, others aim to reduce anger arousal. One woman, for example, reported that, when she was severely angered by her children, she used 'level B of the relaxation I learnt for the birth of my babies'. These methods of anger control, therefore, were spread across several of the stages suggested by the model.

In our case-based study adolescents referred to the probation service for their continual involvement in violent incidents, relating the model of aggression to the real world has already illustrated various differences between clients. In one case a lad's judgement that his dismissal from work was an act of victimization led to his visiting the works at night and wrecking the place. In another case, however, repeated acts of aggression seem to be due to the weakening of inhibitions brought about by the consumption of vast

quantities of alcohol. For many of the probation clients we have
seen, however, different stages of the model seem to provide the
most appropriate explanations for different incidents.

In dealing with these cases one is repeatedly faced with the fact
that, in many environments, aggression is functional. If you're
brought up in the Gorbals, as was Jimmy Boyle (1977), for example,
the frequency of provocative situations makes it adaptive to
develop as many aspects of the aggression apparatus as you can: it
makes sense to be alert to dangerous situations – even to be in
command of them by precipitating them; to interpret them accordingly – even to be over-anxious to see them as provocative; not to be
inhibited about standing up for yourself – even to reduce this
inhibition by testing your abilities; and to react in a physical and
violent way – even to over-react in the way best guaranteed to build
a reputation of your continued prowess.

Attempts at Control

The model of aggression incidents put forward in this chapter has
certain implications for the control of violent and aggressive acts. It
is as well to remember, first of all, that the discussion has concerned
only anger aggression. Much criminal behaviour that is violent or
destructive, however, is committed in the pursuance of instrumental ends. One obvious way in which it might be possible to
control such behaviour is through the increase of inhibitions by the
threatened use of various forms of punishment. Yet a good deal can
also be done to reduce the opportunity for crime by altering the
situation itself. R.V.G. Clarke (1977) has quoted, as one example of
this, the law making steering wheel locks compulsory on motor
vehicles in West Germany; this led to a staggering reduction in the
number of crimes of 'taking and driving way'.

Other situational changes make the risk of detection more likely
and thereby increase inhibitions. Well-lit streets, for example,
reduce the incidences of vandalism and 'mugging'. When the
wearing of crash helmets by motorcyclists in the UK was made
mandatory, this had the unforeseen side-effect of greatly reducing
the number of motorcycle thefts. If people make it less obvious that
they are carrying large sums of money, then the appraisal of the
situation as one of high potential gain will be reduced and the
likelihood of aggressive attack will be lessened thereby.

Some violent acts are predominantly hostile or angry behaviours. Fights between youths are one example of this, and another is family violence. According to the model, if the pathway is broken at any point, then, theoretically, the final stage of aggression will not be reached. It may prove most effective in individual cases, therefore, to develop particular training programmes that aim to change appraisals, to develop a high level of inhibition or to teach methods of anger avoidance and anger control. Novaco (1976a, b, 1977) has demonstrated the use of cognitive methods as a means of modifying aggressive behaviour. The avoidance of those situations likely to lead to anger is another aspect that may be the focus of useful counselling. Naturally, such methods are by no means mutually exclusive, and the most effective approach is likely to be one in which several or all of the stages are considered in the therapeutic setting.

Thus the control of anger aggression can be conducted in a number of ways. At the simplest level of analysis we can say that an attempt can be made to prevent someone experiencing anger, or we can concentrate on preventing the behavioural expression of anger that is experienced. Current efforts may be seen as concentrating on the latter type of strategy; the attempt is made to distance emotional experience from behavioural expression by the construction of externally based barriers or inhibitions. In many cases, however, the former approach may be more effective, or may, at least, be a useful additional focus for intervention. In theory, the processes at this level are amenable to control, and what is now needed is the development of particular and realistic techniques that enable the ideas to be put into practice.

REFERENCES

Bandura, A. 1973: *Aggression: A Social Learning Analysis,* Englewood Cliffs, NJ: Prentice-Hall.

Boyle, J. 1977: *A Sense of Freedom,* London: Pan Books.

Buss, A. 1961: *The Psychology of Aggression,* New York: John Wiley.

Clarke, R.V.G. 1977: 'Psychology and crime', *Bulletin of the British Psychological Society* 30: 280–3.

Frude, N. 1979: 'The aggression incident: a perspective for understanding abuse', *Child Abuse and Neglect* 3: 903–6.

Frude, N. and Goss, A. 1979: 'Parental anger: a general population survey', *Child Abuse and Neglect* 3: 331–3.

Frude, N. and Roberts, W. 1980: Occasions of violence', Unit 4 of Course

P253, 'Conflict in the Family', Milton Keynes: Open University Press.

Kaplan, A. 1964: *The Conduct of Inquiry*, Aylesbury: Intertext Books.

Maccoby, E.E. and Jacklin, C.N. 1975: *The Psychology of Sex Differences*, London: Oxford University Press.

McKellar, P. 1949: 'The emotion of anger in the expression of human aggressiveness', *British Journal of Psychology* 39: 148–55.

Novaco, R.W. 1976a: 'The functions and regulations of the arousal of anger', *American Journal of Psychiatry* 133: 1124–8.

Novaco, R.W. 1976b: 'Treatment of chronic anger through cognitive and relaxation controls', *Journal of Consulting and Clinical Psychology* 44: 681.

Novaco, R.W. 1977: 'Stress inoculation: a cognitive therapy for anger and its application to a case of depression', *Journal of Consulting and Clinical Psychology* 45: 600–8.

CHAPTER 11

Treatment of Aggressive Adolescents

Masud Hoghughi

Aggression and violence have become almost hackneyed subjects in the literature of the social sciences. Practically everyone has something to say about them. In this sense, the topic is like 'punishment', with which it has interesting conceptual connections.

Reflecting the importance and the complexity of the subject, the literature on aggression and violence is one of the most voluminous, encompassing contributions from anthropology, ethology, psychology, sociology, psychiatry and many other disciplines. The major reason for this interest in aggression should be sought in society's preoccupation with the control of deviant behaviour.

SOCIAL CONTROL

Every society's prime concern is its own survival. Therefore, it develops expectations and organizations conducive to this end. These expectations and organizations can be construed as falling under the rubric, 'social order'. Anything that threatens this social order beyond a shifting limit is regarded as undesirable or unacceptable, and therefore as a fit subject for curbing and elimination.

All 'anti-social' acts fall into this category. Such acts as stealing, disrupting other people's lives and even suicidal behaviour are regarded as unacceptable because they threaten, directly or by implication, personal safety and integrity. In this sense, aggressive acts can be regarded as the paradigm of anti-social acts. Indeed, it has been argued (e.g. by Lorenz 1966) that the whole process of social and biological evolution, from the primitive 'id' to the advanced 'superego', has been aimed at developing internal controls and external reinforcements for ensuring the basic observance of the sanctity of other people's lives and their individual and group life spaces.

Aggressive acts pose the most direct threat to individual life and social order. They are, therefore, justifiably the greatest source of social concern and subject of social control. The academic study of aggression can be regarded as an adjunct to and extension of social control. Unless aggression is defined as a social problem it will not merit such widespread study, and unless society thinks it worth studying, it will not authorize the financial and manpower expenditure that research studies reflect.

Social intervention has a number of facets, including the enhancement of what is good, the maintenance of the *status quo* in areas that do not warrant change, and the curbing, containing and elimination of whatever is deemed unacceptable. The more critical the behaviour, the more likely it is to be subject to this mode of control. 'Treatment' is a sub-category of this latter form of social control. It is, therefore, legitimate to assess the value of theoretical and empirical work on aggression from the viewpoint of its usefulness in coping with this form of unacceptable behaviour.

Such coping, and the modes of intervention to which it gives rise, can be construed in the form of the conceptual model shown in figure 11.1. This is a model of purposive, organized and systematic social intervention in the life of any person who presents or experiences problems. It has been applied to a range of services for disordered, including severely aggressive, youngsters, and has been extensively discussed elsewhere (Hoghughi 1979a,b,c, 1980a,b, Hoghughi *et al.* 1980). Its elements are as follows:

1. *Referral*: a problem (person) must be referred or identified before any attempt at coping can take place.

2. *Management* entails curbing and containing the problem so that the threat posed by the problem (aggressive) person becomes tolerable and a state of equilibrium between the subject and his (coping) environment prevails. In this sense it is necessary first to neutralize the aggressive person before anything else can be done

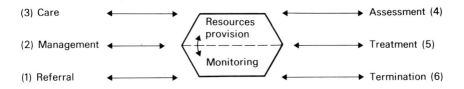

Figure 11.1 A conceptual model of social intervention.

with him. It is not this necessity, but rather the methods of achieving it, that frequently give cause for concern.

3. *Provision of care* is aimed primarily at ensuring the physical survival of the aggressive person. Only when this is achieved may such other aspects of caring, such as social integration and personal enhancement, be attempted.

4. *Assessment* is concerned with the process of determining what is wrong (amiss, undesirable), and what should be done about it.

5. *Treatment* entails the complex process of translating what should be done into ways and means of alleviating the problem(s).

6. *Termination:* when the condition no longer falls outside the latitude of tolerance, because of a reduction of either its frequency or its intensity, the involvement with the person is terminated.

All the above processes require material and human resources and a body of knowledge and practices that enables the intervention and its monitoring at various levels of complexity to take place.

From this point of view, theoretical and empirical contributions to the study of aggression are evaluated in terms of their utility for the control of aggressive behaviour. Utility is, of course, an ambiguous term, which is in practice partly a function of the competence of those who seek to utilize the scientific contribution. As will emerge later, even setting aside the relatively little competence in scientifically aided social control, most theoretical and empirical contributions to the study of aggression are not vastly helpful to its control. With the above comments in mind, it may now be worthwhile to look at the phenomenon of aggression.

APPROACHES TO AGGRESSION

Like so many other definitional tasks, defining aggression has proved problematic. This is because of the intra- and inter-personal and cultural variability of what is deemed to be 'aggressive behaviour'. Side-stepping these difficulties, the *core* of any definition of aggressive acts may be regarded as behaviour that is intended to, or is perceived as intended to, hurt.

Such a formulation, also proposed by others (e.g. Berkowitz 1962, Feshbach 1970), has been criticized by Bandura (1973) on the grounds that it limits the functional purpose of aggression to just hurting others, whereas in reality aggressive acts have many purposes. This criticism is legitimate when directed at the early and limited formulations (e.g. Dollard *et al.* 1939). But most subsequent workers have shown an awareness of the multiple purposes that aggressive acts serve. They have, however, quite rightly asserted that 'hurting', whether intended or perceived, is the core element to which all other meanings and purposes are appended.

It is important, however, to warn, as Bandura does, against rigid adherence to simplistic distinctions such as 'instrumental' and 'expressive'. Not only are these difficult to determine in practice, but they also frequently break down in everyday acts of adolescent aggression, where self-assertion or 'machismo' (Toch 1972) is related to the maintenance of a particular personal identity.

A major sociological criticism of psychological approaches to aggressive behaviour is that the act is divorced from its wider, molar, social context. Whatever the merits of this criticism, it certainly appears that, even from a purely psychological point of view, workers have tended to treat this problem behaviour in isolation from the multiplicity of other problems that aggressive people experience or present.

Although for purposes of scientific convenience it may be necessary to isolate aggressive acts, from a social (control) point of view the acts can be and are seen only as having been committed by whole human beings. These human beings operate in the context of environmental and personal characteristics which, even if tangentially related to the aggressive act, determine what is done with the aggressor.

Classification of deviant (or problem) behaviour has been frag-mented across professions of medicine, law, social work, psy-chiatry, psychology and a host of others. Each profession has developed its own theory and practice in relation to the specific deviance: medicine deals with physical ailments; law and its enforcement with anit-social behaviour; social work with indi-vidual and family dysfunction; psychiatry and psychology with everything but particularly abnormal and maladaptive behaviour. And yet, their different explanatory and ameliorative powers are frequently invoked to deal with the same problem people. At the same time the distinct orientations and professional language create a picture of the same whole person that is fragmented and akin to that created by the six blind men who were asked to draw an elephant from the examination of particular parts of its body.

A further difficulty in adopting an approach that integrates aggressive behaviour in a whole context of the person has been the preoccupation, particularly in psychiatry, with 'understanding' and, therefore, with the differential 'diagnosis' of the aggressive act. But the logical and empirical problems associated with diagnosis are legion (e.g. Feinstein 1977, Hoghughi 1978a, Kanfer and Saslow 1965). These problems are particularly acute in the case of non-physical problems or those for which physical treatments (and, therefore, tests of hypotheses) are not available. Such difficulties seriously reduce the value of traditional psychiatric diagnostic approach to the control of aggressive behaviour.

In the light of the above comments, it appears desirable to adopt an approach to aggression that (1) enables an evaluation of aggressive acts in the context of the total, integrated person and (2) adopts a non-diagnostic, descriptive approach to problems. Such an approach has been developed by the author and his colleagues in relation to disordered and dangerous youngsters (Hoghughi *et al.* 1980). It has features in common with other descriptive approaches, such as Weed's (1969) and the variety of methods usually referred to as 'behavioural assessment' (e.g. Hersen and Bellack 1976).

The 'Problem Profile Approach', as it is called, suggests that adolescents become the subject of social intervention because they present or experience problems. 'Problems' are defined as unacceptable conditions. The 'unacceptable' implies that what is acceptable in one setting or by one person (e.g. the gang) may not be acceptable in another (e.g. the school). The idea of 'profile' suggests that as a person or the perspective from which he is viewed changes, so does the perception of his problems.

Problems are manifested in six functional areas: *physical,* encompassing the body and its subsystems; *cognitive* – aspects of intellectual, educational and vocational functioning; *home and family* – everything to do with the external and internal functioning of family members, collectively and individually; *social skills* – all aspects of small group behaviour; *anti-social* behaviour – covering not only all transgressions against property and aggression against person but also disruptive acts such as absconding and self-destructive behaviour; *personal* – aspects of personality structure, emotional tone and its control, moral development and problems of self-concept. The rationale, critique and consequences of this approach are presented elsewhere (Hoghughi 1978b, Hoghughi *et al.* 1980). Its chief merits, however, lie in its descriptive nature and integrated view of adolescents' problems.

Studies of aggressive adolescents have shown that they suffer from a multiplicity of problems (e.g. Bandura and Walters 1959, Farrington 1978, Hoghughi 1978b, Lefkowitz *et al.* 1977). These problems include a range of bodily ailments; intellectual and scholastic difficulties; severe problems associated with poverty, overcrowding of the home, poor parenting and other adverse parental factors; social incompetence and inability to derive satisfaction from social activities; a wide spectrum of other forms of anti-social behaviour in addition to aggressive acts; and frequently deviant personality structures and maladaptive personal and moral concepts.

Faced with the wide diversity of adverse personal and social factors associated with aggressive acts, some workers have attempted to develop all-encompassing theories which, they claim, account for all forms of aggressive behaviour. David Downes, in chapter 3 above, summarizes the sociological perspectives on aggression, and Bandura (1973) presents a valuable conspectus of psychological theories. The search for a distinctive theoretical contribution is understandable and worthwhile. Certainly, each new theoretical perspective provides another point of view which may make sense of what was previously less well understood. But logically, the notion of 'understanding' is complex, and acceptable only within major probabilistic constraints. Even the testing of a hypothetico-deductive system does not provide proof of the validity of that system. At best it can only fail to provide falsifying evidence (Popper 1972). This is why it is so difficult to understand the vigour with which the claims of one 'theory' against others are pursued.

Many of the so-called theories of aggression are not theories at all in the specific scientific sense, but rather are wide-ranging generalizations. Most of them, particularly the sociological ones, do not lead to unambiguous hypotheses that can be falsified. Those theories that can (e.g. Social Learning Theory, or Frustration Aggression Theory) are a series of short-range hypotheses which are loosely connected by a series of experimental and operational practices rather than any integrated conceptual networks. Most of the theories seem to be aimed at generating yet more theories, which would necessitate further research. This creates a type of scientific regression that can never be terminated. Furthermore, most theories are static and do not centrally allow for the rapidly shifting frequency and severity of aggressive acts in particular settings.

The major reason for the above deficiencies is that our knowledge of human behaviour is, broadly speaking, so limited that it is not at present possible either to satisfactorily theorize or to choose between theories of aggression. What is more, although theoretical 'explanations' may underlie intervention and aid understanding, they are not necessary to effective social control. This is borne out, for example, by much physical treatment in medicine, such as psychotropic drugs.

In view of this it may be more useful to attempt to look at models of aggression that simply present a particular version of the inter-relationships of concepts and processes without suggesting that the model is a reflection of reality. It may be even more useful to use the phrase 'conceptual map' rather than 'model'. This phrase would imply directly that the map is intended to help the reader or the peruser to get from one area or landmark to another. It encompasses the notion that the map and its contour would change according to different perspectives and that, as the knowledge of the terrain increases, so the complexity of the details on the map become increasingly refined and modified. It is in this sense that the following conceptual map of aggression is presented.

A 'MAP' OF AGGRESSION

Aggression, like other behavioural forms, is a product of the *inter-action* of two sets of factors – personal and environmental. Each set comprises a number of individual elements that inhibit or facilitate aggressive outcomes. Most of these factors, such as height, weight, daring, overcrowding, provocativeness, etc., are continuously variable; some, such as gender and the incidence of an extra Y chromosome, are discrete.

It is reasonable to assume that the continuous variables are 'normally distributed'. Within and between cultures, roughly two-thirds of the population are of average height, weight and daring, and the same proportion of settings are of average crowd density and potential to provoke. Just as each element is normally distributed, so the interaction of the elements with each other may be assumed to create one broad dimension which is itself normally distributed.

On this basis, taking the two broad personal and environmental dimensions, *most* personal characteristics are neither conducive to nor inhibitive of aggressive behaviour. But as the two dimensions are (orthogonally?) interacting, a high level of enviromental provocativeness would take relatively little personal predisposition before an aggressive act results. Similarly, a person with strong predisposition to aggressive behaviour (which may be the result of one or more personal features) would take relatively little provocation before he lashes out aggressively. A similar idea in relation to general criminality, though without assumptions of normality, has been presented by Clarke (1977) and is hinted at by other authors, e.g. Bandura (1973).

This idea may be described graphically as in figure 11.2. Such a conception would suggest that *potentially* everyone can be a murderer or a saint. It also accounts for the fact that people's aggressive potential changes in the course of their maturation or altered circumstances. It is not a theory, in that it does not reflect reality, but it does aid alternative hypotheses about what may facilitate an aggressive outburst. It has no theoretical allegiance and in this sense is open-ended. It can accommodate new findings and, most crucially, it enables the understanding and determination of thresholds of aggressive behaviours – the straws that break the camel's back.

Despite the impossibility of logically eliminating one or the other set of factors, under social pressure we often speak as if the motivation for aggressive acts were either purely personal or purely environmental. This is borne out by much of the writing on aggression where either the interactive nature of aggressive acts is ignored or else such scant acknowledgement is made as to suggest that the writer's own concern is of prime importance.

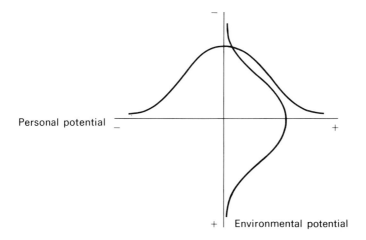

Figure 11.2 A map of aggression.

Personal Factors

Personological and personality research has tackled almost every aspect of human behaviour. It has only recently been recognized that the nature/nurture controversy in terms of exclusive either/or is idiotic and futile. With this realization, writers have begun acknowledging that it is not possible to evaluate even genetic factors in the absence of certain social conditions. However, a number of statistical and other techniques have become available which make it possible to determine, even if only grossly, the relative significance of personal, compared with social, factors. A rapid scanning of the review literature (e.g. Bandura 1973, Feldman 1977, Geen and O'Neal 1976, Goldstein 1975) would suggest that personal factors include genetics (e.g. XYY syndrome), physio-logical or constitutional states (e.g. sexual arousal, hunger); personality structure (e.g. high excitability or pain threshold); attitudes (e.g. coping style or prejudices); perceptual style (e.g. risk estimation) and self-concept (e.g. self-esteem), all of which con-tribute directly to whether a person is likely to engage in aggressive acts or not. These factors have varying short- or long-range effects. They also interact with each other and, in terms of their interactions and individual force, vary in intensity and impact.

Environmental Factors

The distinction between personal factors and environmental factors, as has already been suggested, is primarily one of degree, and for convenience rather than indicative of absolute differences. Given this qualification, the following factors may be highlighted as environmental contributors to aggressive acts: frustrating or threatening environments; provocation, which overlaps with frustration and threat; the 'legitimacy' or appropriateness of a setting, e.g. football ground versus a church; opportunity, e.g. bedroom versus office; 'culture' or subculture of violence, e.g. gangs versus volunteer helpers; availability of weapon, e.g. guns or knives; probability of retaliation, e.g. by a big, burly person; and availability of victim. This latter is a particularly complex phenomenon because it involves the legitimizing relationship of the victim to aggressor, e.g. member of family or lover; and media's role in portraying an ever-increasing range of probable victims.

Bringing together the notion of two interacting factors and the normal distribution of elements making up each factor, it is possible to visualize two dimensions ranging from minus through zero to plus, where the high proneness of one factor may be interacting with the low elicitation potential of another, e.g. being severely taunted by someone who is big and mean-looking – such a situation, in all probability, would not lead to an aggressive act at that particular time. At the other extreme, the high propulsiveness of one element, e.g. sexual arousal, with the ready availability of a little girl in a field, may lead to a sexual assault. Between these two extremes there are degrees pertaining to the combinations of different elements.

This is a valuable way of looking at aggression as a social phenomenon that should be curbed. It enables the description of each set of variables, and the likelihood that they may impinge on a person. It therefore helps towards a cautious prediction of how likely a person is to act aggressively. If, for example, a youngster becomes violent whenever he is called a 'bastard', and he lives in a setting in which such appellations are commonplace, it is reasonable to predict that he is likely to act violently in the future.

AGGRESSIVE ADOLESCENTS

By common consent, adolescence is a turbulent time, and is perceived as becoming more turbulent all the time (although, judged by the most rigorous criteria, there is inadequate evidence to suggest that our own times are worse than those bygone). There are enough elements from criminal statistics, media accounts and personal experiences to support the view that adolescents and young adults now represent the most serious anti-social group in terms of offences against both person and property.

Acquisition of aggressive behaviour seems to be part and parcel of survival in most, particularly Western, societies. A good deal of common aggression in the form of horseplay, pranks, fights and fisticuffs is accepted even among quite respectable communities. Youngsters who engage in such behaviour are not labelled as aggressive, and almost all grow up to be average citizens. A very small group, however, stand out because of the frequency and severity of their aggressive behaviour and their unresponsiveness to normal, interpersonal measures of control. Such youngsters gradually acquire the reputation of being aggressive. However, the definition reflects a set of standards and contextual features that are rarely made explicit. It is only when an adolescent's behaviour can no longer be tolerated in his normal social setting, e.g. home or school, or alternatively when he has committed a grave act such as murder, rape, arson or serious injury, that he is referred for professional assessment as a prelude to effective social control. The core task of assessment is (1) to highlight the adolescent's problem(s) in terms of extent, intensity, duration, etc., and (2) to suggest, according to what may be known, what should be done about those problems and where.

Much of the information provided for assessment is retrospective, and therefore fundamentally susceptible to halo effect and other distortions. Other than when grave acts are committed and detailed police statements are available, it is not possible to determine the exact conditions under which aggression took place. The social environment of the adolescent is not suffused with people trained in the intricacies of 'behavioural assessment'. Even in specialized assessment agencies, the complexities of assessment are not always understood or observed (Hoghughi 1979a).

There are, as yet, no universally shared frames of reference for assessment. It is, therefore not possible to be even moderately confident that in the majority of instances the results of assessment are not more indicative of the idiosyncracies of the assessment agency than of the problems of the adolescent.

At the present time in the United Kingdom, aggressive adolescents are assessed in penal (detention and remand centres), psychiatric (inpatient and outpatient units), educational (child guidance clinics, school psychological services) and social services facilities (a range of day and residential 'observation and assessment' centres). In this sense, the place, method and outcome of assessment of an aggressive adolescent are the major determinants not only of what are seen as his problems but also of where and how those problems may be alleviated.

TREATMENT

Treatment is one form of social control. It can be defined as the 'alleviation of problems', i.e. the reduction of the frequency or severity with which a problem is presented. Although frequently used in a medical, psychiatric, context, treatment is not, nor does it need to be, any more medically biased than 'assessment' is linked to fiscal matters.

The core activities of treatment are (1) translating the outcomes of assessment into treatment objectives, and (2) carrying them out. Bearing in mind the central role of treatment in the social control of deviance, remarkably little work has been done to elucidate the concept and its implications. Even recent major publications (e.g. Rutter and Hersov 1976, Wolman, Egan and Ross 1978) leave this area untouched.

There are three major prerequisites to carrying out treatment:
1. an appropriate theory or orientation which states, explicitly or otherwise, that there is a problem of a particular kind, which warrants intervention of a particular sort;
2. a range of methods – i.e. systematic ways of carrying out certain prescriptions and achieving particular objectives;
3. resources – i.e. materials, equipment and human beings, of particular numbers, personal qualities and professional skills to carry out the treatment tasks.

Each element needs to be explicated and monitored to discover its relevance and efficiency in relation to the desired outcome (Hoghughi 1980a,b).

Treatment of Aggression

Aggression is picked out as an undesirable feature in every age group. It is usually transitory and, among growing children, is dealt with by retaliation or adult sanctions. Only a small minority of such children continue to persist in aggressive acts until they commit an offence with which they are charged. Not all aggressive adolescents commit offences, nor are all who commit offences processed in the justice system. But these are the ones on whom any significant body of information is available.

Other than in minor instances, the social control system, including that for juveniles, does not differentiate aggressive youths from others who have committed offences. Given the relatively high level of institutional structure, there are usually only marginal differences in the treatment of aggressive youngsters compared with others. Treatment settings can be characterized according to the degree of emphasis they lay on particular elements. These elements or dimensions include the following:

child – adult
individual – group
general – specialist
formal – informal
day – residential
open – secure

Treatment disposals fall into one of the four broad categories: (1) *court disposals*, ranging from non-custodial sentences to absolute discharge and from probation orders to custodial sentences (these include placement in detention centres, borstals, young persons' prisons or general or special hospitals); (2) *medical disposals*, in terms of child guidance clinic (CGC), treatment by general practitioner, outpatient and inpatient clinics in general and specialist units; (3) *educational disposal*, including the use of CGC, school psychological services, transfer from one school to another, placement in 'sanctuaries', placement in special schools and, eventually, exclusion; (4) *social service disposals*, ranging from support at home to (if adequate care and control is not available from the adolescent's own family) increasingly serious disposals of fostering, placement in family group homes, hostels and community homes with education, with or without secure facilities.

All forms of social control, including treatment, are founded on implicit assumptions about costs and benefits of intervention. The costs include the obvious expenditure of financial and manpower resources as well as personal, social and ethical costs. These costs are justified on the basis of putative benefits, which may be gained from preventing further exacerbation of the problem or from an actual improvement. In this context, the estimation of risk presented by an aggressive adolescent is a major component of the decision-making process. Risk estimation, related essentially to predicting dangerousness, is deeply affected by political and social considerations (Steadman 1976, Walker 1978).

Treatment of Aggressive Adolescents – Some Ambiguities

What follows is a brief and uncomprehensive evaluation of what is known about the treatment of aggressive adolescents. No attempt will be made to review the relevant literature, most of which has been or will be incidentally mentioned. Emphasis is laid on the difficulties and ambiguities of treatment, because these have to be overcome before any treatment is undertaken and before what is being done now can be improved. The ambiguities will be discussed in terms of the three previously mentioned prerequisites of treatment.

Theoretical and Value Orientations

There are probably as many 'theories' and individual conceptions of aggressive behaviour as there are people who think about it. For expediency and professional convenience, there is a tendency to divide these among academic disciplines, e.g. sociological, psychological; to characterize them as short-, medium- or long-range and in a variety of other ways. This book itself is a testimony to the diversity of these orientations. This diversity, combined with the varying levels and frequent opacity of the viewpoints, makes it difficult to evaluate the relative merits of the approaches to aggression.

The relationship of public attitudes and politics to professional and personal orientations of those who deal with aggressive adolescents is not known. Undoubtedly, a professional can operate only if his views can be accommodated by the public. But how much each affects the other, and, in turn, the *practices*, of the professional remain ambiguous.

There is considerable and intense public ambivalence regarding aggressive adolescents. On the one hand, the more knowledgeable and sympathetic members of the public recognize the transience of much aggression and the social and personal pressures that generate it. On the other hand, they feel profoundly threatened by aggressive adolescents who, even without being aggressive, arouse confused and conflicting emotions among adults. It is not, therefore, possible to discern any constancy within or between the public, and the professional enactment of its views.

This becomes even more evident in the judicial and professional determination of what should be done with an aggressive adolescent. The disposal of the adolescent is affected by both his personal characteristics, e.g. his social class, past history and self-presentation, and discernible environmental pressures towards aggressive behaviour, e.g. an unsatisfactory home. Judgements of past actions are no more based on rigorous criteria than are predictive estimations of future risk. This accounts for the apparently random nature of disposals. Random disposal would be helpful to research if it were deliberate. As it is, however, because the bases of evaluation are unknown and it is not possible to ensure similar disposals for like offenders, one cannot relate the process and outcome of disposal to the original condition of the aggressor.

Adolescence is a major developmental landmark. For well-known physiological reasons, people are more reactive and turbulent during this phase of their lives than before or after it. Much adolescent deviance is transitory and settles down due to both maturational and social factors during early adulthood. There is, therefore, a good deal of emotional and professional confusion regarding the need for the particular mode of treatment for behaviour that, if not reinforced or labelled, may well subside to a tolerable level.

This confusion is evident in the law and its operation. Depending on the age of the youngster, the law can deal with him with varying degrees of severity. Because of the conflict between individualized and tariff approaches to sentencing, there is no consistency in the relationship between the offence and the sentence. However, public protection remains a major element in court disposals. Undoubtedly, the most seriously aggressive adolescents are placed in the care of the local authority, if under the age of 14. Between 14 and 16, either penal or social services disposals are possible. Above

16, almost all sentences for aggressive acts are either penal or quasi-penal (e.g. probation supervision orders). There is a special category of child care legislation (Sec. 53, 1933 CYPA) reserved for those youngsters who commit grave crimes (homicide, arson and serious assaults) and who are placed in the care of the Home Secretary for appropriate (usually treatment-orientated) disposal.

The law concerns itself primarily with the evaluation of the offence. How much note is taken of the totality of a youngster's problems (which can only result from coherent and comprehensive assessment) is not known. Nor is it known whether the disposal is made on the basis of only the aggressive element of the adolescent's problems or the total profile. The same uncertainty is reflected in the orientation of those to whom the task of treatment is entrusted.

'Punishment' remains a major element in judicial and other disposals. Punitive reactions are widespread among the general public from whom the staff of 'treatment' agencies are drawn. No one seriously suggests that, pretensions and assertions to the contrary, prisons and borstals are for treatment rather than punishment. Indeed, punishment (such as deprivation of liberty and undergoing coercive procedures) is inextricably bound up with treatment, even when the latter is not used covertly as a euphemism for the former. Given the 'them' and 'us' perceptions of most habitually aggressive youngsters, it is naive to imagine that they would not interpret such treatment as punishment and react to it accordingly (Hoghughi 1969).

Theoretical orientations can be evaluated in terms of the ease and degree of their translatability to appropriate methods and procedures. It is quite evident that there are major variations among theories of aggression in this respect, and that the vast majority (particularly sociological ones) cannot be translated into small-scale individual and group practice. Although each theoretical orientation may aid greater understanding (and some simply exacerbate our present confusions) from a strictly social control point of view, they are not of much use. In this sense, broadly speaking, the behavioural approaches seem less deficient, because, while developing a great deal of detailed and methodologically rigorous procedures, they maintain a relatively loose tie to a particular theory (e.g. Patterson and Gullion 1968, Patterson, Cobb and Ray 1973, in relation to 'Social Learning Theory'). Because of the loose ties between theory and its practical implications, and also because other major sources of variance frequently are not taken into account in research applications of the theories, it is at present not possible to pick out one or another as having greater validity.

Last but not least, the major determinant of society's action is its perception of how much of its resources may justifiably be spent on various forms of treatment of aggressive adolescents, particularly in relation to its other priorities and the relative costs and benefits of different forms of treatment. The appropriate conceptual and theoretical tools for such an approach are only in an early stage of development (e.g. Glass 1976). One aspect that has received relatively greater attention concerns the ethics of treatment – particularly in relation to behavioural methods (e.g. Blackman 1979, British Psychological Society 1974). But there are wider and more fundamental ethical issues. If aggressive behaviour has developed as a means of adaptation to unfavourable social and personal circumstances, then it is morally questionable to punish such behaviour or to try to alter it, because, if it were to be altered, the aggressive adolescent would be less well adapted to his social circumstances: to make an aggressive child in a highly provocative subculture less aggressive is dramatically to reduce his ability to survive within that environment. It is a matter of moral judgement whether it is not better for society to tolerate the youngster's aggression than seek to change him in a way that would render him maladaptive to his environment. If we accept that, for the sake of society's survival, social order must be asserted, and if we are prepared to set aside some anxieties about the politics of social control (e.g. Taylor, Walton and Young 1973), then the only legitimate approach to treatment of aggressive adolescents seems to be one that replaces the aggressive behaviour patterns with others that are equally or more adaptive in the adolescent's *normal* environment.

Methods

Methods can be regarded as systematic ways of achieving objectives. In the treatment field these can be characterized broadly as falling somewhere in a complex network of dimensions such as penal–therapeutic (remember the cautions), individual–group, general–specialized, molar–focal, psychodynamic–behavioural, short–long time span, concentrating on the adolescent–involving the wider social context.

Although most treatment agencies have multi-professional teams, their orientation derives from the primary professional group operating within them. Broadly, these can be divided into psychiatric, penal, educational and social services personnel. The major determinant of the treatment methods used is, therefore, the dominant professional group rather than the empirically established treatment needs of the client/patient/inmate population. As allocation to a particular agency is frequently a matter of chance and non-treatment-related factors, the relationship between treatment needs and methods used becomes even more tenuous.

There is a great deal of writing about the treatment of delinquent and aggressive adolescents. It has already been suggested that the two groups are rarely distinguished. Most writers have been anxious to advocate the merits of their own orientation. This suggests that (a) the effects reported are due only or mainly to treatment given, and that (b) the differences between treatments are greater than the similarities between both the approaches and the settings in which they are carried out. In any setting, the 'treatment' (whatever it is) is only a minor part of the total daily programme, which is taken up with a great deal of humdrum routine to ensure the management and care of both the client population and the treatment agency. Even when there are major differences in avowed orientation, it is not possible to say whether the similarities are not greater than the differences.

With a small number of notable exceptions, studies of particular methods are methodologically weak in terms of definition of the population, control groups, the technicalities of the treatments given and individual evaluations of response to treatment. Even the methodologically sophisticated (e.g. Patterson's) projects exclude some particularly difficult youngsters as being unsuitable. It is not, therefore, possible to evaluate the relative merits of the methods in general terms of outcome, comparing those who deal with selected populations with those who take (e.g. Hoghughi 1979b,) or have to take (e.g. borstals), unselected, extreme groups.

This is related to another, even more complex, point. Those who write on particular methods have a tendency to separate out the method from the people who use the methods. In this context, the range, diversity and complexity of the settings and the personnel are of vital importance. A method that may be highly productive in the hands of a skilled practitioner may become worse than useless when practised by a less skilled worker. Even in a widely replicated and standardized approach such as the Achievement Place Project (Phillips *et al.* 1973), there are major differences in the 'success rates' of individual establishments. It is not, therefore, possible to disentangle the method from its practitioners. It would be particularly enlightening if studies of methods were matched by studies of people who practise those methods, so that the relative contributions of each may be evaluated.

As indicated in the foregoing paragraphs of this section, there are too many unknowns in the use of methods in treating aggressive adolescents to make any reasonable evaluation possible. Bandura (1973) and Feldman (1977) provide excellent summaries of the available literature.

If the above reservations were to be set aside, it may be suggested that a wide range of behavioural methods is beginning to emerge as more powerful, efficient and robust (see for example the *British Journal of Criminology,* October 1979; Feldman 1977) than the older dynamic approaches. The proponents of the latter, however, are affected by neither the weight of the evidence against their own methods (e.g. Rachman 1972) nor that for behavioural methods (e.g. Carney 1976).

In general terms, the long-range outcome of all methods of treatment *in terms of reconviction* is broadly similar and similarly depressing (e.g. Griffiths 1974). The qualification in terms of reconviction is necessary because (1) offending is largely unrelated to personal pathology; (2) offending and reconviction have a complex and ambiguous relationship; (3) personal improvement (which is the objective of treatment) has little to do, conceptually or otherwise, with further offending; and (4) there are too many loose ends and assumptions about the objectives and settings of 'treatment' (e.g. Cornish & Clarke 1975) to warrant ruling out those long-term results of treatment not related to delinquency. At the present time, the diversity of methods, *where explicit,* is justified in view of the differences in populations, social pressures and resource constraints (Barker 1968).

Practice

Both theory and methods, with all their problems and potential, ultimately find their proof in the practices associated with them. These relate to what is done by whom, how, to whom, when and where, and with what costs and outcomes. Of all the three areas, paradoxically, this is the one that has received the least attention, almost as if it is beneath the intellectual dignity of thinkers and writers to concern themselves with the details of how theories and methods are put into practice. And yet, it is in the practice that some otherwise attractive propositions come to grief.

It is perhaps for the above reason that rarely in the treatment literature are the actual nuts-and-bolts details of what is done spelled out. Even when they are, the practice frequently diverges from the blueprint, though it would be untidy and intellectually disconcerting to take account of all these in the final evaluation (e.g. Hoghughi 1979b; cf. Jesness and DeRisi 1973).

The practice of treatment results from the perceptions of and constraints on staff interacting with the environment of which the actual adolescent is a variably significant part. There is no logical possibility of isolating all the (important) elements with a view to evaluating their interaction. At best, snapshot evaluations may be done whose wider applicability remains uncertain.

In practice, the agents of treatment have varying levels of competence, specialism, authority in carrying out or instituting what they believe should be done with the adolescent. Frequently those with the greatest specialism or authority are the ones who are in the least contact with the adolescent. How far they are able to inculcate their own orientation, competence and delegated authority in their colleagues remains a vague and, so far, unresearched area.

What is clear is that, given a normal distribution of personal characteristics and professional skills, the majority of those who carry out the actual treatment tasks are not exceptional. Their primary task is personal and professional survival, and this is rarely tied to carrying out particular forms of treatment, even if the latter could be sufficiently closely monitored to make such evaluation possible. In the case of aggressive adolescents, personal survival is even more than commonly a priority. What, therefore, appears necessary is to provide usable and effective methods of *managing* aggressive behaviour as a prelude to treatment. With some minor and elementary exceptions (e.g. Hoghughi 1978b, Nethercott 1978), little information is available in this area, and even less of it is taught. In reality, therefore, much of what goes by the name of treatment is an aspect of management of aggression.

In the West, there is currently considerable controversy regarding approaches to juvenile crime (e.g Romig 1978, Tutt 1978), and the venues for any treatment that may be undertaken. There is a strong body of opinion against residential, and for 'community', treatment of offenders. Without opening this particular Pandora's box, it should be noted that society's primary concern is with the maintenance of social order and the control of anything that threatens it in as fundamental a fashion as aggressive behaviour. Maybe in the course of time, pharmaceutical and other physical approaches to the control of aggression will become more acceptable than they are now. Until then, not only for public safety but also for its peace of mind and salving of its conscience, most of the worst aggressive adolescents will continue to be 'put away' in establishments with varied commitments to the ideal of treatment.

What, therefore, appears necessary is the development of a 'practice theory', generated by and geared to what is and can be done, given all the limitations of shifting values, competencies and availability of resources. This may then make possible a humane and productive approach, which, at worst, would not harm the adolescent but would create a benign environment in which normal maturation and beneficial learning may take place; at best, the environment may so closely and sophisticatedly monitor its input, process and outcome that an eventual science of treatment may become more than a theoretical possibility.

SO WHAT CAN BE DONE?

In the light of the above comments, it appears that it may be more sensible to concentrate, at the present stage of knowledge, on containing, curbing and reducing the impact of aggressive behaviour on society rather than on attempting to treat it. This is essential if the public is not to adopt a jungle mentality which promotes self-protection and, therefore, the infliction of debilitating damage on those who threaten social order. To this end it may be necessary to promote rapid feedback to the aggressor and immediate punishment of aggressive behaviour in an empirically and socially acceptable manner. It is not within the scope of this paper to open up the difficulties of the concept of punishment and problems associated with its just and proportional administration.

The psychology of punishment is as complex as its philosophy. Optimal use of punishment requires a large variety of conditions such as valued context, reduction of provocation, feedback, immediacy, articulation of what is being punished and the presentation of rewards for good behaviour at the same time as punishment for less acceptable acts. Otherwise, all that will happen is that punishment will beget hostility and resentment, and will legitimize the use of punishing behaviour by the aggressor on others for real or imagined provocation.

In the case of functionally adaptive aggression, it is necessary to teach aggressive youngsters alternative coping skills so that they may perceive the possibility that a situation may deteriorate to such an extent that they would need to behave aggressively. Such sensitivity training and inculcation of alternative coping skills, such as assertiveness, has been successfully carried out in a number of specialized settings where skilled personnel have been available closely to plan and execute programmes of re-sensitization of the aggressor to a different set of cues and probable responses. But the methods and resources should be sufficiently unesoteric as to make the treatment more widely available than the minority luxury it is at present.

Both in the short and in the long term, it is also necessary to reduce social pressures towards aggression. These pressures have been cited already. From among these the role of the mass media, particularly television, should be singled out. There is now considerable portrayal of aggression which, through a paradigm of social learning, encourages and inculcates such behaviour among vulnerable sections of society. It seems essential that there should be a gradual de-escalation of such portrayals in the media with a view to not triggering off and vicariously reinforcing whatever aggressive tendencies there may be on the part of groups of vulnerable youngsters.

In the long run perhaps the most important measure would involve a process of educating all members of society but particularly the youngest, towards developing the necessary competencies for citizenship and parenthood. One essential aspect of social education would be the development of skills for refraining from and coping with aggressive behaviour. Such a process would also emphasize the transfer of locus of control from environmental constraint to self-restraint. Given the large body of concerned and sophisticated people around, it should not be beyond our wit to achieve these ends with a large measure of professional and public support.

REFERENCES

Bandura, A. 1973: *Aggression – A Social Learning Analysis*, Englewood Cliffs, NJ: Prentice-Hall.
Bandura, A. and Walters, R.H. 1959: *Adolescent Aggression*, New York: Ronald Press.
Barker, P. (1968): '"The impossible child" – some approaches to treatment', *Canadian Psychiatric Association Journal* 23.
Berkowitz, L. 1962: *Aggression: A Social Psychological Analysis*, New York: McGraw-Hill.
Blackman, D.E. 1979: 'Ethical standards for behaviour modification', *British Journal of Criminology* 19(4): 420–48.
British Psychological Society 1974: *Current Guidelines for the Professional Practice of Clinical Psychologists*, London: British Psychological Society.
Carney, F.L. 1976: 'Treatment of aggressive parients', in *Rage, Hate, Assault and Other Forms of Violence*, ed. D.J. Madden and J.R. Lion, New York: Spectrum Publications.
Clarke, R.V.G. 1977: 'Psychology and crime', *Bulletin of the British Psychological Society* 30: 280–3.
Cornish, D and Clarke, R.V.G. 1975: *Residential Treatment and Its Effects on Delinquency*, London: HMSO.
Dollard, J., Doob, L., Miller, N., Mowrer, O and Sears, R. 1939: *Frustration and Aggression*, New Haven, Conn.: Yale University Press.
Farrington, D.P. 1978: 'The family backgrounds of aggressive youth', in *Aggression and Anti-Social Behaviour in Childhood and Adolescence*, ed. L.A. Hersov and D. Shaffer, Oxford: Pergamon Press.
Feinstein, A.D. 1977: 'A critical overview of diagnosis in psychiatry', *Psychiatric Diagnosis*, ed. V.M. Rakoff, H.C. Stancer and H.B. Kedward, New York: Bruner Mazel.
Feldman, M.P. 1977: *Criminal Behaviour: A Psychological Analysis*, Chichester: John Wiley.
Feshbach, S. 1970: 'Aggression', in *Carmichael's Manual of Child Psychology*, vol. II, ed. P.H. Mussen, New York: John Wiley.
Geen, R.G. and O'Neal, E.C. (eds) 1976: *Perspectives on Aggression*, New York: Academic Press.
Glass, G.V. (ed.) 1976: *Evaluation Studies Review*, Beverley Hills: Sage.

Goldstein, J.H. 1975: *Aggression and Crimes of Violence*, New York: Oxford University Press.

Griffiths, K.S. 1974: *Review of Accumulated Research in the California Youth Authority*, Sacramento: State of California.

Hersen, M. and Bellack, A.S. 1976: *Behavioural Assessment*, Oxford: Pergamon Press.

Hoghughi, M.S. 1969: *The Aycliffe Attitude Study*, London: Home Office Research Unit.

Hoghughi, M.S. 1978a: 'Diagnosis of children's disorders – a critique', paper read to the Irish Branch of the Association of Child Psychology and Psychiatry.

Hoghughi, M.S. 1978: *Troubled and Troublesome – Coping with Severely Disordered Children*, London: Burnett Books/André Deutsch.

Hoghughi, M.S. 1979a: 'Assessment: myth, method and utility', *Social Work Today* 10(29): 11–17.

Hoghughi, M.S. 1979b: 'The Aycliffe token economy', *British Journal of Criminology*, 19(4): 384–400.

Hoghughi, M.S. *et al.* 1979c: 'What do we do with disturbed youngsters?' papers read to the 3rd International School of Psychology Colloquium, University of York.

Hoghughi, M.S. 1980a: 'The sequential treatment system', in *Aycliffe School Special Unit – The First Year*, ed. M.S Hoghughi, Aycliffe: Studies of Problem Children.

Hoghughi, M.S. 1980b: 'Empirical social work', *Community Care,* April 3, 10 and 17.

Hoghughi, M.S., Dobson, C.J., Lyons, J., Muckley, A. and Swainston, M. 1980: *Assessing Problem Children: Issues and Practice*, London: Burnett Books/André Deutsch.

Jesness, C.F. and DeRisi, W. 1973: 'Some variations in techniques of contingency management in a school for delinquents', in *Behaviour Therapy with Delinquents,* ed. J.S. Stumphauzer, Springfield , Ill.:C. Thomas.

Kanfer, F. and Saslow, G. 1965: 'Behavioural diagnosis', *Archives of General Psychiatry* 12: 529–38.

Lefkowitz, M.M., Eron, L.D., Walder, L.O. and Halesmann, L.R. 1977: *Growing Up To Be Violent*, Oxford: Pergamon Press.

Lorenz, K. 1966: *On Aggression*, New York: Harcourt Brace Jovanovich.

Nethercott, R.E. 1978: 'Dealing with disturbance', M. Ed. dissertation, University of Newcastle upon Tyne.

Patterson, G.R., Cobb, J.A. and Ray, R.S. 1973: 'A social engineering technology for retraining the families of aggressive boys', in *Issues and Trends in Behavior Therapy,* ed. H.E. Adams and I. Unikel, Springfield, Ill.: Charles C. Thomas.

Patterson, G.R. and Gullion, M.E. 1968: *Living with Children: New Methods for Parents and Teachers*, Champaign, Ill.: Research Press.

Phillips, E., Phillips, E., Wolf, M. and Fixsen, D. 1973: 'Achievement Place: development of the elected manager system', *Journal of Applied Behavioural Analysis*, 6: 541–61.

Popper, K. 1972: *The Logic of Scientific Discovery*, 3rd edn, London: Hutchinson.

Rachman, S.J. 1972: *The Effects of Psychotherapy*, Oxford: Pergamon Press.

Romig, D.A. 1978: *Justice for Our Children*, Lexington, Mass.: Lexington Books.

Rutter, M. and Hersov, L. (eds) 1976: *Child Psychiatry – Modern Approaches*, Oxford: Basil Blackwell.

Steadman, H.J. 1976: 'Predicting dangerousness', in *Rage, Hate, Assault and Other Forms of Violence*, ed. D.J. Madden and J.R. Lion, New York: Spectron Publications.

Taylor, I., Walton, P. and Young, J. 1973: *The New Criminology: For a Social Theory of Deviance*, London: Routledge & Kegan Paul.

Toch, H. 1972: *Violent Men*, Harmondsworth: Penguin.

Tutt, N. (ed.) 1978: *Alternative Strategies for Coping with Crime*, Oxford: Basil Blackwell.

Walker, N. 1978: 'Dangerous people', *International Journal of Law and Psychiatry* 1(1): 37–51.

Weed, L.L. 1969: *Medical Record, Medical Education and Patient Care*, Cleveland: Case Western Reserve University Press.

White, A. 1962: *Explaining Human Behaviour*, Hull: University Press.

Wolman, B.B., Egan, J. and Ross, A.O. (eds) 1978: *Handbook of Treatment of Mental Disorders in Childhood and Adolescence*, Englewood Cliffs, NJ: Prentice-Hall.

CHAPTER 12

Violence in Prisons

John McVicar

Unlike, I suppose, the other papers in this book, mine has had a rather chequered career, and its origins lie in even less respectable fields than a university campus or a police station. I want to touch on these origins, because I take to heart Alvin Gouldner's strictures about objectivity in sociology.

Our attitudes and values inescapably influence what we study and, more important, how we study it. We study the social world with much of the same resources that we use to live in it, so consequently our social theories secrete elements of our attitudes and values. It is, therefore, part of the aims of sociological enterprise to discover what draws the researcher away from the ideal of objectivity. This is vital because, as Gouldner reminds us, 'every social theory facilitates the pursuit of some but not of all courses of *action*, and thus encourages us to accept the world as it is, to say yea or nay to it. In a way, every theory is a discreet obituary or celebration for some social system' (Gouldner 1973: 47).

Possibly my version of the 'okay' world has contaminated my research to such an extent as to invalidate it. At any rate, I am going to elucidate briefly the provenance of this paper in order, perhaps, to do the invalidator's work for him.

Nine years ago I restarted a 26-year jail sentence, and that kind of foreclosure on the future tends not only to concentrate the mind but also to encourage one to pull something out of the bag. I decided that the best rabbit I could come up with was a university degree. Consequently I took the academic trail with all the enthusiasm of a new convert, in search of something to impress the

Parole Board. I came up first with a sociology degree from London University, but, unfortunately for me, sociology degrees don't cut much ice with the sort of people who sit on Parole Boards. On the principle of if at first you don't succeed, try again, I looked round for a topic that would sustain a postgraduate degree. I'd read some of the penological literature while doing my first degree and got the impression that it wasn't up to much. This impression was especially strong in relation to the way prison researchers dealt with the subject of violence.

I knew that most prison violence, both between prisoners and between warders and prisoners, was a perfectly normal phenomenon. That is to say, it wasn't usually the result of, say, some psychopathic disorder, or, of frustration being expressed in an aggressive outburst – as much of the literature that I'd read suggested. It was as normal, for example, as the law-abiding citizen calling the police when he himself is assaulted.

In 1977 I started working on a thesis to correct, as I saw it, both the flaw in the literature and the Parole Board's mistake in not letting me out. Whether it was the thesis of my embodiment of the 'try, try again' maxim I don't know – or care, for that matter – but the next year the Parole Board let me out to finish it. The following year I spent in Leicester University.

When I chose violence as a subject for sociological investigation I was fully aware that most social scientists study it with the express aim of using their knowledge to prevent or control violence and aggression. In contrast, the purported knowledge about criminal and convict violence that I offer you does not contain any policy implications that would facilitate preventive intervention. Indeed, what I shall attempt to demonstrate is that the high level of personal violence that characterizes the worlds of the criminal and the convict is an integral feature of those forms of life; moreover, that this violence – certainly in the case of the convict – is a necessary aspect of a greater degree of freedom than would otherwise be the case.

It is almost a truism to say, as does J.E. Thomas, that it is the researcher's commitment to prison as a place of reform that makes for the kind of flaws that I reacted to when I first read the literature. Thomas writes of this commitment being the literature's 'generic weakness' (1972: 1). Indeed, criminology generally could be said to suffer from the commitment of so many criminologists to the acquisition of knowledge that will facilitate the control or prevention of crime instead of attempting to understand it. Polsky also picks up this point in *Hustlers, Beats and Others*. He says, for example, that he has nothing against social workers, probation officers, policemen or anyone else trying to keep others from breaking the law: 'If a man wants to make that sort of thing his lifework I have no objection; that is his privilege. I suggest merely that he not do so in the name of sociology, criminology, or any other social science' (1967: 141). One of the books that have recently been published on an English prison is almost a treatise on prison management: the only way I can recommend King and Elliot's *Albany* (1977) is as a lesson in how not to conduct prison research. When I am confronted with such books, though, I take heart from Dr Johnson's observation: 'Let fanciful men do as they will, depend upon it, it is difficult to disturb the system of life.'

With that preamble out of the way, let me, first, summarize my theoretical position and then go on to outline some of the evidence that I adduce to support it.

THEORY

In most of the literature about maximum-security prisons for men, there is an acknowledgement of the importance of violence or its threat in regulating interaction among convicts. In what is still, I suppose *the* book on such establishments – *The Society of Captives* – Gresham Sykes says: 'violence runs like a bright thread through the fabric of life in New Jersey State Prison and no inmate can afford to ignore its presence' (1958: 102). To anyone like myself who has served time in such institutions, this is another truism. To know such things, though, is a long way from explaining them.

Being a sociologist who learned his trade at Leicester University, where Norbert Elias lays down the law on such things, I looked for an explanation for this phenomenon in the way that male prisoners were typically *interdependent*. What seems crucial in the sort of configuration formed by their interdependence was the way they were bound together by a common rejection of the authorities. Prison staff are part of the forces that the state brings to bear on the problem of law and order. By rejecting prison staff – that is, by establishing at the heart of the convict code a rule that convicts do not collaborate with warders – the inmates rejected the services of the state in regulating their own affairs. In particular, they rejected drawing on the police or the courts when facing a law and order problem. Moreover, since they didn't institute from within their own ranks any authority or body for dealing with conflict, they were in effect placing themselves into a subculture that has affinities with a feudal society. In such a society, there are no institutions that legitimately monopolize force, and there is no central body that functions to enforce the law. In their absence, the individual must do it on his own or with what allies he can muster – or submit to injustice. The member of a subculture that rejects the encompassing society's law enforcement institutions cannot turn to such an institution when his rights are encroached upon or his dues are not rendered. Members of such subcultures are clearly in a different position from the members of anarchic or feudal societies where there *are* no central institutions for enforcing law and order, since they have, as it were, reneged on what Jean Jacques Rousseau conceptualized in his *Discourse on the Origin and Foundation of Inequality among Men* (1755) and *The Social Contract* (1762).

Rousseau presents an imaginary reconstruction of how, in moving from a 'state of nature' to a 'state of society', man relinquished certain liberties for the good of the group or the whole. This, of course, is the famous social contract, which brings the state into existence. What is particularly pertinent for my purposes is the relinquishing of 'natural man's' right to use force. In order for something approximating what we call a state to exist, the means of violence must be largely monopolized by a sector of the state. We can imagine the position of members of the subcultures that I am dealing with by thinking of them as having *repossessed* from the state the right or power to use force which the state usurps when it comes into existence.

Where one has convicts or criminals who are committed to the rule of non-co-operation with law enforcement agencies – a rule that lies at the heart of the morality that many of these people espouse – there will be rules that define the protocols of violence. The person who uses violence according to these protocols will certainly acquire greater prestige and status than someone who goes against them. Nevertheless, as the law and order lobbyists continually remind us, morality doesn't amount to much unless there are institutions that can draw on the state's monopoly of force to encourage backsliders. Such is the potency of violence in human affairs that the advantages of using violence to expendite one's interests are likely to gainsay the moral condemnation that falls upon a person who breaches rules that ideally regulate its use. However, it bears reminding ourselves that, as in all societies, the convict has a morality, which lies at the centre of the cultural resources that enable him to engage in and participate in the construction of a form of life.

PRISONER–PRISONER CONFLICT

I want to analyse the courses of action open to a prisoner who faces some injustice – for example, one who is assaulted by another prisoner. This victim faces three choices of action: first, he can decide that discretion is the better part of valour and do nothing; second, he can resist by assaulting his attacker and, indeed, escalate the violence in order to deter further attacks; and third, he can inform the authorities, and leave it to them to punish his assailant.

The third course of action breaches the non-co-operation rule of the subculture. In the United States the informer will be condemned as a 'rat'; in the UK, as a 'grass'. These labels will identify him as something lower in the code-following convict's list of evildoers than even the warders or convicted sex-offenders. The informer in prison more often than not will seek the protection of prison authorities rather than risk the possibility of attack or face the hate and contempt of his fellow convicts. When he does seek protection, what often he find is that the prison authorities place him in cellular confinement, this being the easiest way of isolating him from the rest of the prison community.

I am going to use some extracts from John Irwin's fine book (1970) on prison life, *The Felon*, to illustrate what I mean by the convict code and to show how it works in the area of personal disputes. Irwin himself was once a convict, but after release obtained academic qualifications and gained a lectureship. The two extracts that I use are culled from interviews that he conducted in San Quentin and Soledad. I have picked both for the very graphic way they show how the 'settle your own disputes' standard operates. In view of Officer Galea's riveting account of New York gangs (see chapter 13), perhaps the ground has been prepared for the rich and colourful language of these extracts.

The first one is from a con in San Quentin in May 1968:

The convict code isn't any different from that stuff we all learned as kids. You know, nobody likes a stool pigeon. Well here in the joint you got all kinds of guys living in the yard together, two to a cell. You got nuts walking the yard, you got every kind of dingbat in the world here. Well, we got to have some rules among ourselves. The rule is, 'do your own number'. In other words, keep off your neighbour's toes. Like if a guy next to me is making brew in his cell, well, this is none of my business. I got no business running to the man and telling him that Joe Blow is making brew in his cell. Unless Joe Blow is fucking over me, then I can't say nothing. And when he is fucking over me, then I got to stop him myself. If I can't I deserve to get fucked over [Irwin 1970: 83]

This offers us a very succinct summary of the convict code: if someone encroaches on a convict's rights, he must stop himself or accept it.

The other interview that I want to quote from Irwin's book is from a young prisoner in Soledad. The prisoner describes an incident in which he attacks another prisoner for being too forward in asking that a debt be honoured.

Con: I was talking to my friend and this dude came over to us and wanted to know when I was gonna give him the two cartons I owed him. I told him I was busy talking to my friend here and I would straighten him out later. He kept on and started getting salty. This got me hot, not 'cause he wanted the cigarettes, 'cause I righteously owed him the stuff. But the motherfucker was gettin' on my nerves. So I finally told him 'You know what, man, I don't owe you no cigarettes.' He told me, 'Listen man, you be here with the stuff in an hour.' I told him, 'I'll be here.'

Interviewer: So what happened?

Con: Well, I went and got my stuff [weapons] and met the motherfucker.

Interviewer: What happened?

Con: I piped him. Laid his head open. He didn't fuck with me after that. [Irwin 1970: 26]

Convicts committed to the non-informing rule or non-betrayal rule create a society that has some affinities with a feudal society or a stateless African one. In both of these forms of society, either because of a breakdown of the centralized state or because no central law enforcement institutions have developed, no sector of the state handles the problem of crime. In these societies the individual faces the problem of what to do when another person encroaches on his rights. Indeed, one of the brute facts of life in such societies is that, unless one has the power to enforce one's rights, one is extremely vulnerable to injustice.

It is no coincidence, then, that one of the best descriptions of code-following prisoners' attitudes to violence comes from an anthropologist's comment on the Nuer, a stateless African society.

> It is an ideal standard of conduct, rather than a rule, that every man should be quick to retaliate against an offence, either to his honour or to his rights. It is taken for granted that a man who was afraid to fight for his rights need not hope that they would be respected. Yet the knowledge that a man who considers himself wronged will not hesitate to fight, though at first sight may seem to indicate a condition of lawlessness, is in fact what maintains the law. People know what actions are infringements of other's rights, although they may not agree in particular cases that someone's rights have in fact been infringed. [Nair 1962: 40]

There are three points that I want to make in relation to Nair's comments on the Nuer. First, again, it is probably not a coincidence that certain qualities found in the typical male members of the Nuer are similar to those found among dominant prisoners. For instance, both are extremely touchy about personal insult, take great pride in gladitorial prowess, and brook no authority. Doubtless the cluster of traits that make up the 'macho' personality are waiting for some enterprising psychologist to investigate.

Second, although the Nuer and the Prison world that I am describing are characterized by a high level of personal violence, they are not as violent as the outsider would suppose. These worlds are not lawless. Hostilities are held in check by a sort of balance of terror which develops when violent men come together in a situation where the fruits of live-and-let-live outweigh the spoils of domination.

Third, like people everywhere, the man in these violent worlds are subject to the same constraints that all human groups come up against. Intrinsic to the group's endurance is the notion of crime or its equivalent. Murder and theft are discouraged in all societies and the societies that I am discussing are no exception. A sense of justice lies close to the heart of being human, but men can only pursue it with whatever power they possess and in whatever institutions they live. The convict knows what justice is, and, by his own light, his world is imbued with a sense of morality.

THE INMATE CODE

As I've already said, the cornerstone of the convict or inmate code is the rule that, whatever you do, you don't go to prison staff for help in any dispute with another prisoner. One is led to question where this rule comes from. In the literature there is some controversy about whether the code is indigenous or imported. Sykes, who for me is still the best prison researcher, plumps for the indigenous explanation. He argues that the inmate code, the prison sub-culture, is something that arises in response to the 'pains of imprisonment'. Now I'm not going to draw the battle-lines for you on this controversy, as I'm sure you don't need telling that, like all such things in the social sciences, they stretch a long way. All I want to say is that I feel the theorists who argue for the importation explanation are correct.

The hard core of dominant prisoners in any prison that punishes the sort of criminals that the advanced capitalist nations lock up come from either those who specialize in 'heavy' property offenses like robbery, or gangsters. It is generally these sort of offenders who make up 'the wheels' or 'the movers' in a maximum-security prison. Since they run whatever show that prison regime allows, it isn't surprising that the form of social relation that they impose upon the convict world is very similar to that found amongst such criminal groups in outside society.

The salient concern of the full-time criminal is undoubtedly the avoidance of arrest and conviction. This consideration tends to have an even greater phenomenological urgency in the mind of such criminals than does the much vaunted profit motive in the mind of the entrepreneur. One of the most dangerous threats to the criminal who must work with others in the commission of his crimes is the risk of betrayal. He has to trust and rely on other criminals in order to commit crimes, so their loyalty is a primary condition of him remaining undetected. Clearly, such criminals would be seriously handicapped in their chosen profession if confederates were prepared to betray whenever circumstances made it in their interest to do so. So fundamental is this threat that all full-time criminal groups develop a cultural defence against it, i.e. a no-informing rule.

This norm is so basic to the protection of the criminal enterprise that it becomes a vital part of the criminal's morality. The fully committed social criminal absorbs this standard into his self-image and, because it is so prominent in his moral field, it impresses itself through interaction into his identity. We must remember that important rules not only are ideals of behaviour but also reflect measures of esteem, so it is not surprising to find that 'rightness' for a thief or a gangster is one of the most important dimensions of self-image. Anyone who has talked to such men for any length of time cannot fail to be struck by the way they harp on this point in any discussions touching on matters of right and wrong. Not surprisingly, because it is such a basic ingredient of the right criminal, non-informing gets generalized into an across-the-board ban on criminals co-operating with law enforcement agencies. Again, therefore, like the convicts we've already discussed, criminals cannot draw on the facilities of the state to settle disputes with their own kind, but must settle their differences themselves. They can involve such sanctions as gossip, ridicule, contempt, ostracism, monetary penalties and so forth; but also in the criminal's armoury is violence. He lives in a culture in which violence is a *legitimate* and *proper* and *manly* sanction to invoke. This follows from the pattern of relations in which he is enmeshed, the sort of bonds that typically bind him to other criminals, and the kinds of sanction that necessarily underpin the criminal's morality.

The attitudes, beliefs and values – the culture – that criminals bring into prison will shape the social world they create inside. Obviously, the pains of imprisonment will set up pressures to select the more adaptive patterns of response possessed by the inmates. However, power is a particularly potent cultural resource – especially when that form of power is force. In human affairs, violence has a finality that is denied to other forms of power. In Ortega y Gassett's phrase, it is 'the standard that dispenses with all others'.

Committed criminals who habitually use violence come into prison not only experienced in the use of force but also as part of a subcultural group that legitimates its use. In any fight for dominance among prisoners, there are clearly going to be contenders. Moreover, criminal morality is also structured around the non-betrayal rule which has great adaptive potential in prison.

Professional criminals, committed to a norm of non-co-operation with the authorities, come into prison and are presented with a similar array of authority to the one that they rejected outside. To the professional criminal who suffers one of his occupational hazards – imprisonment – there are no good warders, only ones marked by varying shades of badness. The professional criminal's inflexible rejection of prison staff, though, usually takes the practical bent of developing an underlife of rackets. These rackets undermine the regime by offering illicit services, and thereby go some way to mitigating the pains of imprisonment.

PRISON VIOLENCE AND PRISON RACKETS

In the final section of this chapter I want to link up the notions of violence being a legitimate form of power for the code-following criminal, with the underlife of rackets that characterize prison life. I also want to round off with a couple of portraits of prison 'heavies' in order to flesh out my analysis.

Korn and McKorckle have floated the theory that the reason for the virulent rejection of warders by convicts is to avoid the implications of being a condemned criminal. It is the principle, therefore, in their much quoted words, of 'rejecting the rejectors'. By rejecting the warders and the judgements implicit in being locked up – that is, that one deserves to be locked up because of one's wrongdoing – the convict preserves a high opinion of himself.

There may be some of this in the convict's rejection of staff. However, I feel that a fuller explanation lies in looking at the realities of imprisonment and the focal concerns of the convict. The first point to make is that by and large people don't like being in prison. The architecture of prison is a tribute to how much this dislike of being locked up motivates people to get out. The second point is that, whatever the regime allows a convict, life can always be made better by circumventing some of the restriction.

Most of the action in prison revolves around opening up the

system. Getting more food, better clothes, uncensored communication with the outside, money, drugs, pornography, and so on. Whatever criminals enjoy outside and are denied inside they attempt, when in prison, to obtain illegally. These are the secondary adjustments that convicts spend their time on in prison – they are not very interested in learning a trade or educating themselves or reforming their character. They may do these things in order to impress bodies like parole boards, but what their hearts are in is getting as close as they can to the things they do outside.

Who is going to be the bookmaker inside? Who is going to smuggle in 'grass', hashish and LSD 'tabs'? Who is going to corrupt warders, in order to arrange illicit channels for mail and money? In other words, who is going to run the rackets? Well, since such rackets are also lucrative for the people running them, these are likely to be the most powerful and criminally sophisticated. It is hardly suprising that it is the heavy, professional criminals who are dominant in such prison enterprises.

And don't let us pretend, along with all the other prison researchers who have held their hands up in horror at what they saw in prison, that the rest of the prisoners don't get any benefit from this arrangement. They can place a bet on the horses, they can buy dope, they can get an uncensored message outside – *because there are prisoners running rackets*. So, although they may come from a cultural background that is inhospitable to the morality of the gangster and the robber, they pay lip service to it because they know they are better on balance with it than without it.

The first portrait that I want to present is of an American prisoner, and the account comes from a book written in 1972 by a man who gave evidence against a number of Mafia strongmen. His name is Vincent Teresa and the book, *My Life in the Mafia*. He begins by describing his entry into prison before he became an informer:

> When you arrive at Lewisburg, it doesn't take long to find out the power of Mafia Row. . . . Now the *Capo di Capi Tutti* of Mafia Row is Lillo. . . . He's a stone killer. I think he took care of at least eighty hits himself. He's about five-foot-three, bald-headed and he walked around with a mean look on his face.
>
> Inside Lewisburg, Lillo was the boss. The warden ruled nothing. . . Lillo did. At the snap of his fingers, he could have

turned that prison into a battlefield. Instead he was Mr Law and Order. He ruled G Block with an iron fist, and there were 150 long-term prisoners there. . . .

On G Block everyone lived Lillo's law. . . . [Teresa 1972]

Lillo's real name was Carmine Galante, and one interesting prediction that Teresa makes about Lillo is that he will take over the New York Mafia when he is released. Well, Mr Galante was released in 1974 and did as Teresa predicted. Indeed, in copybook Mafiosa fashion, he was eventually gunned down by four masked gunmen in a Brooklyn restaurant on 12 July 1979. According to the FBI's bugs, Carmine Galante had offended his colleagues by muscling in on their rackets and selling Mafia membership, and was planning on making his daughter a member as well!

The other portrait of a prison leader comes from my own research and experience and is the nearest example I found to a Lillo. His name was Don and I met him during my eight years in Leicester's special wing. A robber, serving 18 years, Don – 6ft tall and 15 stone – presented a menacing and threatening presence with his aggressive posture and habitually belligerent expression. Don's first significant act was to set the tone for the way he served the rest of his time in the wing.

The procedure with all incoming prisoners was to go through whatever effects that they had in their possession and to restore them, with one exception, to the owner as quickly as possible. The exception was such items as record players and radios, which were held back to be checked by the electrical engineers for illicit VHF equipment. This usually took a day.

After receiving the rest of his effects, Don began asking for his record player. After some initial evasion, he was told by a warder that he would have it tomorrow and told the reason for the delay. Don's reply was: 'Governor, I've had that record player in my possession for three years and I haven't done anything that entitles you people to take it away from me. Now I want my record player. I didn't ask to come here. But I'm prepared to accept that but what I won't accept is you people taking liberties with me'. The principal officer with whom this exchange took place began taking great pains to disassociate himself from the decision that had separated Don from his record player. 'Don, if I could get you your record player, I would do it this instant. But there is nothing anyone can do. Head office make these rules and we have to abide by them. I personally will take your record player over to the engineers first thing in the morning and see that you get it as quickly as possible.'

Don, as was his way, listened impassively to this and then answered as if it had never been said. 'I want my record player by tonight and I either get it by tonight or there is going to be trouble. All I want is what I'm entitled to. I'm not asking you cunts' – suddenly his voice went up a number of octaves and doubled in decibels – 'to let me go home for the night. I'm asking for my record player which I've had in my possession for the last three years.' He glared challengingly at the warder for a few moments, then stalked back to the remainder of the wing's residents, who'd marshalled by the kitchen door, some five or six yards back from the office, in mute support of Don's action.

The next two hours witnessed a number of similar confrontations between Don and various prison officials who tried unsuccessfully to reconcile Don to the loss of his record player for the night. Sometimes Don would state his case flatly and rationally; other times he would scream, rant and threaten. The threats would be accompanied with all the movements and postures of a fighter about to throw a punch. Whenever he did the latter, staff backed down and turned to appeasing him rather than arguing the toss about the record player rule.

Eventually the security officer came over and effected a compromise which was really an official capitulation. What was agreed upon was that Don would let him look at the record player to examine it for VHF equipment in the knowledge that he wasn't an expert and could damage it. I think the only way it could have got damaged during the search was through the official's nervousness. Don, needless to say, agreed to this and came back to the rest of the prisoners to announce with a triumphant smirk on his face: 'I'm getting my record player tonight.'

A few months later another prisoner in the wing had a run-in with the same principal officer who had been so ready to placate Don. Harry had gone to the office for some utensils that were kept locked up. The warder told him to wait and, because of the urgency with which they were neeeded, precipitated this response from Harry: 'you cunts will be all right, you'll go too far with me one day and you'll never do it again.' He turned away; however, the warder took umbrage and shouted at him, 'Don't make remarks like that to me.' Harry turned round in a fury and screamed, 'Come out here and tell me that, you cunt. Come out here and say it.'

This is precisely what the warder did. He fumbled with his keys as he unlocked the gate of the office and was clearly under strain, but he walked up to Harry and very close to his face said: 'Yes R———, what are you going to do? Just calm yourself.' Harry ranted a bit but in the end he backed off, refusing the gauntlet that everyone witnessing the incident knew has been thrown him.

Harry had shot and killed three policemen; Don was only a robber. To the outsider, the former would probably have appeared a more dangerous person, but to the warder the crucially relevant difference between the two convicts was that Don had a record of assaults on warders while Harry didn't. Don had shown that he was prepared to take his beatings off the warders and still come back, a risk that Harry had never been prepared to take.

Don's violent behaviour, and particularly his readiness to use violence against warders, made him the embodiment of an ideal that even non-criminal convicts tended to admire. Don was a folk hero, and in the many discussions among convicts concerned with 'the compilation of a demonology and hagiology of the prison world' (Cohen and Taylor 1972), tales of his victories figured prominently.

CONCLUSION

Let me quickly recap the main points of what I've been saying. Violent behaviour among convicts is in certain circumstances a perfectly normal kind of behaviour. It is integrally linked to a form of life in which such people are involved. Certainly for the prisoner it plays an important part in combating the pains of imprisonment. It has disadvantages – but this is merely another way of saying that we live in an imperfect world. Many of us use motor-cars, accepting that part of the price we have to pay for the advantages of personal transport is 8,000 deaths from motor-car accidents. A high level of violence in the prison world is the price convicts have to pay for having people who can fight the regime and develop and maintain rackets. Prison violence is an integral part of the system of social relations that are the most adaptive for combating the pains of imprisonment.

REFERENCES

Cohen, Stanley and Taylor Laurie 1972: *Psychological Survival,* Harmondsworth: Penguin.
Gouldner, Alvin 1973: *The Coming Crisis of Western Sociology,* London: Heinemann.
Irwin, John 1970: *The Felon,* Englewood Cliffs, NJ: Prentice-Hall.
King, R.D. and Elliott, K.W. 1977: *Albany,* London: Routledge & Kegan Paul.
Nair, Lucy 1962: *Primitive Government,* Harmondsworth: Penguin.
Polsky, Ned 1967: *Hustlers, Beats and Others,* Chicago: Aldine.
Sykes, Gresham 1958: *The Society of Captives,* Princeton: University Press.
Teresa, Vincent 1972: *My Life in the Mafia,* St Albans: Panther.
Thomas, J.E. 1972: *The Prison Officer since 1880,* London: Routledge & Kegan Paul.

CHAPTER 13

Youth Gangs of New York

John Galea

In this chapter I am not going to talk about theory. I am going to talk about the experiences that I have had as a New York City police officer working with youth gangs.

From the period after the Korean War to the end of the 1950s, we had a 'gang problem' in the city of New York. The gangs were characterized at that time as *fighting* gangs, and they fought mainly over 'turf' – an arena up to about three blocks in radius which they regarded as theirs. Or they fought over the girls in the group; or it was an ethnic struggle. During this period there wasn't what we would term any aggression acted out towards the community: most of the action was directed towards other members and other youth gangs. This pattern of gang activity eventually declined. Since the early 1970s, however, we have witnessed a resurgence of youth gangs in New York City, which appears to have followed in the wake of the Vietnam War.

No one can really say what it was that stemmed the tide of gang activity in the 1960s. But we do know that there was an influx of drugs into the country and we had an enormous number of 'junkies'; this probably turned the kids away from fighting each other and brought them together in a unified drug culture. Also, after the Vietnam War kids who had been in the army were coming back to conditions of high unemployment. These were trained killers, and when they came back they had no jobs. What they did was to form gangs in order to survive, and in 1971 or thereabouts we saw a great resurgence of gang activity in New York City. But whereas years before the gangs were mainly 'fighting' gangs, today the pattern has changed. The game is survival, and this means committing crimes for profit – robbery, harassment, burglary, dangerous weapons.

Now, as a result of this increased street gang activity, especially in the Bronx, there was a need to know more about the identities and activities of gang members. For this reason the first Gang Intelligence Unit was established in the Bronx by the Youth Aid Division of the City of New York. Soon after that Manhatten, Brooklyn and Queens also set up Youth Gang Units.

New York is a city that has over eight and a half million people, of which some two million reside in Brooklyn. It is composed of five boroughs – Manhattan, Richmond, the Bronx, Queens and Brooklyn. The Police Department divides Manhattan and Brooklyn into two separate units – Manhattan South and North and Brooklyn South and North. There are 73 police stations in the city of New York, of which 24 are in Brooklyn: 9 in Brooklyn North and 15 in Brooklyn South. In the whole of the city there are at present 130 'delinquent' gangs with a total of 10,300 members. Eighty of these gangs are in Brooklyn, with a total of over 5,800 members. Of these 80 gangs, 40 are in the Brooklyn South area, with a total membership of 3,400. In addition, there are 113 other gangs under investigation in New York City, 97 of which are in Brooklyn and 52 of those in Brooklyn South.

As a member of the Gang Intelligence Unit No. 3, I am responsible for gathering information relating to the Brooklyn South area, so my responsibility is to keep tabs on 40 active gangs with 3,400 members, and to investigate 52 other 'gangs' to determine if they are, in fact, gangs. In the city of New York we have 6 officers assigned to Gang Units: one in Manhattan, one in Queens, one in the Bronx and three in Brooklyn. I am the only one assigned to Brooklyn South. We have another officer assigned to Brooklyn North and one assigned to do a lot of the clerical work.

To give you a base for comparison with other cities, in Detroit they have 85 gang information officers (plus a number of social workers); in Chicago they have 125; in San Francisco they have 47 (plus sheriffs and social workers); in Los Angeles there are 55 (plus sheriffs and social workers); in Philadelphia they have 90. In New York City we have just six.

I'd like to concentrate on the activities of the street gangs in Brooklyn, because that's the area that I am most familiar with, and

East New York, Brooklyn, July 1980.
(Photo by Peter Marsh.)

to give you some idea of the nature of the area in which the gangs live and reside. In order to do that I have singled out one group, called the Sexboys. The Sexboys is a group that we can regard as fairly representative of all the other groups in the city of New York. Anything that you can attribute to the Sexboys you can attribute to the other gangs as well.

In the early 1970s, when gangs had proliferated to a great degree, there was a group called the Ghetto Brothers. The Ghetto Brothers was a group of Hispanics and blacks and they had well over 200 members in Brooklyn, but they also had divisions in the Bronx, Manhattan and Queens. The rival gangs were the Tomahawks, which was a black gang, and the Crazy Homicides, which was an Hispanic gang. In 1972 the Ghetto Brothers split up and one of the young fellows, a kid by the name of Ralphie, took a group of kids from the corner of Pitkin Avenue and Essex Street, which is in the East New York section of Brooklyn, and named them the 'Sexboys'. They took the 'Es' off the 'Essex Street' signs on the corner where they had their club house, leaving 'Sex Street', and hence the name. At the time just after Ralphie had formed the group there were about 50 or 60 members. Of these, between five and ten could be called the real 'motivators', and these were the kids you would always see around the street.

In 1973 Ralphie left the group – he got locked up and was gone. It was then that Leftie became the leader. Leftie, whom I knew personally, was a nice kid. But he was killed in 1975 in a pool. Some of our parks have pools in them and this particular park was not in Leftie's area. He had ventured out, and he was in the turf of another group by the name of the Bikers, and he was killed. After Leftie died, Danny became the leader, and has remained the leader up until very recently. At this moment however Danny is in gaol, locked up for a homicide. Ralphie has now been released from gaol and has assumed leadership of the group again.

To give you some idea of the violence that is a feature of gang activity, I'd like to recount a few incidents in which I have had a personal involvement, starting in 1972 with the Ghetto Brothers, who were the forerunners of the present Sexboys.

In those days there was a black in charge of the Ghetto Brothers. There was again an internal struggle, and eventually he was shot. He didn't die, but subsequent to that shooting we descended upon Pitkin Avenue and entered the clubhouse building. In the process

Members of the Sexboys, Brooklyn Police Station, May 1978.
(Photo by Peter Marsh.)

of doing this one of the police officers was shot. In the return of fire two of the Ghetto Brothers were killed and numerous others wounded. This was when the breakup of the Ghetto Brothers began.

Around 1973, when Ralphie was the leader of the Sexboys, there was a homicide. This came about as a result of Danny being stabbed in his ear, or around the ear portion of his head, by a rival gang member. The gang member unfortunately stayed in the area, and went on to a social club. He had been in the social club for a short time when some of the Sexboys appeared. The rival gang member was shot dead. Two other people in the social club were also shot – a woman was shot in the leg and a man in the arm. Three of the Sexboys were subsequently arrested on the basis of information supplied not only by the people in the social club at the time but by myself and other officers in the Unit. (We have a good relationship not only with this particular group but also with the other groups. If we want to know about the Sexboys we ask members of the Crazy Homicides, their main rivals. The gangs tell us about themselves and about each other mainly because we represent someone they can talk to as friends. But we are also their foe.)

We arrested three members of the Sexboys, but unfortunately there was a foul-up. Ralphie was under 16 at the time, and he was questioned by the District Attorney without either of his parents being present. As a result, his confession was thrown out and he wasn't even locked up. Just one kid was actually put away and he is still away now. His name is Chico.

After that, there was a Roman Catholic Church where the priest was killed and the place robbed. There were no arrests, but from the drawings that we have of the possible perpetrators, they strongly resemble at least three members of the Sexboys. The priests who were there will not give any evidence, and because they will not testify this case will never be solved.

In the same area on Pitkin Avenue there was a social club that was used as a hang-out for the Sexboys. A man came into this club to use the pool table, and while doing so he took out some money. One of the Sexboys – Ralphie again – saw the big wad of money that he had taken out. Ralphie then went to one of the rival gangs, the Crazy Homicides, and set this particular man up for what they call a 'geese'. This is nothing more than a robbery. He set it up that way because everybody knew the Sexboys in that area, so he felt that if

Sexboys' colours, May 1978.
(Photo by Peter Marsh.)

the Crazy Homicides, who they happened to be on friendly terms with at this particular time, came down and committed the rip-off, or the 'geese', the two groups could split the money and nobody would be the wiser. Unfortunately, the owner of the social club in which the robbery was taking place interrupted it, and as he fought some of the Crazy Homicides he was shot and killed. As a result of his shooting, Ralphie and two members of the Crazy Homicides were locked up. This is one of the few times that Ralphie actually went to gaol. However, while the funeral was going on, members of the Sexboys politely went to the home of the man being buried and burglarized his apartment.

In 1975, while Ralphie was in gaol, Leftie became the leader. As I have already described, he was stabbed in a city pool in another part of Brooklyn in the territory of a rival gang called the Bikers, and died as a result of the stabbing. What is interesting about his death is the fact that there was a funeral procession of gang members. They actually took the casket and walked with it through the streets of East New York. It was dressed with the gang colours and had Leftie's jacket draped over. Just as, when somebody dies, they go through the block in a hearse, the gang actually walked the casket through the area.

A good deal of violence in the same area of Brooklyn has also been attributed to the Crazy Homicides. One grisly homicide that was attributed to them was of a young fellow, 16 years of age, who was found in an abandoned building, his head partially shot off with a shotgun. They had defecated on him, tied his hands behind his back and burnt his body.

The Sexboys and the Crazy Homicides have had an ongoing feud for years. In 1977 they had a classic shoot-out. The Sexboys had been getting the worst of it in their fighting with the Crazy Homicides. So they decided they would set up the Crazy Homicides and put them in the hands of the police officers. They told the police officers, 'We are going to meet with the Crazy Homicides and they are going to be "dirty" ' (in other words, they are going to have their weapons on them). So along with a few other officers I was present as some of the Sexboys converged on the territory of the Crazy Homicides. To their surprise, however, the Crazy Homicides were laying an ambush, and shots were fired all over the place. Two of the Sexboys were shot but nobody died. I took one guy to the hospital who had a hole in him – he was shot in the side with a rifle. There were nine or ten arrests, all Crazy Homicides, and at least 11 rifles and shotguns were confiscated. Everyone arrested in this particular shoot-out has by now been acquitted.

Most recently, the new leader, or should I say one of the older leaders, of the Sexboys, Danny Rivera, was arrested for homicide. He was also arrested for arson and assault. Four members of the Sexboys had purchased some marijuana from two blacks and felt that they were being given short measure. An argument ensued which spilled out on to the street, and the Sexboys assaulted the two blacks. About five or six other blacks happened to be walking down the block at the time: they intervened and chased the Sexboys away. The Sexboys came back 15 or 20 minutes later but, much to their surprise, these black fellows were waiting for them. Out of the garbage cans came some shotguns, shots were fired, and one of the Sexboys, a deaf-mute, was shot in the rear. The Sexboys again retreated. The following night a van was stolen and four members of the Sexboys followed two female blacks down the block. These two girls entered a building where the blacks who the Sexboys had the problem with allegedly lived. When the two girls went in, the Sexboys apparently threw kerosene bombs into the building with a cry of 'Fire, fire, fire'. The men in the building came out, and as they did so they were shot down by youths said to be members of the Sexboys. One of them died and another was badly shot but lived. The girls were burnt but they weren't shot.

As a result of this particular incident, the Police Department arrested Danny, who happened to be the leader at the time. We know that there were four individuals involved and we know who they are. Only one, however, was identified by eye-witnesses: that was Danny, and that's why he was the only one arrested. While Danny was in Riker's Island, which is a city facility, he tried to hang himself, and now he can only remember things that happened before 1975. He has no conception of 1976, 1977 or why he is in gaol. He is at the point where Leftie died. I have no reason why that is.

Now I would like to tell you something of the functions that I perform as a police officer in the Gang Unit. As you see, I work with some very aggressive individuals. I have two roles: I am their friend, but also their foe. Sometimes I don't understand why they even talk to me, because I personally am responsible for many of them being locked up. When anything happens as far as crime is concerned in the East New York area, and the Sexboys are mentioned, whatever the unit, – be it the Homicide Squad, the Robbery Squad or the Rape Squad – they always come to me, to help them bring whoever it is, or whoever they think it is, into the office.

To give you an example, just recently two members of the Crazy Homicides committed a homicide: while they were robbing a transit booth clerk, they shot him and he died. Now in New York City we are going through a big financial crisis, and we are very short of police officers. We have a high crime rate within our subway system, and the Police Commissioner of New York, in order to aid the Transit Police Commissioner, has put members of the Police Department at the latter's disposal. The Transit Commissioner has taken his detectives off special assignments and put them in the subways in uniform, in an attempt to provide some protection for those who ride the subway. This experiment had lasted for about a month and a half, and during that time we had had no crimes of violence in the subway system. On this particular night, two Crazy Homicides shot and killed this one transit clerk, and this became a big, big thing: the first incident after New York City Transit and Police Departments had got together and tried to make the subway system safer. Well, these two individuals happened to be guys that I have known for years, and in the street the word was out who had committed the crime. It was also out that the Homicide Squad was definitely after them and that they were to be considered extremely dangerous. We knew that they were armed and that they were going to be no chances taken in arresting them.

The youths involved knew me and they got in touch. Through my intervention they were subsequently brought in, and nobody was hurt. This is one of the services that we provide for the gang members. They know that if I come for them, or if one of the other members of my Unit comes for them, they don't have to worry about any sort of physical harm. Nor do they have to worry about a weapon being planted. (This is a favourite cry of all criminals – that the police plant weapons on them.)

Some of the other services that we provide for these kids include getting them jobs. We know that they are a part of society but they just can't cope with the rest of society. It can be very difficult to deal with them, but we try. I have got kids back into school; we have got a couple into the armed forces. We do whatever we can to help them; our office is one that they can walk into at any time, sit down, relax and just talk. They know that if they commit a crime they are going to be arrested. But they also know that they can come and talk about it to us. We treat them as individuals, and they in turn treat us as individuals. They know that we are the establishment, but they don't really see us as such. We are allowed to go into their club houses. We don't socialize with them, but while we are on duty we do actually go out with them, just to see what's going on.

I personally find something new about these kids all the time. Every day is a new adventure – a new slang word, different habits. Recently we drove a mother of one of the kids to hospital. It was getting late and we were about to go off-duty when she asked us to drive her there. So we said OK. We went through a few red lights while driving and she said, 'Oh, wow, you ate that light!' – this was one of the new words on the street. That's how we pick up phrases like that, by being around these kids.

Recently, I have been involved with a group by the name of the Inner City Round Table Youth, or ICRY. This is an organization of former youth gang members who are committed to community service. The director of the group is a man by the name of Nazim el Fatah who happens to be a former president of one of the largest youth gangs in history, the Blackstone Rangers in Chicago. In the Chicago area gangs tend to be enormous. You have maybe two or three gangs, and each has a very large membership, whereas in the city of New York you have more gangs but with a smaller number in each. On every block in New York, you will find a gang. In the Williamsburg section of Brooklyn you have South 1st Street, South 2nd Street. . . up to South 9th Street. On each block there is a different group of the gang called the Bikers. So you have South 1st Street Bikers, South 2nd Street Bikers, South 3rd Street Bikers and so on. Then after that you have the Unknown Bikers and the Deadly Bikers. These gangs are sometimes peaceful with each other but at times the South 1st Street Bikers are fighting the South 6th Street Bikers. This is the way gang life is in New York.

Nazim, being the director of ICRY, got in touch with my office and arranged a meeting with us and with the Justice Department. At this meeting we were very enthusiastic, and it gave me, as an officer, an opportunity to pay the kids more than just a little

Members of Savage Riders and Sandman, employed by ICRY, July 1980.
(Photo by Peter Marsh.)

'Rival' gang members, now involved together in ICRY, July 1980.
(Photo by Peter Marsh.)

lip-service. For years now I have been responsible for making sure that some of them go to gaol. I have been like a Herbert Hoover to these guys. Now I think with this particular group, ICRY, I am in a better position to give a better service to the kids. The end result should be that we are here to help rather than to put away.

The ICRY is made up of two boards. One board consists of prominent businessmen and public figures in the city of New York, such as the Honourable Judge Bruce Wright. He is affectionately termed 'Cut 'Em Loose Bruce'. He is a very liberal judge – liberal in the sense that, if the person in front of him has roots in the community, he will give that person bail; will let them go on his own recognizance. We have had instances where police officers have been assaulted: in the most recent incident a police officer was stabbed in the neck, and the individual was let out on Judge Wright's own recognizance.

The other board of ICRY is composed of the youth gangs in New York, and at the head of this group is a gang member by the name of John Flynt. He happens to be the leader of a motorcyle gang called the Chingalings, which is composed entirely of ex-service-men. The ICRY is trying to bring all the gangs in the city of New York together under one umbrella – together in terms of talking about training for the future and training for a vocation. Not only is this an ideal aim, but we think the climate is right for it. We also think that, with our knowledge of the street gangs, and with the contacts that we have, we should be able to bring most of the kids into this particular programme. We have had meetings with the New York City Youth Board and the Division for Youth in the State of New York; we have had meetings with the Justice Department; and all these meetings are part of an effort to fund some sort of programme so that we can actually help these street gang members into a more positive way of life.

Contributors

Dr Len Berkowitz is Vilas Research Professor in Psychology at the University of Wisconsin, USA. He is very well known for his experimental social–psychological work on aggression, and his books – which include *The Roots of Aggression* and *Aggression: A Social Psychological Analysis* – are internationally recognized texts in the field. More recently, he has been conducting non-laboratory studies of violent prisoners and his concern with the limitations of rule-based explanations of violent behaviour is the theme of his chapter.

Dr Anne Campbell is well known for her work on female delinquency and aggression and completed a doctoral dissertation in this field in 1976. She is the author of *Girl Delinquents* (Blackwell, 1981). Currently, she is conducting research on female gang members in New York.

Dr David Downes is a senior lecturer in social administration at the London School of Economics and Political Science and is best known for his classic book *The Delinquent Solution*, published in 1966, which is seen as a definitive text in the field, and for his numerous contributions to a more radical style of criminological enquiry.

Professor Robin Fox is Professor of Anthropology at Rutgers University, New Jersey. He is also Co-Director of the Harry Frank Guggenheim Foundation, New York. His books include *Kinship and Marriage, Encounter with Anthropology, The Red Lamp of Incest* and, with Lionel Tiger, *The Imperial Animal.*

Dr Neil Frude is a lecturer in clinical psychology, University College, Cardiff. He took an M.Phil. in clinical psychology at the Institute of Psychiatry in 1970 and a Ph.D. in 1973. His current interests include aggression theory and explanations of violent incidents, particularly family violence.

John Galea is a police officer presently assigned to the Gang Information Unit, Youth Aid Division in New York. He has a B.A. in criminal justice and is currently reading for a Master's Degree in public administration. He is an active member of a number of organizations including the New York State Juvenile Officers Association and the National Black Police Association. His work with New York street gangs has been the subject of various radio and television programmes and he has lectured on the subject at colleges and high schools in New York City.

Hugh Gault is a tutorial fellow at University College, Cardiff. He has an M.A. in child development from Nottingham University. His current interests include aggression in young children and the psychology of violent young offenders.

Dr Paul Heelas studied social anthropology at the University of Oxford. He is currently a lecturer in the Department of Religious Studies at Lancaster University. He has published widely on a number of subjects and is currently concerned with indigenous psychologies and the relationship between psychology and anthropology.

Dr Masud Hoghughi is the Principal of Aycliffe School, a regional children's centre in Durham. He has spent his professional life as a clinical and educational psychologist, working mainly with adults and adolescents in a variety of settings. During the past few years he has been particularly concerned with creating a comprehensive service and developing advanced techniques for the assessment and treatment of severely disordered adolescents. He is a lecturer at the universities of Durham and Newcastle.

John McVicar is in a position to speak with considerable authority on the subject of violence in prisons since he has spent a good deal of his life in penal institutions. He came to the attention of the general public following his dramatic escape from Durham Jail – a feat which resulted in an extended sentence of 26 years following two years at liberty. Whilst in prison he gained a B.Sc. in sociology and is currently studying for a Ph.D. at Leicester University. He is the author of *McVicar by Himself*.

Peter Marsh is best known for his work on the social behaviour of young football fans. His books include *Aggro: The Illusion of Violence* and *The Rules of Disorder*, which he wrote with Elizabeth Rosser and Rom Harré. He has also been involved in research concerned with non-verbal communication and has written on the subject of gestures with Desmond Morris and others. He is now Senior Lecturer in Psychology at Oxford Polytechnic and is conducting further research on aspects of aggression.

Dr Rachel Meller took a degree in neurobiology at Sussex University and a Ph.D. on 'Sexual and Aggressive Behaviour in Talapoin Monkeys' at Cambridge. At present she is a junior research fellow of the Mental Health Foundation, extending this research on monkeys to investigate the neuro-chemical basis of such behaviours in their social groups.

Dr Graham Murdock studied sociology at the London School of Economics and Political Science and at the University of Sussex. He joined the Centre for Mass Communication Research at Leicester in 1968 where he has specialized in the political economy of communications, the sociology of cultural production and the impact of mass media on youth. He is the co-author of *Demonstrations and Communication* (1970) and *Mass Media and the Secondary School* (1973) and has written over 40 articles on the sociology of communication and youth. He is currently preparing books on youth culture, media ownership and the media–violence debate.

Name Index

Wolfgang, M. E. 92, 101
Wolman, B. B. 186, 199
Wright-Mills, C. 115

Yin, P. P. 82, 90

Young, J. 34, 45, 79, 86, 90, 191, 199
Young, S. K. 121, 135

Zuckerman, S. 120, 136

Subject Index